Donald Watson

Bird Artist and Writer

Edited by Roger Crofts

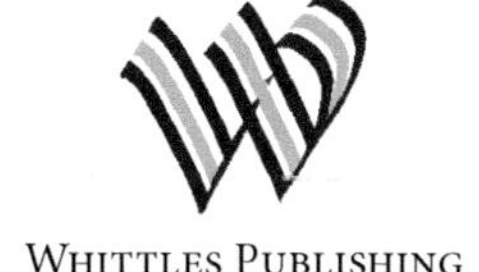

Whittles Publishing

Whittles Publishing Ltd,
Dunbeath,
Caithness, KW6 6EG,
Scotland, UK

www.whittlespublishing.com

ISBN 978-184995-592-8

Printed by Halstan

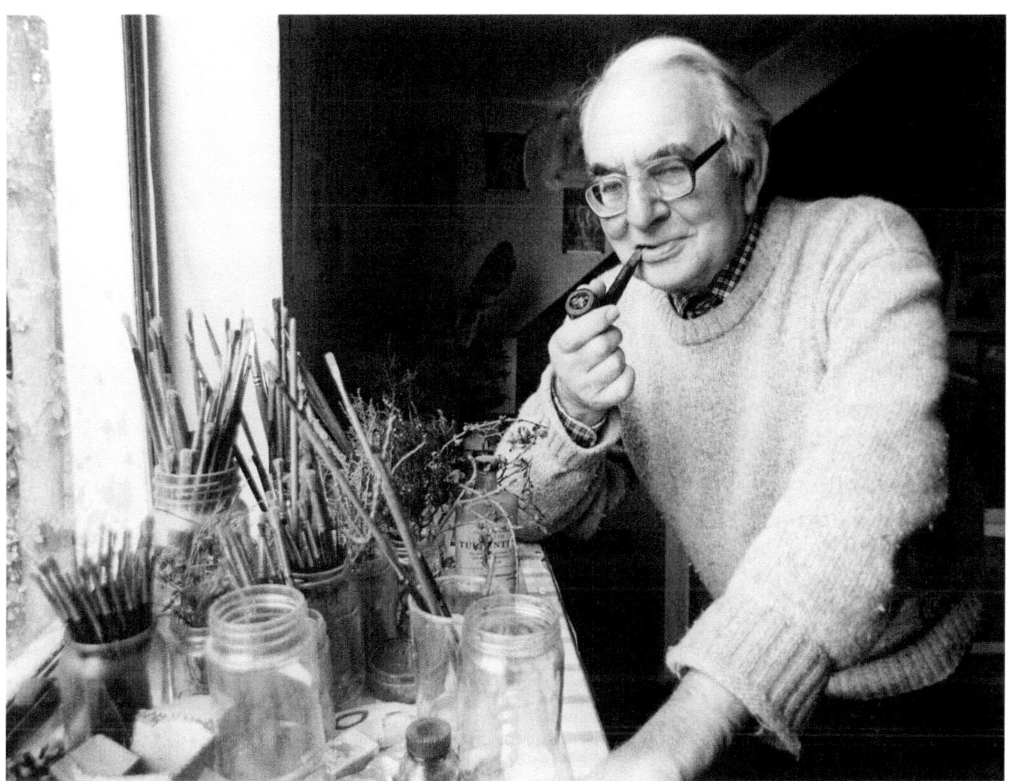

Donald Watson at his painting table in his studio at Barone

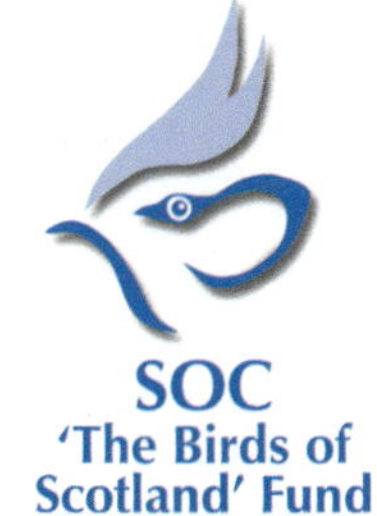

This publication
has been produced
with the generous
support of the Scottish
Ornithologists' Club
(SOC) through its
Birds of Scotland Fund
www.the-soc.org.uk

Contents

Foreword

I never met Donald Watson, but I greatly warmed to him through his writing and his art. This book is reassuring in that the tales told of him by colleagues, friends and family all reinforce the impression that he was a fine man, as well as being talented.

Watson's *The Hen Harrier* is within reach now as I sit at my keyboard. It was one of the first Poyser books I owned, and was given to me as a Christmas present in 1977. I had seen a few hen harriers at that time, but they were few and far between, so each sighting was a treat. This book, my introduction to Watson's writing and drawing, was a treat too. Watson had not just seen hen harriers – he had watched them, and watched them with an artist's eye as well as with a naturalist's eye. The artwork showed me the bird that I had seen a few times and which I wanted to see much more often. The bird was faithfully placed in the habitats in which it occurred. The author clearly knew this bird very well, and the accounts of his studies inspired me not only to study birds in the field but also to communicate about nature.

Watson's paintings and drawings still work on many levels. For the birdwatcher in me these are real hen harriers, ring ousels, shelducks or greenshank, clearly seen and known to the artist. To the ecologist the birds are in their proper places in the habitat, and so often the depicted landscape – whether it be Aberlady Bay, Caerlaverock or the hills of Dumfries and Galloway – transports you directly to a remembered view. And they are beautiful.

Watson was uncomfortable about the changes he saw around his long-term home in Galloway. We see from this book some of his attempts to bring these problems to the attention of bodies who could act to limit the damage. Of course, we find public and less obvious examples of his writing about persecution of birds of prey, but Watson knew, from experience and observation, that his hen harriers suffered from afforestation, disturbance from walkers, the attentions of golden eagles, cold winters and the reduction of food supply caused by heather burning. However, gamekeepers were firmly in his sights. He was an effective communicator of the problem of wildlife crime linked to the game-shooting industry.

I enjoyed reading his letter to his member of parliament, Ian Lang, in December 1987, on the subject of afforestation of his local hills. Donald's letter provides an insight into his thinking, displays his marvellous use of words and is a good model of a constituent using local examples to alert their parliamentary representative to important national issues. One would not normally have the privilege to read such a letter so long after the event.

He wrote about the loss of waders as silage replaced hay crops, of acidification of watercourses, of egg collecting, of stock densities and lack of carrion for scavenging ravens. These were well observed concerns, the result of knowing an area well and being a careful, as well as caring, observer of change.

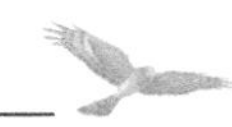

This book of nine chapters by seven authors reveals much about the life of Donald Watson as a family man, an artist, a writer and a conservationist. These touching tributes are sprinkled with anecdotes and stories, and they paint a picture of Watson as a rounded individual and not simply a talented artist. And he was not only a talented artist – one of the best – but also a talented observer of wildlife.

Mark Avery
North Northamptonshire, December 2023

Contributors

Mark Avery: Foreword

Mark is a scientist by training and a naturalist by inclination. He writes about, and comments on, environmental issues. Mark worked for the RSPB for 25 years until standing down in 2011 to go freelance. He was the RSPB's conservation director for nearly 13 years. Mark lives in rural Northamptonshire and is a member of the RSPB, the Wildlife Trusts, the British Trust for Ornithology (BTO), the National Trust for Scotland and the Labour Party. He is a trustee of the World Land Trust.

Roger Crofts – 1: Introducing Donald Watson; 7: Donald Watson the writer and illustrator; 8: A conservation campaigner; 9: Watson Birds – a legacy project

Following training and research in geography and geomorphology, Roger worked in the Scottish Government covering many issues: economic development, rural areas and local government finance, and finally nature conservation and countryside. He was the founder chief executive of Scottish Natural Heritage 1992–2002, where he worked with Jeff Watson, Donald's son. He has been living part-time in St John's Town of Dalry for 17 years and was the instigator of Watson Birds. He is an environmental adviser, writer, speaker and advocate for better care and management of nature working in Scotland and in Iceland especially. More details at www.rogercrofts.net.

John Threlfall SWLA – 2: Donald Watson the artist

Like Donald, John is a member of the Society of Wildlife Artists (SWLA) and has also had the good sense to make Dumfries and Galloway his home. Similarly, it is wildlife in its habitat that is the inspiration for his work, and extensive field studies the primary resource.

John is an experienced and enthusiastic tutor, running wildlife drawing courses for the Field Studies Council and Artsafari, teaching weekly classes in life drawing, portraiture, still life and landscapes as well as specialist workshops in pastel techniques. He was a tutor on John Busby's Seabird Drawing Week for a number of years. He has published two books of his paintings and writings: *Between the Tides* and *Drawn to the Edge*.

Louise Watson – 3: Donald Watson, my father

Daughter of Donald and Joan Watson, Louise grew up with her three siblings, Pam, Jeff and Kate, in the family home of Barone in St John's Town of Dalry. She attended local schools in Dalry and Kirkcudbright before studying English at the University of Edinburgh. Her subsequent career has been centred on the world of books: she worked in publishing for several years in London and Cheltenham before taking up a position in an independent bookshop. Since the early 1990s she and her partner, Andrew, have lived between the rivers Severn and Wye in a beautiful part of Gloucestershire. Whenever possible, they take advantage of the opportunity to watch wildlife on their doorstep.

Vanessa Watson – 4: Donald and Jeff

Vanessa was Jeff's wife. During Jeff's early research into the golden eagle and beyond, she often accompanied him in his field work and still continues to monitor golden eagle territories that he had monitored. As a family member, she also came to know Donald well – as did their son, Ronan – and understood the significance of Donald's influence in Jeff's life. Vanessa works in rural development at Scottish and European levels, with a special focus on the relationship between people and the environment.

Chris Rollie – 5: Donald Watson

Born and brought up in New Cumnock, Ayrshire, Chris has a BSc (Hons, Biol.) Stirling, and was a science teacher for ten years. He was an RSPB conservation officer in Dumfries and Galloway from 1991, and area manager from 2000 until semi-retirement at end of 2018. He has been chair of Dumfries and Galloway Raptor Study Group since 1991, and chair of the UK Ring Ouzel Study Group since 1998. He was a neighbour, close friend and companion of Donald Watson for 20 years. Chris loves hill and moorland birds particularly. He now volunteers on hen harriers, golden eagles and ring ouzels for RSPB. He is a professional tour guide with Naturetrek and Adventure Canada, and undertakes some freelance bird survey work.

Des Thompson – 6: The Hen Harrier from a beginning in the long, fine summer of 1959 – a prescient eye for beauty and danger

With more than 30 years' experience working in government agencies, Des was the principal adviser on biodiversity and science with NatureScot, Scotland's nature agency. Now a Leverhulme emeritus fellow at UHI North, West and Hebrides, his interests include upland ecosystems and science-policy biodiversity decision making. He is a member (and founder chair for ten years) of the Technical Advisory Group on African and Eurasian raptors supporting the UN Convention on the Conservation of Migratory Species (CMS), and is the CMS COP-appointed councillor for climate change. Publishing more than 15 books, he took his first degree at Paisley College (now University of West Scotland), and PhD and DSc from the University of Nottingham. His very first report, 'Notes on Hen Harriers breeding in East Ross-shire' (1976), was cited in *The Hen Harrier*.

Colin Galbraith – 6: The Hen Harrier from a beginning in the long, fine summer of 1959 – a prescient eye for beauty and danger

Colin has a lifelong interest in nature. He has edited several books on raptors and was chair of the UK Raptor Working Group, which undertook the seminal investigation into the ecology of raptors and their interactions with grouse moors and with racing pigeons. He has worked for many years with the United Nations on a range of global conservation issues. Colin is currently chair of NatureScot and was previously chair of the UK Joint Nature Conservation Committee (JNCC). He has a PhD from the University of Aberdeen on eider ducks, and an honorary professorship at the University of Stirling.

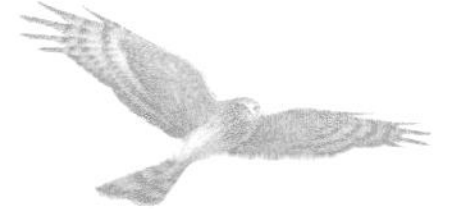

One
Introducing Donald Watson
ROGER CROFTS

> Donald Watson's pictures are delightful and have the great merit of so obviously being painted by an artist who knows his birds in the field – and who knows and can paint that field also.[1]

Donald Watson (1918–2005) is best known as a painter of birds of the highest standard. He painted individual birds, birds in their native habitats, and birds in their natural landscapes. He used pencil, pen and ink, gouache, water colour, scraperboard and occasionally oils. His output was prolific, although it is impossible to even guess the scale of his *oeuvre*. His work was based on meticulous observation of birds in the open air, as an examination of his sketchbooks and notebooks attests. Donald was an illustrator of bird books of his own authorship and those of others, especially in the Poyser series. He provided scraperboard images for many magazine articles about birds and rural life. He was also a leading figure in the nature conservation movement and commented vociferously about the damage to bird habitats, especially of commercial forestry. He was a founder of the Scottish Ornithologists' Club.

At a time when memories seem to become shorter and important people of even the recent past are forgotten, we want to place on record Donald Watson's contributions to birds, nature and the arts. This is why we have brought together a series of essays by those who knew him. We hope that in doing so it will stimulate and inspire current and future generations interested in any aspects of birds, naturally and artistically, to realise their potential and leave their own legacy.

His personal history

A little personal history of Donald is needed to set the scene. He was born at Cranleigh in Surrey on 28 June 1918. His father was a Scot, James George Watson, a banker and financial manager by profession. Interestingly enough, Donald's father spent time in the Congo working for Tanganyika Concessions, alongside the father of his wife-to-be, who worked for Union Minière. His mother, May Vernon Pearson, was English. She was a devoted and talented amateur gardener with greenhouses; and the flowerbeds were legendary within the family. One of three sons (the others being Bruce, the eldest, and Eric Vernon), Donald showed early interest in wildlife and an ability to draw and colour by making a set of Snap cards on different animals at a very young age. An older brother and an aunt and an uncle were all artists so, as he said, 'it was familiar territory for me'.[2]

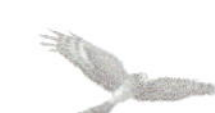

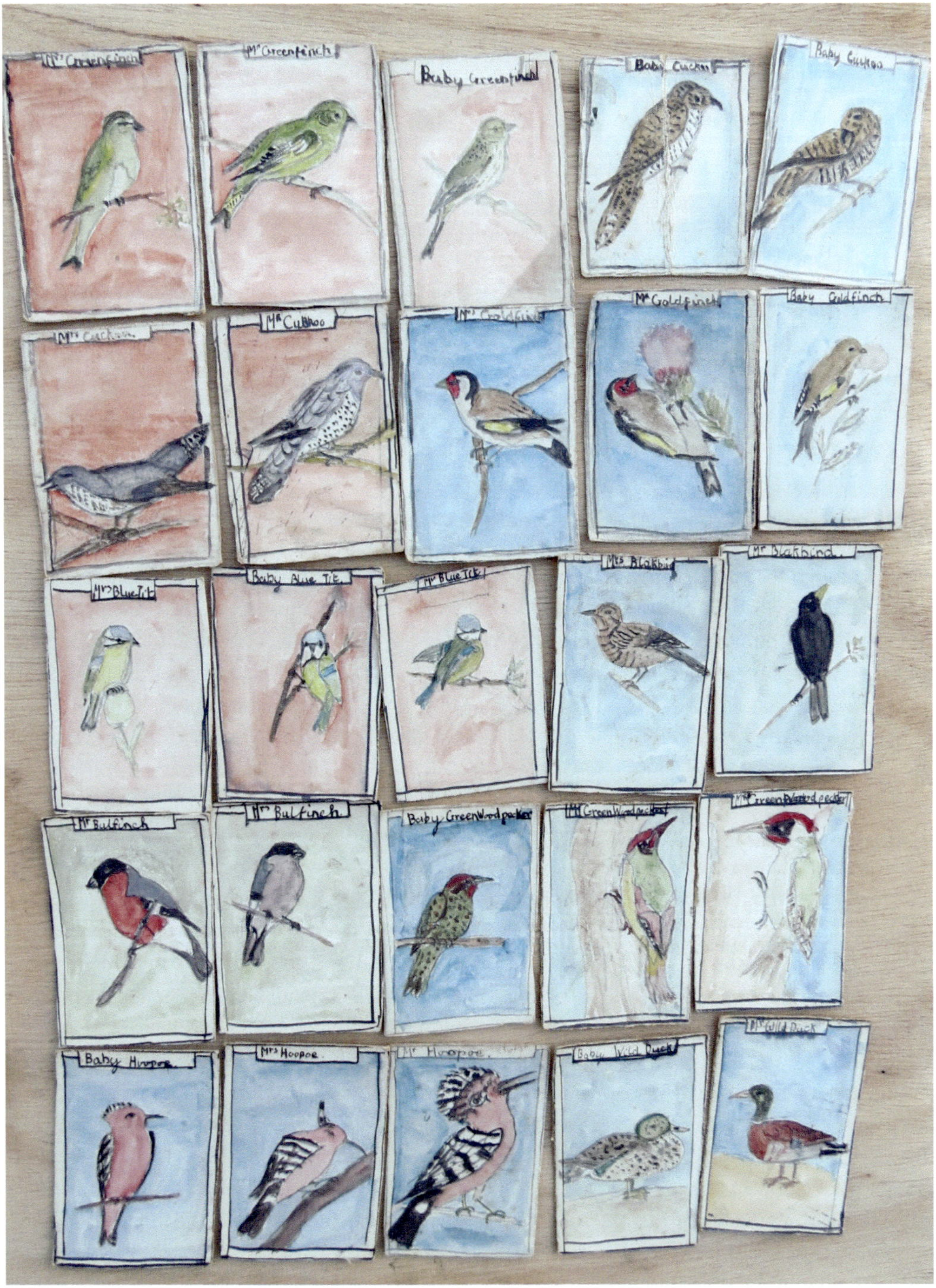

1.1 Above: Snap cards produced at age 8

1.2 Right: Donald Watson painting of rural scene early in his career

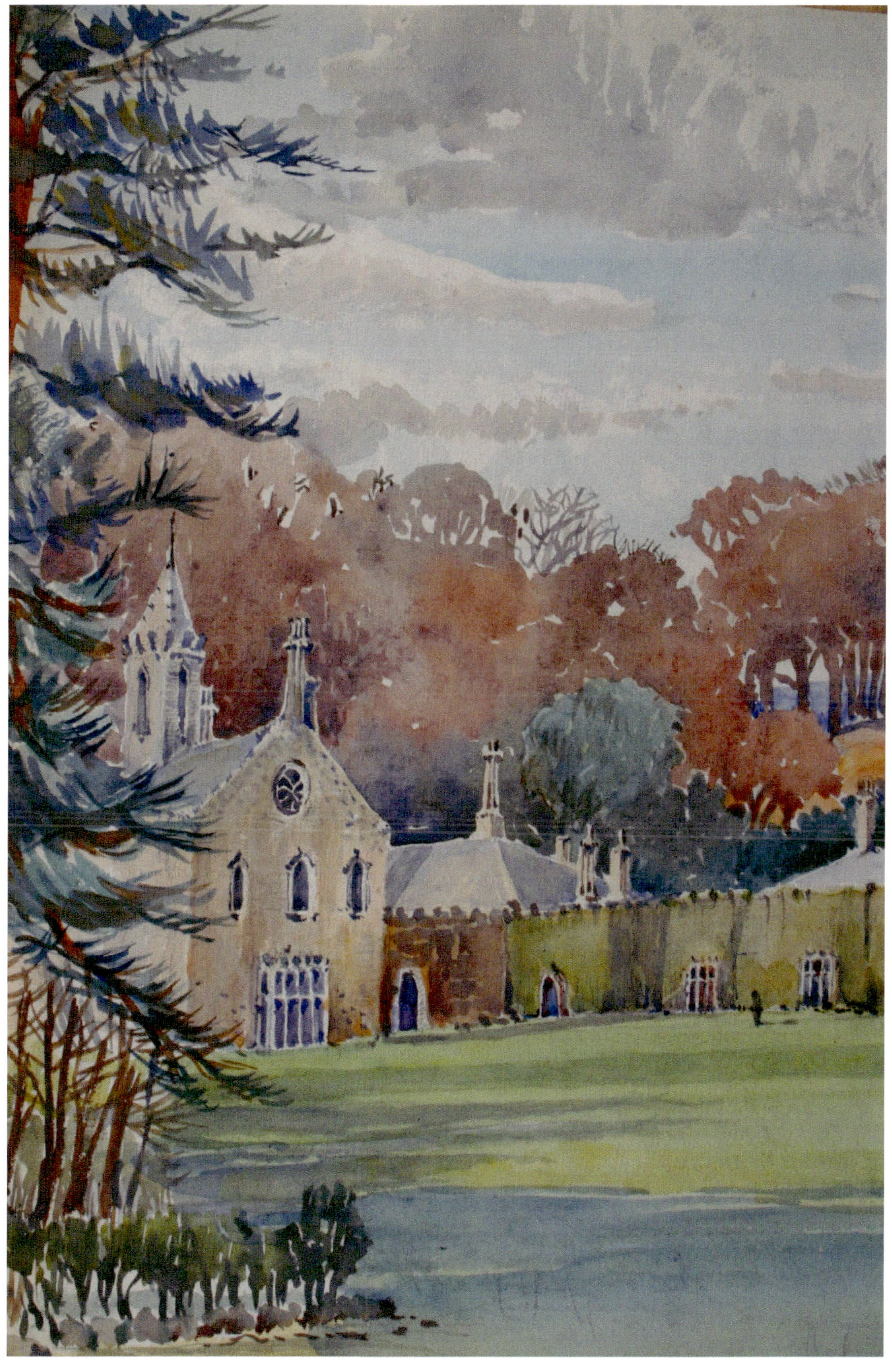

Following his father's death in 1931, his mother moved the family to Edinburgh. At that time Donald was in his early teens, and he spent five years at Edinburgh Academy. Evidence of his academic prowess is easy to discover, given the number of prizes that he won in history and other subjects throughout his time there. In 1934 he won the prestigious RSPB Public Schools Essay Competition, his entry entitled 'Wings and their Uses'. His interest in birds was clearly well known at the school, as his prize for 'the best in Modern History' in Year VII was W.H. Hudson's notable book *Birds and Man*. That he was an inquisitive child is clear from perusal of his copious notebooks from his teenage years.

Despite his ornithological interests, rather than studying biology he stuck to history, the subject that he was best at, and having gained a scholarship to St John's College, Oxford, read for a degree in history there. His interest in art meant that he specialised in the study of Renaissance artists. After graduation, he served in the Royal Artillery of the British Army during the Second World War, based predominantly in India and Burma. There he met others with similar interests in birds and painting, and after being demobbed continued corresponding with them over the years. During his war service, he made the decision to combine art and ornithology as a profession, and in 1946, at the age of 28, began his full-time freelance career as a bird artist. He quickly made an impression in the art world with exhibitions of his paintings at galleries in Edinburgh, Glasgow and London. The rise in his standing in the art world was attested by his first one man show in 1949, set up by Ronnie Wheatley, an art dealer at the Doig, Wilson & Wheatley Gallery in Edinburgh.[3] This was followed by one man shows in many locations around Britain. He was also a regular exhibitor at the Royal Society of Water Colourists and the Royal Scottish Academy. Not surprisingly, given his growing stature in wildlife art, he became a founder member of the Society of Wildlife Artists.

The most momentous period of his personal life was in the late 1940s. As a child he had met Joan Moore in Surrey, and they married in 1950. He was invited by Arthur Duncan, who at the time was the chair of the nascent Nature Conservancy body in Scotland, to stay at the Duncans' farm near the village of Tynron in Nithsdale and paint the birds of the area. In Donald's last book, *In Search of Harriers*, he stated

> I gladly acknowledge the many kindnesses received from the late Sir Arthur Duncan, a Dumfriesshire farmer and landowner who for many years encouraged my painting of birds in landscapes and to whose wide knowledge of natural history I am so greatly indebted.[4]

Donald soon became so entranced by the landscape and bird life of the area that he felt it was a place to set up the family home and studio. Fortuitously, there was a house for sale in the village of St John's Town of Dalry, over the hills from Tynron. A former temperance hotel and originally two separate houses, it was rather larger than he and Joan really needed at the time. In *One Pair of Eyes* he describes his reaction:

> the house was much too big and rambling, but at the back it has an irresistible garden, a slope with a grove of aspens and a mass of daffodils, and an outlook to the Rhinns of Kells … Selfishly I also had my eyes on the doctor's bedroom with a north light for the studio.[5]

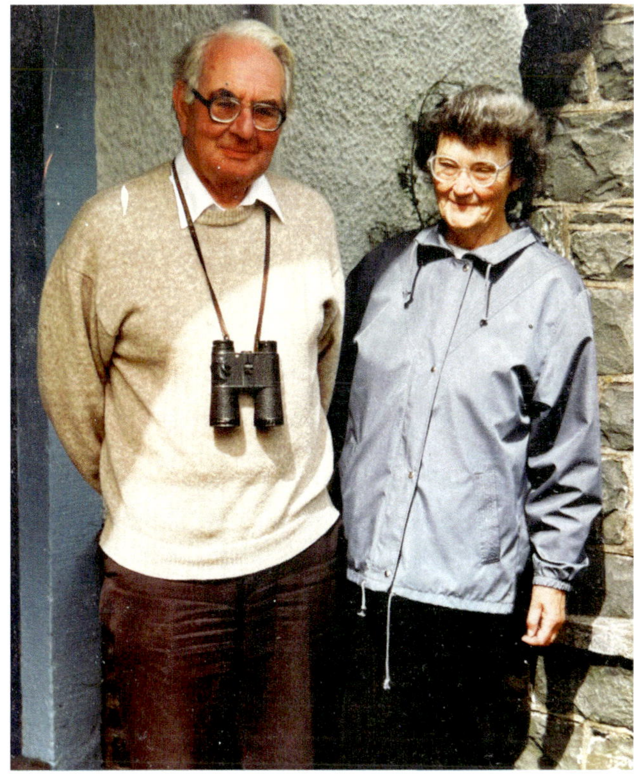

1.3 Left: Donald and Joan at Barone

1.4 Below: Barone: front view with studio window

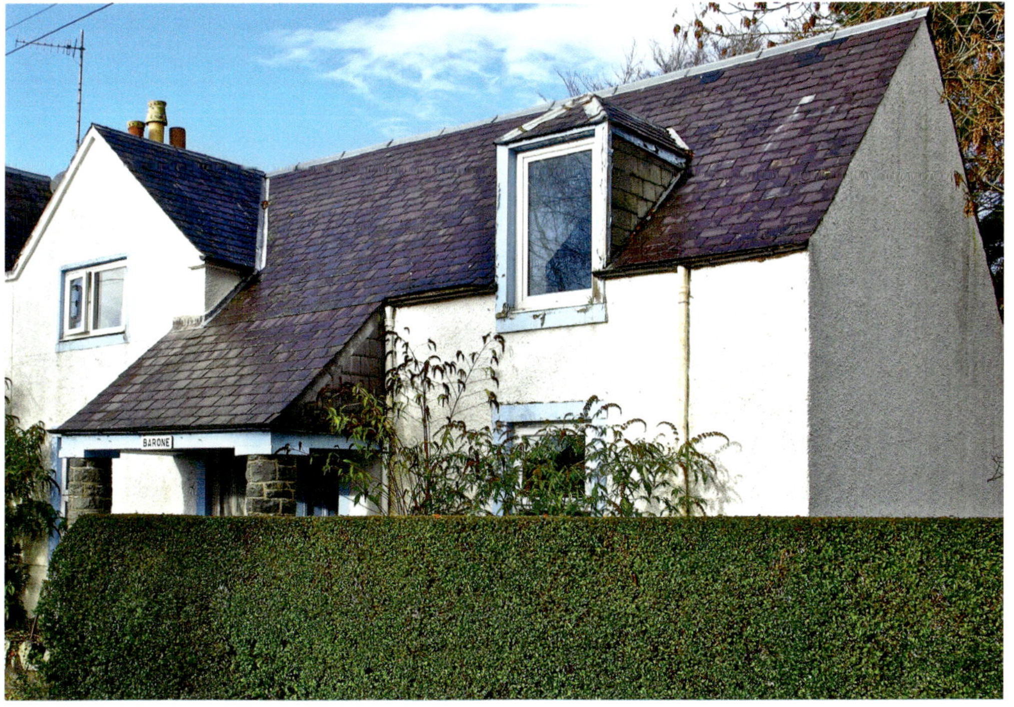

They moved into the house in 1951. Hence began the association with the village, its people and the surrounding area for the rest of his and Joan's lives. It was there that their four children – Pam, Louise, Kate and Jeff – were born. There they grew up before going off to school elsewhere, Jeff to his father's *alma mater*, Edinburgh Academy. That Jeff went on to become the world's leading expert on the golden eagle is partly a reflection of Donald's influence and encouragement, as Jeff's widow reflects later in this book. Donald, in some background notes for an exhibition, described the area as 'a stimulating combination of wilderness and intimacy in the landscape and a rich variety of wildlife'.[6] No wonder he lived in the area for the rest of his days.

An artistic prodigy

Donald clearly was an artistic prodigy and an excellent observer of birds. He says that he began drawing animals, and especially birds, when he was about four years old, much encouraged by his older brother, Eric, who had similar leanings. He went on bird-nesting expeditions, and he copied pictures of birds from books, as well as keeping diaries with watercolour drawings done from observation and memory when he was nine years old. He describes a visit to Archibald Thorburn's studio as a memorable experience, Thorburn being one of the leading bird artists of

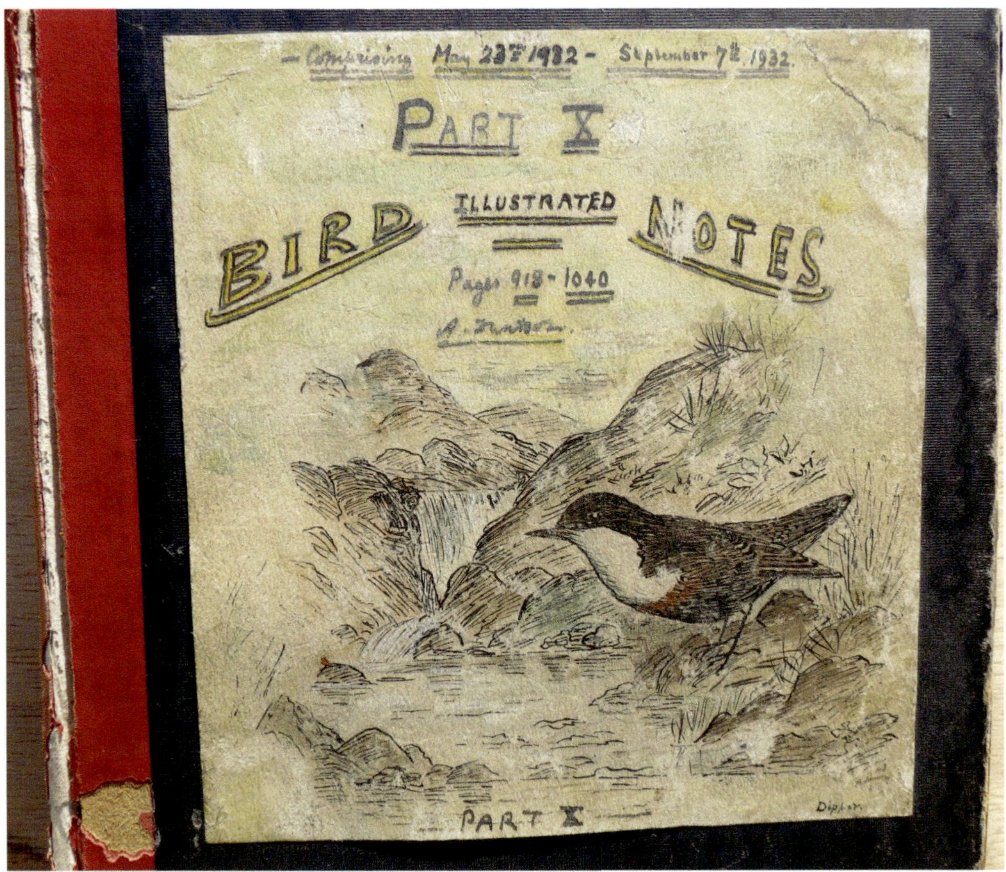

1.5 Page of Granton notebook by Donald aged 14

his day. The notebooks he produced in his early teens, while observing and counting birds on the shore at Granton in Edinburgh, display his extraordinary talent for translating his observations into accurate depictions of the hundreds of species he was seeing.[7]

Once settled in Edinburgh, he seems to have spent a great deal of time on the shores of the Firth of Forth at Granton. Here he honed both his skill as an acute observer of birds and the ability to distinguish, for example, between the many varieties of seabirds that he saw there. Indeed, one of his notebooks has an illustration of 60 species of seabirds, along with two wonderful collections entitled *Glimpses at Golden Eye* and *Impressions of Warblers*. At the same time, he met and came under the wing of George Waterston, a member of the Edinburgh printing family and a doyen of birdwatchers and recorders. Out of that association came Donald's introduction to the bird community of the Lothians, becoming a founder member of the Midlothian Ornithological Club, the forerunner of the Scottish Ornithologists' Club. It was also the start of many visits to the Isle of May, a noted hotspot for seeing migrant species.

Donald's own perspective is given in an undated note:

> I observe wildlife, especially birds, both as an artist and a naturalist. Without the excitement of watching out in the countryside my pictures would hardly begin. The changing colours of the landscape are a great stimulation for my art. Often I prefer a composition in which an animal (frequently a bird) is a vital but small focal interest in spacious surroundings, but the latter can be no more than a richly textured foreground. Tonal truth and lively drawing are high priorities. There is a challenge in the mobility of wildlife subjects. Meaningful, spontaneous postures of flying, feeding or preening birds are testing to do. While delighting in the beautiful patterns and markings of plumage, I try not to let them cancel out the overall softness of feathers. I try to capture the effects of light on colours of wildlife and landscape. Season, weather, a sense of place and atmosphere mean a lot to me.[8]

What an insight into his skills, approaches and experiences.

His career

Through the 1950s Donald Watson studied the work of other bird artists. Bruno Liljefors, widely regarded as the greatest bird artist of his generation, was his inspiration, and Donald closely studied his books.[9] He was also passionate about the French Impressionists, and this is reflected in some of his early paintings, which have an 'impressionist' element to the landscape whilst depicting birds with great accuracy. The stairs leading to his studio exemplified his interest in the work of other artists: Keith Brockie, John Busby, Eric Ennion, George Henry, Cloe and R.B. Talbot Kelly and Archibald Thorburn, among others.

The following 30 years saw him at his most prolific as a bird artist for exhibitions, for private commissions and for illustrations in his own books and those of prominent ornithologists. He produced the plates for *The Oxford Book of Birds*, showing birds in their family groups and set within their habitat. Clearly his reputation as a depicter of birds in their habitat surroundings with verve and accuracy saw him fully established as a leading bird artist in the early 1960s, when he was in his mid-thirties.

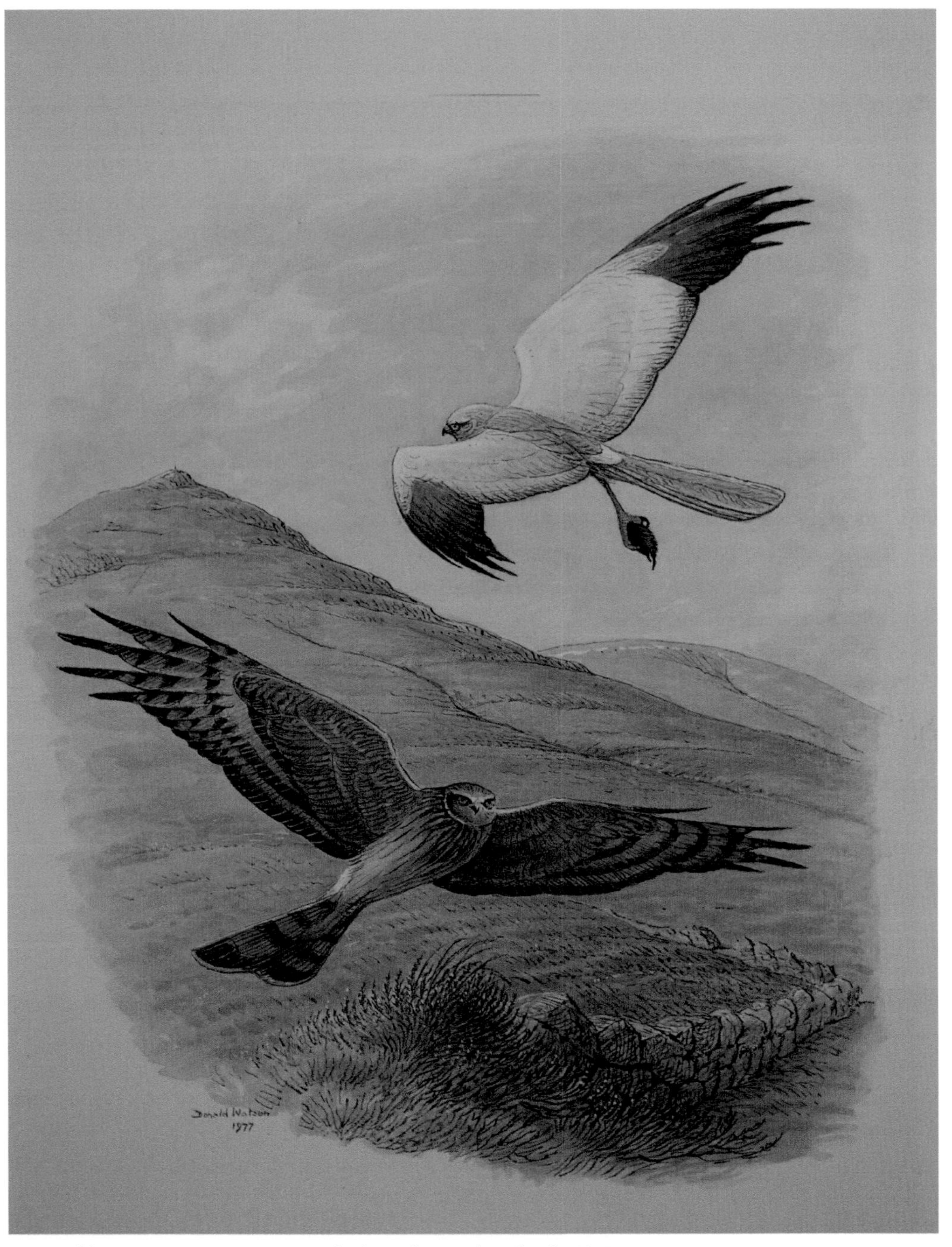

1.6 Donald Watson painting: Hen Harrier food pass from male to female, 1977

Donald went on to produce five more books.[10] His ornithological expertise was, and remains, high through his work on the highly persecuted hen harrier. His monograph in the Poyser series remains the standard work on this bird, to the extent that in 2017 it was reprinted, 40 years after its original publication. Posthumously, his family has had his more personal account of this bird, together with his outstanding paintings, published as *In Search of Harriers*. His knowledge of individual species and his ability to depict them in their habitat surroundings is exemplified further in his book *Birds of Moor and Mountain*. Donald was, however, more than a bird artist and ornithologist. He was also an evocative writer about nature, the influence of light and season, and the importance of watching, sketching and painting out of doors. He was also an observer and – increasingly later in life – a commentator and campaigner about poor land management practices and illegal persecution of species. These traits are well reflected in his two books, *A Bird Artist in Scotland* and *One Pair of Eyes*.

A prolific letter writer, he had a long correspondence with his older brother, Eric. He corresponded with other bird artists, most especially with Robert Gillmor, the leading figure in the Society of Wildlife Artists and a very fine bird artist himself. Donald became friends with David Bannerman, whose classic books he illustrated.[11] This friendship was reflected in a perceptive and kindly tribute when Bannerman died in 1979, reflecting Donald's own attribute of always seeing the best in people. These writers and artists provided great support to Donald when some of his publication ideas came to naught and when earlier contracts were conveniently ignored during takeovers in the publishing world. Fortunately, Donald survived these setbacks.

It is clear from reading *Birdwatchers' Year* and *One Pair of Eyes* that Donald Watson took ventures out of doors as frequently as possible to observe, sketch and take notes on birds. He seemed undaunted by the season, the weather and the time of day or night. He must have been made of stern stuff, and had a strong constitution given his walks on to the Rhinns of Kells and in Grobdale, two of his favourite places where, whatever the weather, he would sit outside until he got a view of birds after many hours of patient waiting. He quotes the protection afforded by what he calls his 'harrier hat' on 7 July in *Birdwatchers' Year*:

> At the first of the two Harrier nests mentioned on 12th June we saw the cock drop prey before we went near. No sign of the hen at first, then as we collected one of the three big young from a ditch, we heard her shrill whickering, and she came at us in a long low dive and thumped the back of my head with her foot. My old 'harrier hat', well holed with claw marks, is some protection. As she banked and turned to attack again, I tried to memorise flight attitudes and the marvellous chequered pattern of her underwings, always more exciting than in anticipation.[12]

The artist

Over the years, Donald became the go-to artist to illustrate several of the monographs published by the redoubtable husband-and-wife team, Trevor and Anna Poyser. Starting with the illustrations for Derek Ratcliffe's scientifically ground-breaking book on the peregrine falcon (published three years after *The Hen Harrier*), Donald and Derek became firm friends and collaborators as the correspondence from Derek demonstrates, as well as his references to his interaction with Donald in his New Naturalist series book, *Galloway and the Borders*.[13] As Donald was the main illustrator

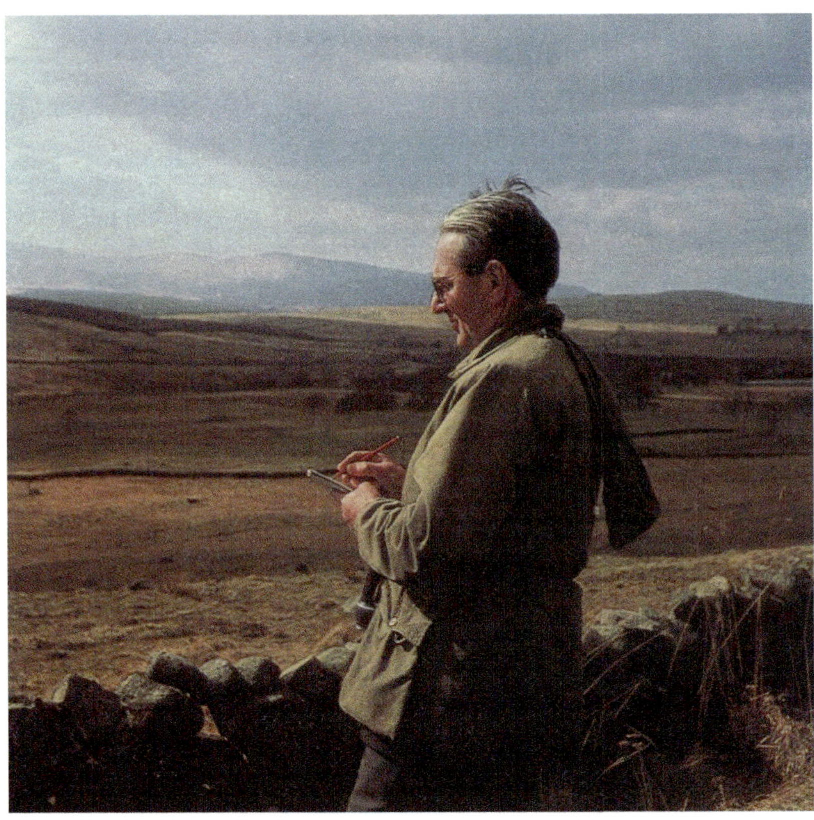

1.7 Left: Donald in the field

1.8 Right: Donald Watson cover painting for *Birds in Scotland*

for the books *Waders* and *Greenshanks*, written by Desmond and Maimie Nethersole-Thompson, they became close collaborators, something that connected their sons, Jeff and Des, who were to become close colleagues in Scottish Natural Heritage. What progeny!

There was a regular demand through the post for commissions for a specific painting; most of these Donald accepted. The response from each commissioner on receiving the painting was unreservedly ecstatic, saying how much they enjoyed being able to see the painting on the wall of their house every day. A typical response is the one from Eric Hosking, the outstanding wildlife photographer, writing in 1979: 'we are so delighted with the paintings and so thrilled to have two of your pictures on our walls. We know they will bring great pleasure in the years to come, and they will take us back to those lovely islands [Seychelles with Jeff]'.[14] If there was ever a comment from those purchasing Donald's paintings, it was that he charged far too little, but his modesty did not allow himself to set prices above what he thought they justified.

It is quite impossible to guess how many paintings Donald created through his career, but it must have been in the thousands. We shall never know how many, either, as any records of purchasers have long since vanished. The nearest we have is the catalogues of exhibitions where he displayed his works. An attempt has been made in Annex 2 to list these, but this list cannot be regarded as definitive. His fame clearly meant that he was asked to exhibit at ornithological conferences around Britain. He also was frequently requested to produce paintings for calendars, some produced by local traders such as a haulage company in Dumfries, and the Curwen Press

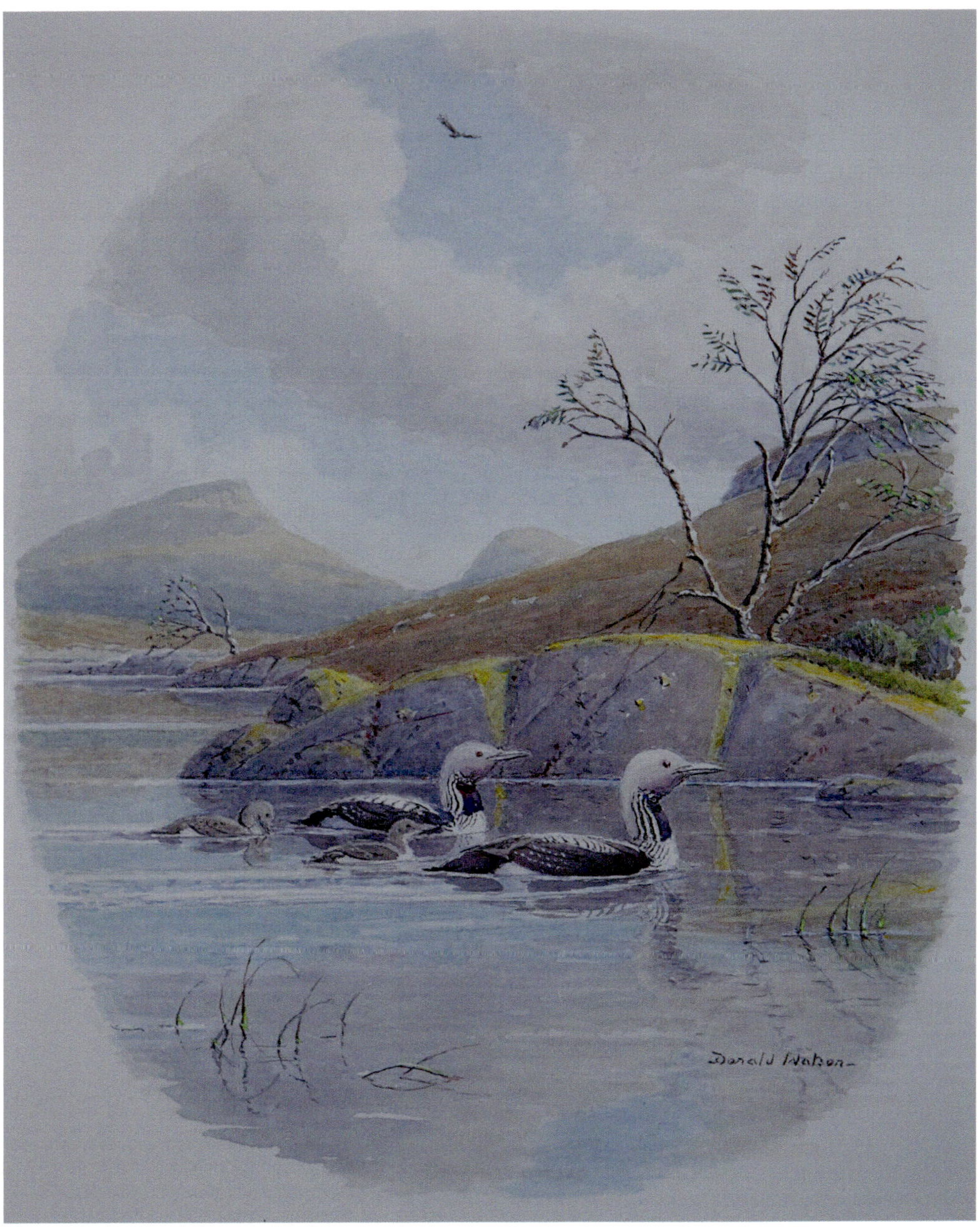

British Wild Life calendars and the BTO calendars. He also had greetings cards printed for his own use and for sale through the British Museum and the BTO. His loyalty to local companies is perhaps best reflected in the fact that he used the same framer, Coopers of Shambellie, near Dumfries, to frame his paintings until they ceased trading, when he used Roger Blamire of Gelston Framers (whose son Leo now runs the framing business). Like most artists, Donald liked to have similar frames for his paintings in exhibitions.

He describes, in briefing notes of an unknown date, the development of his skills.

> One aspect was filling of sketchbooks with on the spot drawings and notes, particularly of birds, but for a long time these were secondary to my love of the landscape. This led me to attempt outdoor painting in almost all kinds of weather except pouring rain and I believe this was of enormous value in teaching me to observe tones, colours, textures, and light effects. I often got lost in the complexity which nature presented and only gradually began to understand the need for more selectivity and simplicity.[15]

Donald's ability to produce, almost at the proverbial drop of a hat, scraperboard images of both birds and rural scenes made him a natural source of drawings for magazines. Over the years he became one of the main illustrators for *The Countryman* magazine, drawing to order illustrations to match articles on many aspects of country life. He was also a frequent illustrator for the mainstream bird magazines in Britain, such as *British Birds*. More recently, his sketches have been a fruitful source for the compilation of a book about walks around Fingask Castle in the Carse of Gowrie: *Jackdaws and Other Friends*.[16]

His paintings are still collected by many followers. Not only do they adorn the walls of the homes of his family and close friends, but they are also on the walls of many houses in St John's Town of Dalry and The Glenkens area of Galloway, where he and his wife Joan lived from the early 1950s until their deaths. His paintings are exhibited in public collections in Belfast, Dumfries and Glasgow. They are still sought after by private collectors as evidenced by sales at, for example, the Wildlife Art Gallery at Lavenham in Suffolk and the McGill Duncan Gallery in Castle Douglas until their recent closure.

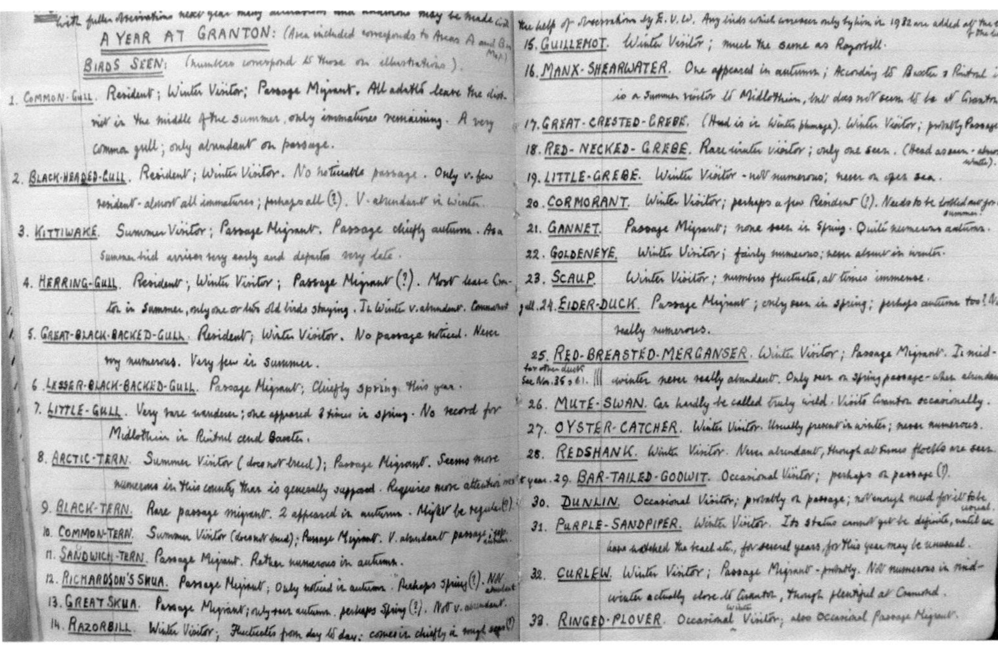

With fuller observation next year many [illegible] may be made with the help of observations by E. V. W. Any birds which were seen only by him in 1932 are added at the end of the list.

A YEAR AT GRANTON: (Area included corresponds to Areas A and B on Map.)

BIRDS SEEN: (numbers correspond to those on illustrations).

1. COMMON-GULL. Resident; Winter Visitor; Passage Migrant. All adults leave the district in the middle of the summer, only immatures remaining. A very common gull; only abundant on passage.
2. BLACK-HEADED-GULL. Resident; Winter Visitor. No noticeable passage. Only v. few resident - almost all immatures; perhaps all (?). V. abundant in winter.
3. KITTIWAKE. Summer Visitor; Passage Migrant. Passage chiefly autumn. As a Summer bird arrives very early and departs very late.
4. HERRING-GULL. Resident; Winter Visitor; Passage Migrant (?). Most leave Granton in Summer, only one or two old birds staying. In Winter v. abundant. Commonest gull.
5. GREAT-BLACK-BACKED-GULL. Resident; Winter Visitor. No passage noticed. Never very numerous. Very few in summer.
6. LESSER-BLACK-BACKED-GULL. Passage Migrant; Chiefly spring this year.
7. LITTLE-GULL. Very rare wanderer; one appeared 3 times in spring. No record for Midlothian in Rintoul and Baxter.
8. ARCTIC-TERN. Summer Visitor (does not breed); Passage Migrant. Seems more numerous in this county than is generally supposed. Requires more attention next year.
9. BLACK-TERN. Rare passage migrant. 2 appeared in autumn. Might be regular (?).
10. COMMON-TERN. Summer Visitor (does not breed); Passage Migrant. V. abundant passage, esp. autumn.
11. SANDWICH-TERN. Passage Migrant. Rather numerous in autumn.
12. RICHARDSON'S SKUA. Passage Migrant; Only noticed in autumn. Perhaps spring (?). Not abundant.
13. GREAT SKUA. Passage Migrant; only seen autumn. perhaps Spring (?). Not v. abundant.
14. RAZORBILL. Winter Visitor; Fluctuates from day to day: comes in chiefly in rough seas (?)
15. GUILLEMOT. Winter Visitor; much the same as Razorbill.
16. MANX-SHEARWATER. One appeared in autumn; According to Baxter & Rintoul it is a Summer visitor to Midlothian, but does not seem to be at Granton.
17. GREAT-CRESTED-GREBE. (Head is in Winter plumage). Winter Visitor; probably Passage
18. RED-NECKED-GREBE. Rare winter visitor; only one seen. (Head as seen - about winter).
19. LITTLE-GREBE. Winter Visitor - not numerous; never on open sea.
20. CORMORANT. Winter Visitor; perhaps a few Resident (?). Needs to be looked out for in summer.
21. GANNET. Passage Migrant; none seen in Spring. Quite numerous autumn.
22. GOLDENEYE. Winter Visitor; fairly numerous; never absent in winter.
23. SCAUP. Winter Visitor; numbers fluctuate, at times immense.
24. EIDER-DUCK. Passage Migrant; only seen in spring; perhaps autumn too! Never really numerous.
25. RED-BREASTED-MERGANSER. Winter Visitor; Passage Migrant. In mid-winter never really abundant. Only seen on spring passage - when abundant. (for other ducks see Nos. 36 & 61.)
26. MUTE-SWAN. Can hardly be called truly wild. Visits Granton occasionally.
27. OYSTER-CATCHER. Winter Visitor. Usually present in winter; never numerous.
28. REDSHANK. Winter Visitor. Never abundant, though at times flocks are seen.
29. BAR-TAILED-GODWIT. Occasional Visitor; perhaps on passage (?).
30. DUNLIN. Occasional Visitor; probably on passage; not enough need for it to be usual.
31. PURPLE-SANDPIPER. Winter Visitor. Its status cannot yet be definite, until we have watched the coast etc., for several years, for this year may be unusual.
32. CURLEW. Winter Visitor; Passage Migrant - probably. Not numerous in mid-winter actually close to Granton, though plentiful at Cramond.
33. RINGED-PLOVER. Occasional Winter Visitor; also Occasional Passage Migrant.

1.9 Page of Granton sketchbook, 1934

His standing

Donald's standing in the bird and wildlife art was extremely high, as attested by reviews of his work described in more detail in Chapter 7. Nicholas Hammond in his book *Twentieth Century Wildlife Artists* includes Donald as one of the 43 'of the world's foremost artists chosen to represent wildlife art of the twentieth century at its very best'. Donald is listed alongside Sir Peter Scott, Bruno Liljefors, Keith Shackleton, Archibald Thorburn, Eric Ennion and Robert Gillmor, among others. Given that Donald met Archibald Thorburn as a young boy when living in Surrey, Hammond states categorically that 'there is something of Thorburn in Watson's own work, but very often his bird paintings are as good as, if not better than, Thorburn. He has a technique that really shows the mouldings of the bird's body'.[17] Additionally, Chris Rollie recounts that Donald always regarded the compliment on his painting of geese by goose expert Hugh Blair as one of the highest he ever received. He was especially proud of this, given Blair saw him as the best painter of geese when both were friends and colleagues of Peter Scott.

Praise also came from Stanley Cursiter, the outstanding Orcadian landscape painter and director of the National Gallery of Scotland. In a letter dated January 1969, he wrote:

> It seems to me that you have the priceless gift of eyes that see things in correct relationship and that all you had to do was to develop that gift and master your technique through experience.

Cursiter strongly advised Donald against going to art college as he would be taught 'a great deal of irrelevant nonsense about their ideas on what constitutes art'. He compares Donald's eyes with those of Henry Raeburn, concluding that

> his [Raeburn's] wonderful eyes allowed him to develop the technique to record what he saw, but it was the precision of his powers of "seeing" that allowed him to do so. You have the same kind of eyes – good luck to them.[18]

Accolades followed. From 1969 to 1972 Donald was elected president of the Scottish Ornithologists' Club, and in 1986, on the society's 50th anniversary, honorary president, a position he held until his death. Also, in 1980 he was only the third person to be awarded honorary member status of the SOC, for his distinguished service to Scottish ornithology. At the same time, Dr John Berry, the founder director of statutory nature conservation in Scotland, was given the same status. The naming of the gallery after Donald at the club's new headquarters at Aberlady in East Lothian in 2005 reflected the esteem which he was, and indeed still is, held in the Scottish ornithological community.

His engagement with the wider ornithological community was intense, partly a result of his own work which led to the publication of his outstanding monograph in *The Hen Harrier*, partly because of his acute ability at recording change and partly because of his growing interest in bird and habitat conservation. As a result, he was a member of the Council of the BTO, contributed to the work of the Rare Breeding Birds Panel of Britain, was a member of the South West Scotland Raptor Study Group and, in the later 1980s, a recorder and compiler of the Scottish Ornithologists' Club's annual bird reports for Dumfries and Galloway.

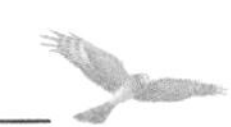

Donald Watson

1918-2005

Born in Surrey, Donald came to live in Edinburgh as a child. He was an acclaimed artist, naturalist and author, best known for his evocative depictions of the Galloway countryside, where he lived most of his life, an[d] his classic studies of the Hen Harrier.

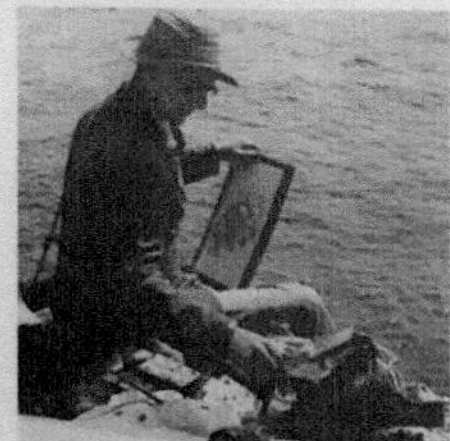

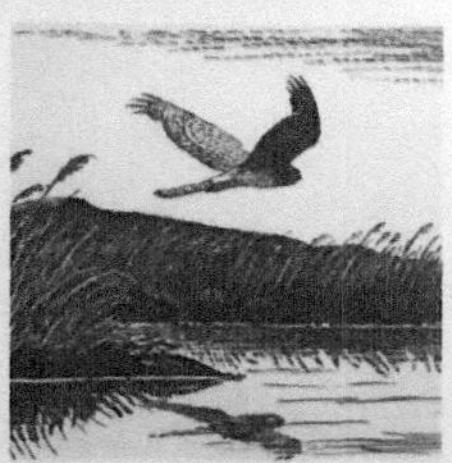

He was a founder member of the Society of Wildlife Artists and the Scottish Ornithologists' Club, of which he was a former President and Honorary President.

This gallery is named in his honour and this plaque commemorates the centenary of his birth on 28 June 1918.

1.10 Donald Watson Gallery plaque at SOC HQ

He enjoyed giving talks to local groups around Scotland, and the audiences certainly appreciated them. Following a talk to the Stirling Branch of the Scottish Ornithologists' Club in 1969 the secretary wrote to him as follows:

> We feel very privileged to have been treated to such a scholastic survey of some of the great bird artists from the earliest days and given such a lucid explanation by one who really knows what makes them great. Crowning it all was the splendid survey which you treated us to of your own work amplified by your explanations of what you are aiming at in the various paintings.[19]

It is clear from talking to fellow residents in St John's Town of Dalry that Donald was a well-known and highly respected member of the community. As Peter Holt puts it:

> Donald and Joan are buried in the peaceful graveyard of Dalry parish Kirk, where Spotted Flycatchers perch lightly on the mossy tombstones and catch insects in the dappled summer air.[20]

Their home was a gathering place for many ornithologists and artists, where Donald and Joan provided warm hospitality. Indeed, it was a place where visiting birdwatchers and ornithologists and artists made a beeline to. Long evenings were had with Donald reminiscing about birds with his pipe filled with Benson and Hedges Mellow Virginia Flake or Condor ready rubbed, and sharing a dram of Whyte & MacKay with his guests, and Highland Park with his friends.

As Jo Miller, a locally born and noted Scottish musician, told me recently, she played the fiddle and Donald danced to her tunes. Joan, his beloved wife, played a vitally important part in their local life, not only bringing up the children, but also teaching domestic science at the local junior secondary school. She is still fondly remembered in the village, with many saying, 'Ah, Mrs Watson taught me, and I still remember her well.' For at least one season in the late 1950s, Donald was appointed by the education authority as an uncertificated teacher of art in Dalry Further Education Centre. Some homes in the area resemble Donald Watson galleries, given the number of paintings owned and proudly displayed by owners. A reaction from one was

> As I write I look at a truly magnificent picture which you painted for me to be given for my birthday. I cannot begin to describe how thrilled I am by it. I have always admired your work and I cannot praise too highly your painting of a view which I know and love.[21]

That is an oft-repeated sentiment in the area. I know how highly these paintings, included the one quoted, are still treasured by their owners.

This book

As will be clear from this introductory essay, Donald had many interests, and this book provides reflections on these. It begins with an appreciation of Donald as a bird artist, by John Threlfall, who knew him well and is a successful bird artist and author himself, formerly living and working in Galloway. The family's perspective is given by his daughter Louise in consultation with her sisters, Pam and Kate. Donald's influence on his son Jeff is reflected by Jeff's widow, Vanessa Watson. Chris Rollie, the former Dumfries and Galloway Area Manager of RSPB and a long-time resident in St John's Town of Dalry, provides deep insights from his many years of talking with Donald and going out in the field with him. Donald's work as an ornithologist, best reflected in his monograph *The Hen Harrier*, is reviewed by Des Thompson and Colin Galbraith, themselves noted ornithological scientists who work in the statutory nature conservation agencies. This is followed by my review of Donald's status as a writer, quoting extensively from reviews of his work published at the time and reflecting on them. I have also written the chapter on Donald's role in conservation and

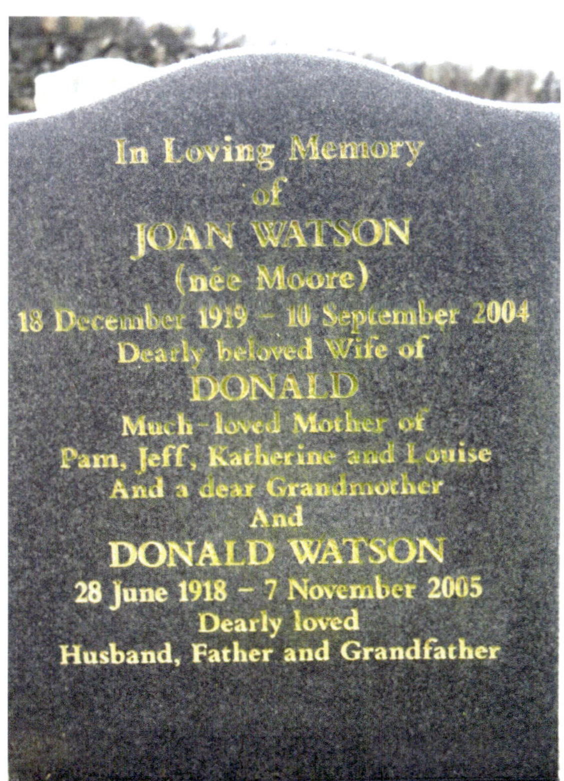

1.11 Donald and Joan Watson's gravestone in Dalry Cemetery

opposing damage to nature, based on the many items Donald wrote and the conversations he had with so many like-minded colleagues in the nature conservation community. Finally, I have introduced the Watson Birds project. Annexes provide lists of Donald's authored works the books he illustrated and, where information is available, the exhibitions where his paintings were shown.

> In my kind of painting I am happiest relating birds to their environment. My eyes respond to colour, tone, light and modelling of forms, whether of living creatures or land masses.[22]

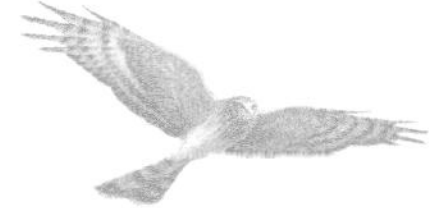

Two

Donald Watson the artist

JOHN THRELFALL

> It is that sense of place, the bewitching atmosphere of a precious moment witnessed and the audacious skill to render that onto paper using a sympathetic medium, a discerning eye for colour, an intuitive gift for composition and all combined with a stringent ornithological accuracy that distinguishes Donald's work from his peers.
>
> John Threlfall[1]

My introduction to Donald

I first met Donald at his home and studio in Dalry back in the early 1980s. At the time I was working for the British Geological Survey and during that summer we were in Dumfries and Galloway, based for a few weeks at nearby Balmaclellan. I had been trying my hand at a few bird drawings, and through a mutual friend a visit was arranged. Donald generously gave up a couple of hours to show me his gallery of paintings on the walls of their home, talking effusively about the ones that were not his! Back then, this was a privileged education for me as someone with very little knowledge of the bird art world. The highlight, though, was to go up the stairs into his studio. There was that big window with its north light overlooking the garden, the book-lined walls, the scattering of sketchbooks, drawings, illustrations and paintings, the jars of brushes and a large oil of a kestrel's nest, with well-grown youngsters, on the easel.

I was a bit lost in awe and wonder, to be honest. It was the first artist's studio of any description that I had visited, and to have this exclusive access into the hidden world of a master bird artist was both daunting and inspiring. I remember his modesty and humility more than any details of the conversation we had. He was troubled by the painting on the easel; it was not quite working for him, and he asked for my thoughts. My only thought was that it looked fantastic! He tried to tease out of me a more insightful critique, but my lack of experience and knowledge was only ever going to be a hindrance rather than a help on that one.

At Donald's insistence, I now had to show him my fledgling efforts. I cannot now recall what I did show him that day, but I do well remember his kind, thoughtful, insightful and generous words that set me on my own bird art path. I left there with a repurposed focus, a clarity and determination … as well as a deep well of gratitude to this great man and artist.

Donald was a founder member of the Society of Wildlife Artists (SWLA) when it launched in 1964, becoming its first honorary member in 2002. Some 43 years later, I was also elected a full member, just too late to relay the news to him and thank him for the wise words and counsel that had helped propel me to that proud moment in my life. I am, though, now perhaps a bit better placed to appraise his work and legacy.

Donald the artist

I moved to Dumfries and Galloway in 1991, and one of the first things I did was to buy and read *A Bird Artist in Scotland*,[2] Donald's autobiographical account of his bird-fused upbringing, his military service years and his eventual move to Galloway. A significant portion of the book is a selection of diary entries for 1987, all beautifully illustrated with his paintings and black-and-white illustrations.

It was those paintings that so evoked the Galloway landscapes I wanted to get to know: 'Golden Eagles over a crag, South West Scotland'; 'Goosanders on the River Ken'; 'Greenland White-fronted Geese by Loch Ken' – these, and many more, only whetted my appetite for the landscapes and wildlife to be experienced. His account of moving to Galloway in 1951, with its 'intimate appeal', is brimming with palpable excitement at what he could discover just within a walk or cycle-ride away from Barone in Dalry. It mirrored my own feelings on moving to the Solway coast 40 years on.

If we look closely at his 1978 painting of shelduck and waders on the Dee Estuary, for example (Fig 2.1), it exudes atmosphere and mood through the subtleties of colour. A glowering sky threatening to overwhelm the sparkle of

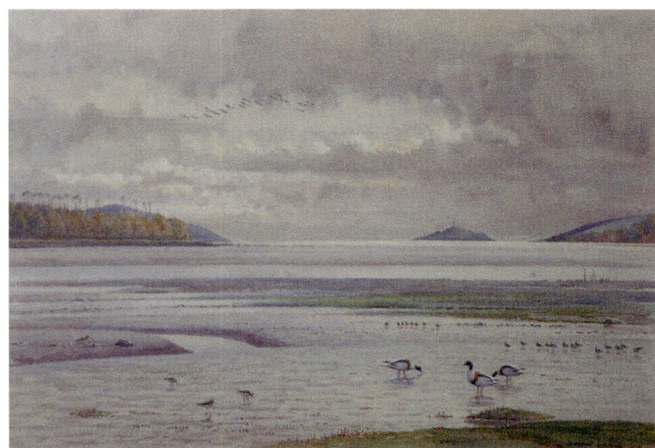

2.1 Donald Watson painting: Shelduck and Waders on the Dee Estuary, 1978

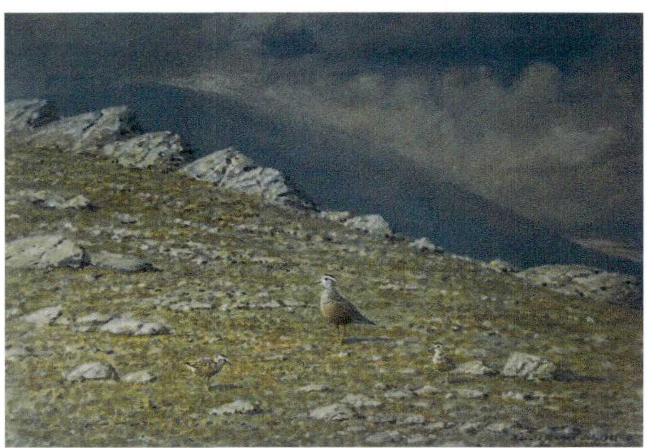

2.2 Donald Watson painting: Dotterel, 1983

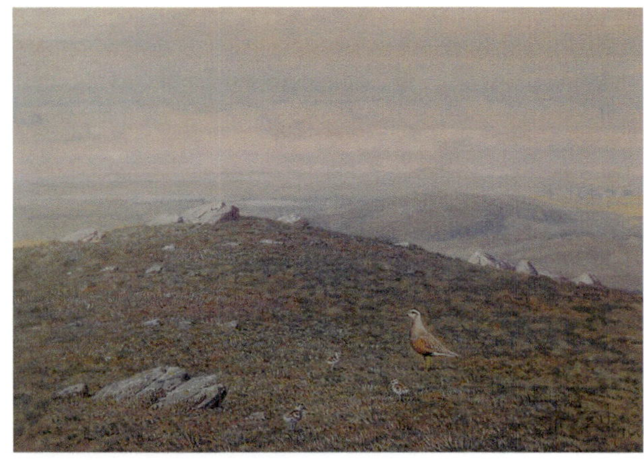

2.3 Donald Watson painting: Dotterel, 1975

sunlight contrasting with the tranquil foreground of quietly feeding and roosting birds. The horizon line that divides the painting in half contravenes accepted compositional conventions, but also adds an edginess to the moment as the imminent change in the weather from the west pulls across the scene. The softness of the gouache-on-paper medium that Donald used to such wondrous effect, and the use of harmonious colours, are challenged by the realities of the place and the day; the vastness of the light-filled estuary space, the restless sky and the tensions within the symmetry of the picture rectangle.

Donald, it seems was not shy of contradicting the accepted compositional wisdoms of the day if it accorded a certain tension and sense of drama to the painting. The dotterel family high on a Galloway hillside (Fig 2.2), caught centre-stage by a burst of bright sunlight on an otherwise dark, maybe even stormy, day. As an art tutor myself, I would never advocate slashing the painting in half with that harsh, jagged diagonal. What that does achieve is to unnerve the viewer, to intensify the feeling of weather-induced foreboding, and further concentrates the attention onto those fragile scraps of life that have to cope with every condition that the mountain environment can throw at them. Here is an artist who has no doubt witnessed this situation and is using all his consummate skills and understanding to not only replicate a vision and feeling in his own heart and mind, but also involve the viewer in that visceral moment as well. The best art creates an emotional response in the viewer, and this does it perfectly.

Contrast that painting with Fig 2.3, again of dotterel. So similar in so many ways, but an altogether gentler experience. One of those high-top days when you do not want to come back down. You can luxuriate in the softness of the day, your relaxed attention wandering into the distance, floating through thin veils of air to distant lochs. When you are ready, you can return to the dotterel family, knowing that they are safe under the always alert and watchful eye of the adult male bird. We can enjoy the precocial independence of the youngsters as they forage for prey items in their just-beginning lives.

I am not aware of any breeding dotterel in the Galloway Hills in recent times, so Donald has given us not only two treasured experiences to savour in their very different ways, but also the documented historical and much lamented demise of these beautiful waders on our mountains.

Ornithologist, writer and artist as one

These paintings are where the ornithologist and the artist meld together with a force that many wildlife artists fail to grasp or attain. From my point of view this is Donald's true legacy, and it elevates him high in the pantheon of European bird art. With his archival observations in both paint and word I suspect that his legacy may continue to grow, our sense of longing for more bird-rich times aching all the more when we review Donald's work. The acute lens of time focuses increasingly on the content of his paintings as much as on the artistic flair of process.

This is particularly true of his Galloway paintings, simply because he was such an adept painter of the landscape. For those who know Galloway well from a geographical perspective, the exact location of each piece is clear; we can go and stand where he stood to paint, and compare the landscape he saw with the realities of today and the change therein. We also have his fascinating diary entries to supplement the artistic output, to flesh out the visual documentation. But when all is said and done, only so much can be said in pencil or paint, and many an artist is equally compelled to make notes or expand upon their thoughts and feelings at greater length through the written word.

Artistic techniques

Two artists who Donald freely admits were a strong influence, the Scot Archibald Thorburn and the Swede Bruno Liljefors, were similarly acute observers of the natural world. Their art in particular stresses the vital importance of habitat and environment just as much as the bird or animal and the indissoluble relationship between them. Indeed, these two artists, born in the same year (1860), were among the first to articulate these relationships onto canvas or paper, and that lineage of influence very much was to include Donald Watson (as well as artists such as Peter Scott, Keith Shackleton and Carl Rungius). As a 12-year-old boy, Donald had in fact been able to visit Thorburn in his nearby studio as they were both then living in Surrey. It was 1930, and Donald had spent some formative years copying Thorburn illustrations out of books. He was fascinated by Thorburn's use of body-colour, an opaque watercolour technique that was superseded by gouache, and it was this medium that Donald adopted for the vast majority of his paintings.

Gouache, when dry, has a matt, chalky appearance, which Donald found ideal for his atmosphere-filled landscapes, but the best quality paints also contain a high proportion of pigment so that their covering power and opacity is excellent. It is thus possible to paint light tints over dark, which helps to explain their popularity amongst illustrators. It was this property that Donald exploited in order to place flocks of birds within a large landscape setting, which, if working in transparent water colour, would all have had to be carefully prearranged. He could paint the chosen landscape on the spot, in one go – *en plein air* – and, if necessary, place the birds into that view back in the studio after some contemplation.

This method can also be used on toned papers, and Donald did so 'especially greys, to obtain an overall unity of tone values'. Any inhibitions he felt about working this way were salved by noting that other prominent artists of the time, such as Joseph Crawhall, Allan Seaby and Eric Ennion, adopted this or similar methods. He liked Ennion's proclamation that he was 'terrified of white paper'!

The entwining of science and art reached its apotheosis for Donald in the 1977 publication of *The Hen Harrier*. His passion for these birds had cast a spell on him many years previously, and in his words 'they turned me into a more specialised kind of birdwatcher and did much to freshen my eye as an artist for the hill country and its wildlife'.[3]

A hen harrier quartering any hill country landscape certainly does quicken the pulse of many a lesser artist or ornithologist. The painting in Fig 2.4, 'Hen Harrier at Court Knowe', illustrates this perfectly. Take the bird out for a moment and we perceive a fine, if moody, landscape. The foreground wall and road lead the eye into the right-hand side of the painting; the telegraph poles elevate the eye to the distant hills, where we travel back left across the scene to the silhouetted trees, which in turn draw our attention back towards the bottom. This lovely swirl of movement … into which the male hen harrier flies. Against a flattened sky it becomes the focal point, the centre of the pictorial vortex. The thing with focal points is that they usually follow a 'rule' of thirds approximating to the golden ratio, i.e., the focal point is often placed a third of the way in from the side and a third of the way down from the top or up from the bottom. Although in this painting the bird is indeed almost a third of the way down the picture rectangle, Donald has almost placed the bird in the centre. This more accurately reflects our excitement of the encounter. We hold that buoyant flight of the harrier slap bang in the middle of our vision, maybe through binoculars, such is our desire to dwell wholeheartedly on this magnificent creature we are

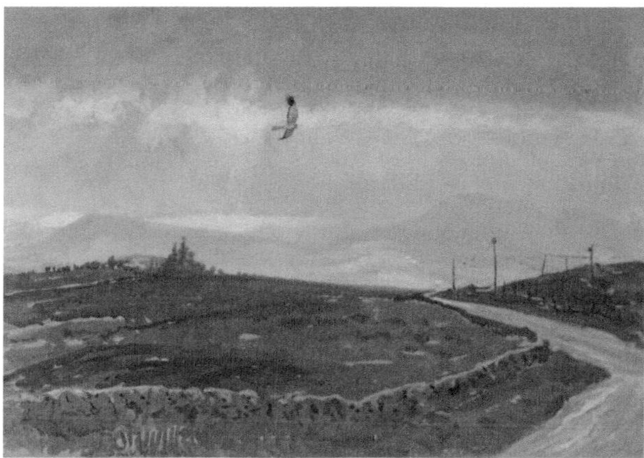

2.4 Donald Watson painting: Hen Harrier at Court Knowe, 1976

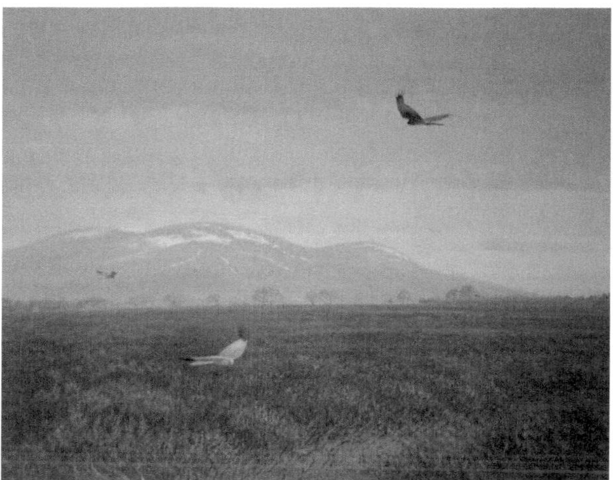

2.5 Donald Watson painting: Hen Harrier at a roost, 1989

so lucky to share this moment with. The artist's own excitement mirrors our own. We are able to associate with the artist's emotions and to recall similar experiences in our own birdwatching lives. There is a mutual understanding. Whatever the minutiae of compositional design, Donald's paintings so often have this effect and thereby lies their enduring appeal, one that entices both bird enthusiast and art lover.

In the painting in Fig 2.5 the pale cock harrier is placed classically a third of the way in from the left-hand side and against a dark background, whilst the brown female harrier is placed a third of the way in from the right-hand side and against the light sky. Our eye oscillates between these two birds – until, that is, we notice the third bird entering from the left in the middle distance. It is this bird, I think, that makes this painting work so well, for it immediately creates depth, a sense of space, pulling our attention into the landscape from where we can explore the scene beyond the lure of the foreground birds. Here we appreciate the skill of the landscape painter, the delicacy of the hues and tones to create that misty haze, and the subtlety increasing the intensity of both as we are drawn back towards the foreground.

Bruno Liljefors worked predominantly in oils, and was not immune to the artistic progressions of his day. There was his Japanese period for instance, and he visited the Paris salon in 1883 to see the work of the leading Impressionists. The colour combinations and brushwork in his later work suggest that he embraced some of their concepts. Donald too was to incorporate some of these into his own painting, though working almost exclusively in gouache rather than oils; it was their colour theories rather than their brushwork that are most apparent in his work. The use of complementary colours in Fig 2.6 is a good example; the pale lilac clouds and distant hills are matched with the warm yellow sky and closest grasses, and the blue shadowed landscape with the orange tints of sky, reflection and middle ground. Or Fig 2.7, where the green of the water complements the warm red-brown of the male wigeon heads, and the yellow ripples complement the lilac-grey of the mud and the male birds. These principles never deserted him. His deep-seated understanding of colour relationships remained ingrained even as he painted late in life.

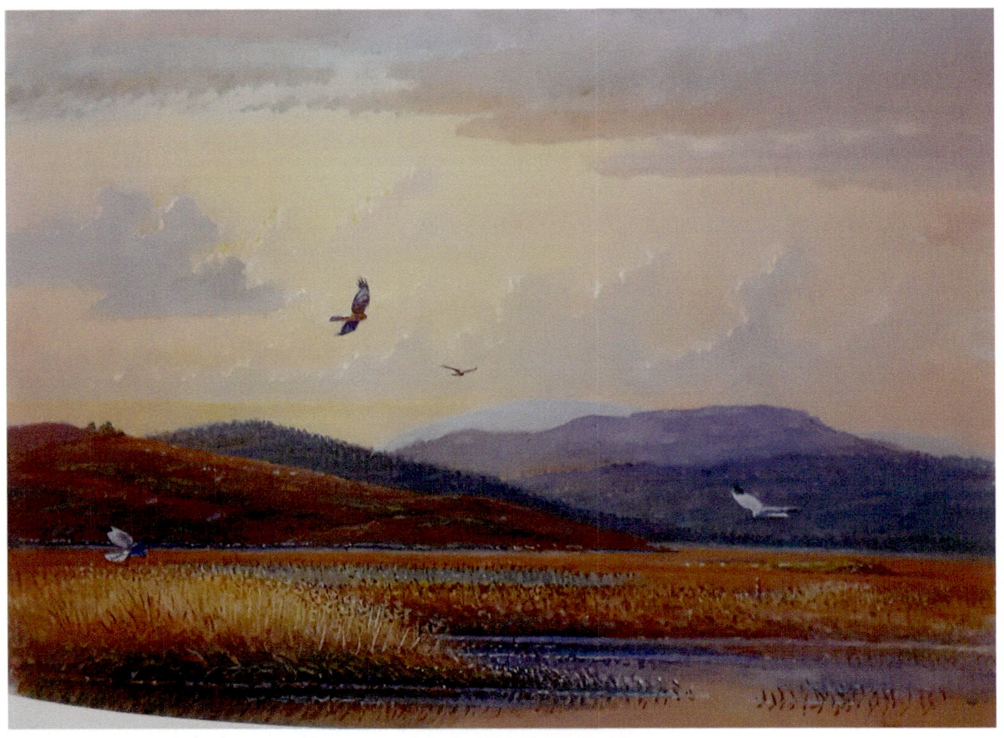

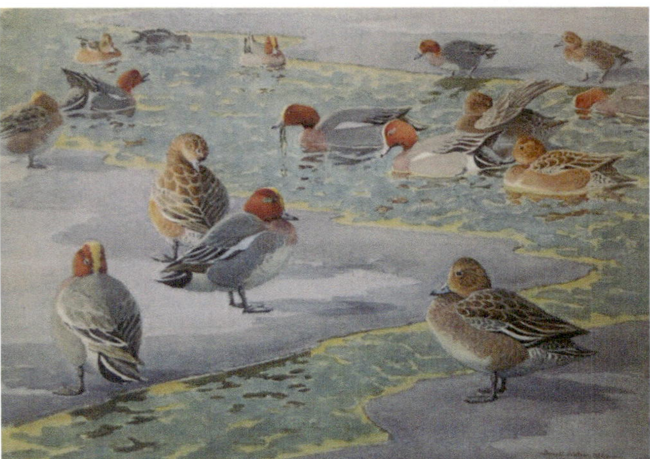

2.6 Above: Donald Watson painting: Hen Harrier Roost at Airie Flow
2.7 Left: Donald Watson painting: Wigeon, 1956

I well remember a painting of a black grouse lek in an exhibition at the Tolbooth Gallery in Kirkcudbright which did not perhaps stand up to close scrutiny, from a 'steady hand' point of view - but the colours - and consequently the atmosphere, the sense of place, of being there, and the quality of the early morning light - were just fabulous! Liljefors liked to paint at both ends of the day, and Donald followed suit with memorable effect.

His paintings always carried that sense of place, though, it has to be said, of having been out there to witness both the birds and the light. He always emphasised that in order to capture these

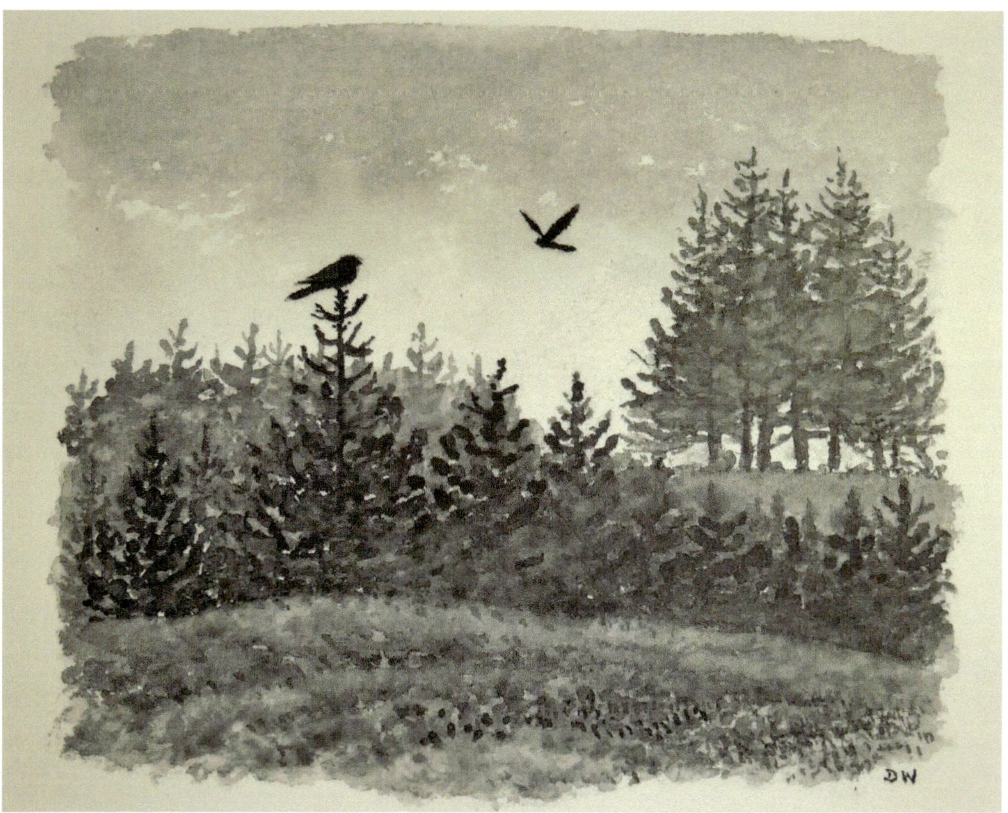

2.8 Donald Watson painting: Nightjars

events as exquisitely as he did there was no other way than to be drawing and painting on the spot, with the subject matter in front of him. There is the initial excitement for the artist, a particular light or view, birds or animals going about their daily lives, and the terrain and habitat to which they are conjoined – and then the desire to reflect, express or document what the artist believes they see and feel at that moment onto paper or canvas. There are then all the problems associated with doing so; the cold, the wind, the rain, the changing light, creatures that do not hang around, the midges that do … maybe even the heat and all-too-bright sun! It can be infuriating and very demanding. Patience, determination and perseverance are needed – and Donald had all those attributes in abundance when required, particularly as he enjoyed painting the winter landscape so much. He writes of carting his large board, easel, paints, brushes and stool (plus all the other materials and paraphernalia needed for a day out painting) whether along a mossy dyke or up a hill, to the same spot each day.

Working *en plein air* was the favoured way of painting for the French Impressionists and adopted by many wildlife artists, including Liljefors, Ennion, Tunnicliffe and others. Donald writes of his dilemma between 'making field sketches to be used for studio paintings and exploiting my new faith in tackling the habitat on the spot'.[4] It was the latter method he most often adopted until later in life, when he relied on 'making only minimal sketches and notes outdoors and using these as a basis for larger studio pictures.'[5]

Those field sketches, however, were the basis for all his bird portraiture, many of them in black and white, which distilled the essential character of a bird and rendered them as living breathing beings onto the page. For this reason, he was increasingly sought after by other ornithologists and publishers to illustrate their texts. He was able to depict the bird alone or in its relevant habitat either in full colour or in monochrome with equal facility as with the nightjars at the edge of a conifer block (Fig 2.8). This meant that relatively late in life he took on increasing amounts of illustration work for books and other publications, and indeed this occupied him for nearly 30 years. These illustrations would fall into a number of categories, including coloured plates, pen -and-ink drawings, scraperboard work and ink wash or paint monochromes.

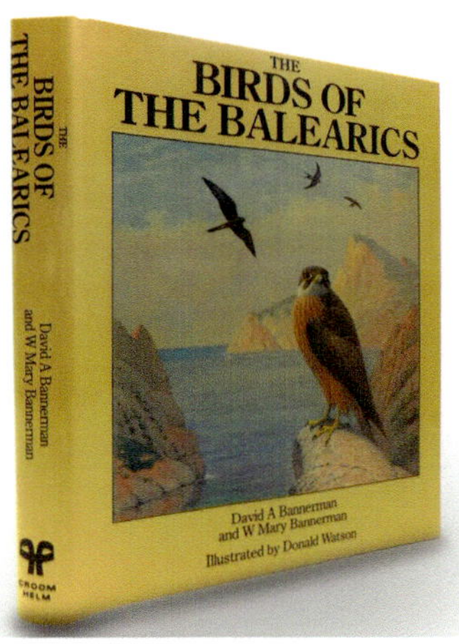

2.9 Donald Watson cover illustration of Bannerman's Balearics book

Illustrator of books

Now Donald had the challenge of working to someone else's brief and to their deadlines. This can be very demanding, and the sheer amount of work and the time it consumes can be daunting. Donald's contribution to *The Oxford Book of Birds*, with 96 pages of illustrations, took a full two years. That is a huge, dedicated commitment.

It may also involve some degree of travel in order to provide authenticity; for example David Bannerman's *The Birds of the Balearics*[6] (Fig 2.9). Not only may the birds encountered be unfamiliar, but the light and colours to be depicted will differ and must be correctly observed, adding further challenges. The design for a coloured plate in these books is a work of art in its own right. These are, again, birds in their natural habitat, in scale with it and with all the other birds illustrated on the same page, obviously within a limited space and to a prescribed format. Artistically, I think that here Donald's work most closely resembles that of Thorburn. The inclusion of local vegetation into many of the plates is beautifully observed and rendered, and adds so much to the sense of place as well as to the attractiveness of each page. Yes, they may be for merely illustrative purposes, but these are fine paintings on their own, with all the subtleties of colour and light and atmosphere that characterises the very best of Donald's output. Here is a painter as illustrator, and not the other way around.

This is also very apparent in his ink wash 'paintings' that so many authors and publishers requested. In monochrome paintings or tonal studies, he was able to 'convey some of the feel and atmosphere of a landscape without using colour at all.'[7] In the case of the Balearics paintings, that is no mean feat. For printing and publishing purposes these paintings would have had to have been on a small scale, but they have all the distinctive attributes of Donald's larger works. I find myself avoiding the term 'illustrations' to describe them, such is the nature of their execution and impact (Fig 2.10). Without the use of colour, however, the artist is compelled to create visual descriptions using, predominantly, tonal values, i.e. shapes and areas of light and dark. As humans, we are predisposed to notice strong contrasts – the darkest dark against the lightest light, a bird in flight against a pale sky – but it is the subtle use of half-tones, those falling between the two extremes, that creates the illusion of space and depth and ultimately brings a sense of

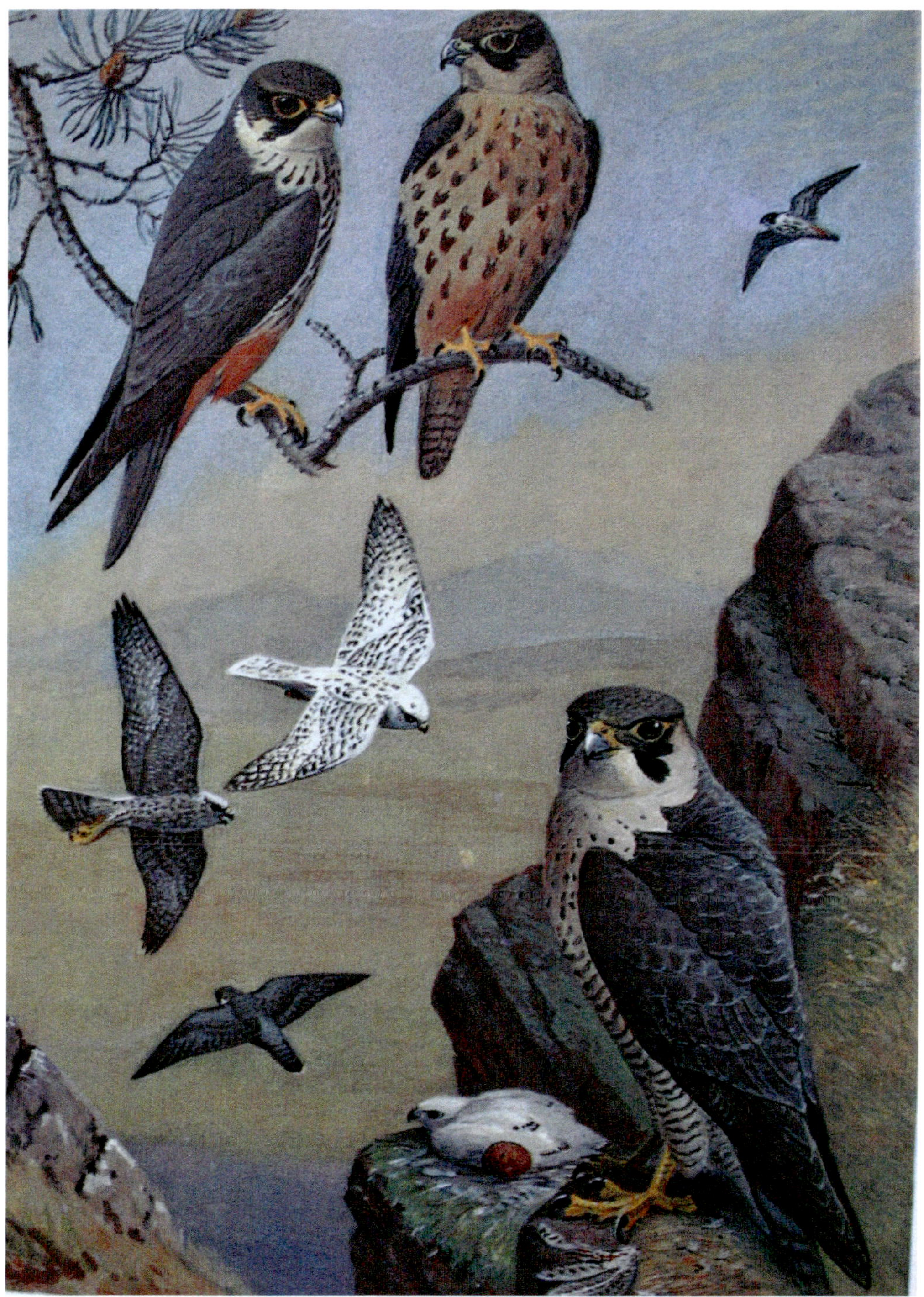

2.10 Donald Watson plate from *The Oxford Book of Birds*

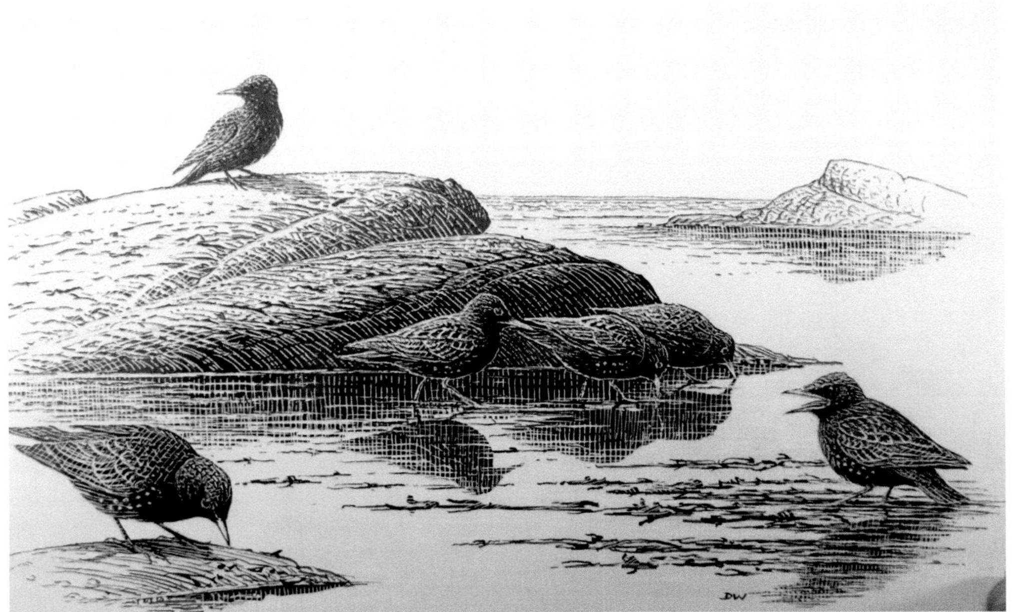

2.11 Donald Watson scraperboard: Starlings by the shore

unity or harmony to the painting, and makes it work. Look at Donald's monochrome paintings in view of this, and see them for the mini-masterpieces that they undoubtedly are.

Donald's illustrations are never overstated. They are very much focused on the 'jizz' (usually translated as 'general impression, size and shape') of the bird, whether in full colour or monochrome. The size can only be conveyed in relation to something else, hence many of the single bird studies incorporate a hint of habitat. Many of them were also done on scraperboard (sometimes known as scratchboard) where black ink is painted onto a white board with a smooth kaolin clay covering, and etched into it using a sharply pointed metal scalpel, needle or stylus, the resulting fine white lines carving form into the inked shapes (Fig 2.11). The finished effect is that of a wood engraving or woodcut. These drawings can easily be reproduced, though this method is not a printing process like woodcuts and engravings.

Donald's contemporary Charles Tunnicliffe was a master of these black-and-white mediums and, using cleverly crafted designs, turned these techniques into an art form. Donald's use of scraperboard seems to have been mostly functional vignettes, but there are some exquisite larger pieces that are much more complex in their composition and execution, detailed scenes with groupings of birds in the landscape (Fig 2.12). For many years it was a popular medium with illustrators, as it is possible to get very precise detail. Donald was a gifted exponent, creating clean, strong images, albeit with a great sensitivity of line based on the keen understanding of his subject matter.

It was not just birds, of course. Some of his earliest scraperboards were done for *The Countryman*, and over time the commissions were far-ranging (Fig 2.13). Commissions are a mixed blessing, as there is the promise of a guaranteed income but there is also the taxing issue of working to an editor's vision and time frame, and often with an unaccustomed theme. The problem-solving aspect of the latter can, however, be a learning experience that can be motivational in its own right, as well as generating confidence in tackling future work. In Donald's case this meant he could be relied upon to produce high quality, accurate, 'true to life' illustrations, and to be entrusted with such work by eminent authors and publishers.

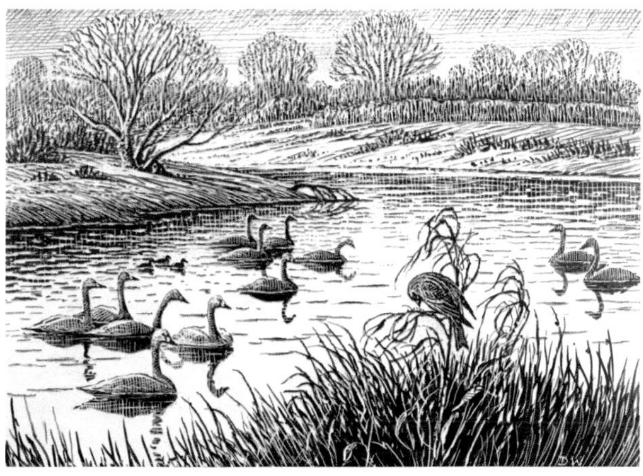

2.12 Donald Watson scraperboard: Whooper Swans

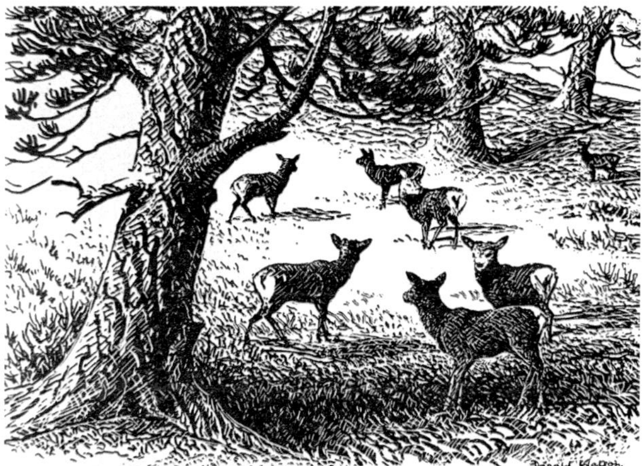

2.13 Donald Watson: Antlerless Stags, scraperboard image for *The Countryman*

His artistic history

All that was in an uncertain future as, despite showing much potential in art through school, he read for a history degree rather than an art qualification. Whilst his twin passions may have waned, he did not completely lose interest in ornithology and bird painting, but his 'private ambition centred increasingly on becoming some sort of writer, although neither writing nor painting seemed to offer any real prospect of a career'.[8] Interestingly, though, he was studying Renaissance art for his degree, so had not abandoned art entirely, graduating in 1940. War service was then to follow. He was stationed in India for training and then to Burma for the Arakan Campaign against the Japanese. Despite the rigours and atrocities of war he found solace, and, whenever a favourable moment arose, 'so much satisfaction in birdwatching, drawing and painting'.[9] The visual impact of a new landscape and its wildlife had reignited those passions that had faded so much in Britain. He was now starting to seriously consider the possibility of becoming a professional artist after the war (Fig 2.14)

A chance meeting with George Waterston led to Donald showing Arthur Duncan and the Reverend J.M. McWilliam, both eminent ornithologists, some of his Burma paintings. On the strength of these, Duncan presented him with the opportunity to work on a series of paintings of 'birds in their habitat' ... and the rest, we could say, is history. If only it was that simple!

However, in 1947 he was invited to organise a small exhibition of Scottish bird art to coincide with a big conference in Edinburgh sponsored by the Scottish Ornithologists' Club. This opened further doors for the aspiring artist, not least an association with the Rowland Ward Gallery in London that was to last 10 years. Much of his work to follow was then destined for exhibitions and galleries, and it is for these wonderfully evocative paintings that he is best remembered.

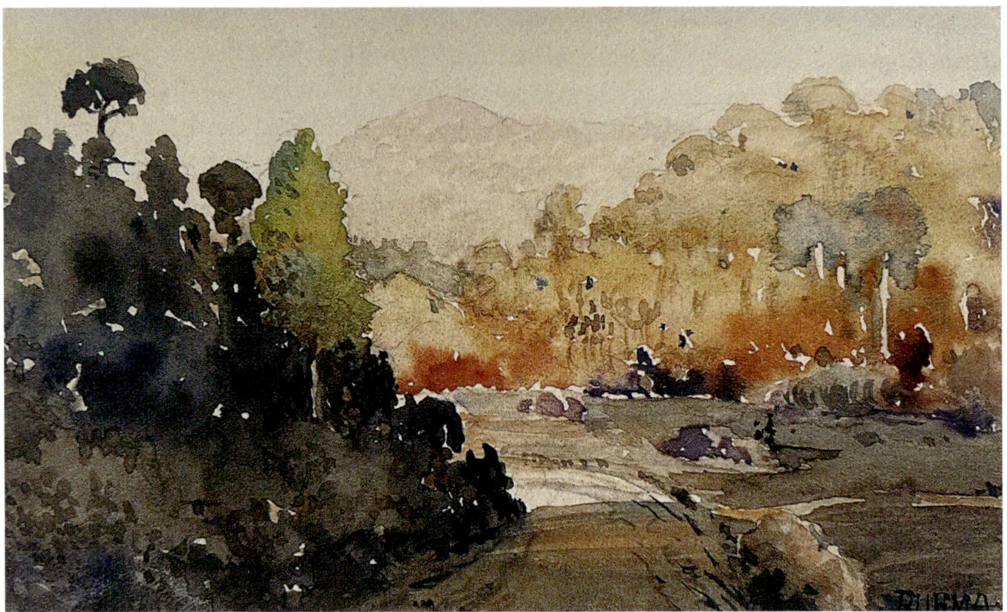

2.14 Donald Watson painting: Burma

Overview

So let us conclude this chapter by looking admiringly at a few other examples of the master bird artist in his prime.

The 1958 painting 'Goosanders, River Ken' (Fig 2.15), which I mentioned earlier, is a beautiful, softly illuminated late autumn/early winter view. A hint of frost lingering in the shaded contours of the land allows the artist to contrast the dominant warm colours with a subtle counterpoint of cool ones. The ripples created by the two birds in the foreground are also cool blues, thus helping to generate a movement of the eye through the painting. Our viewer's wandering eye, though, is very much held within the frame by the simple device of 'blocking' all four corners, in this case with foliage. Again, we witness the use of complementary colours so beloved of the Impressionists, the oranges played against the blues, the tints of mauve against the yellow-green sunlit fields. The restlessness of the goosanders belies the overall feeling of this painting as joyfully serene – that slight, but deliberate, tension that Donald brought to so many of his best works.

The painting of a pair of hen harriers in Fig 2.16 plays with similar juxtapositions; the pale cool grey of the male against the warm foreground, and the warm colours of the female against the cool shadows cast by the hillock. Our eye wants to follow those walls, especially that sinuous diagonal slanting away into the distance, but then the top of the conifer block tends to move us away left, where it contrasts with the darker shadowed hillside. That curving hill against the pale sky brings our eye back to the right and down into the picture again. At least that would be the case if we could just tear ourselves away from the hen harriers, the aerial buoyancy of their flight so perfectly captured that we are almost floating with them. (An artist's note to consider, closely and enviously, the way Donald has painted those conifers!)

We must have a look at Fig 2.17, because I think he had a lot of fun with this composition. It certainly makes me smile, at any rate. In many ways, it has a similar configuration to the previous painting, the foreground harriers holding our attention with their gorgeous shapes and aerobatics, and the meandering dyke from the bottom left angling towards the middle of the picture rectangle before swinging back left again. Of course, Donald does not want to lead us out of the painting in this way, so he deftly introduces the train and the vertically rising steam to prevent that happening – and that just so happens to lead us to the higher bird by way of bringing the focus back round. The contours of the landscape do the rest. Brilliantly conceived, but with a hint of mischief, I think!

It does, however, cast us back in time again, placing Donald's artistic *oeuvre* in its historical context; in 1963 Beeching did for the Dumfries to Stranraer railway line. Viewed in this light, there is a poignancy to much of Donald's Galloway portfolio of paintings and illustrations. The loss of so many breeding birds and general biodiversity, whatever the reasons for that decline, is undeniably lamentable. As an antidote, what we can do is to appreciate Donald's work as a joyous celebration of the beauty and the wildness of the Galloway landscape and its wildlife from that era. In our days of 'shrinking baseline syndromes', Donald grants us a pictorial account of a richer, stronger, more diverse reference baseline that we would do well to comprehend.

In his 1986 book, *Twentieth Century Wildlife Artists,* Nicholas

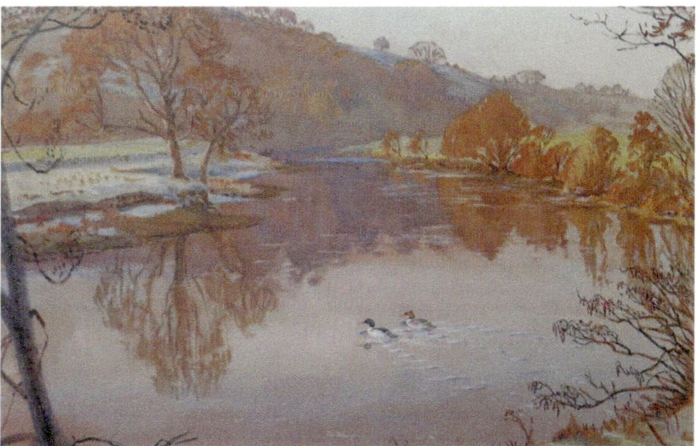

2.15 Donald Watson painting: Goosanders, River Ken

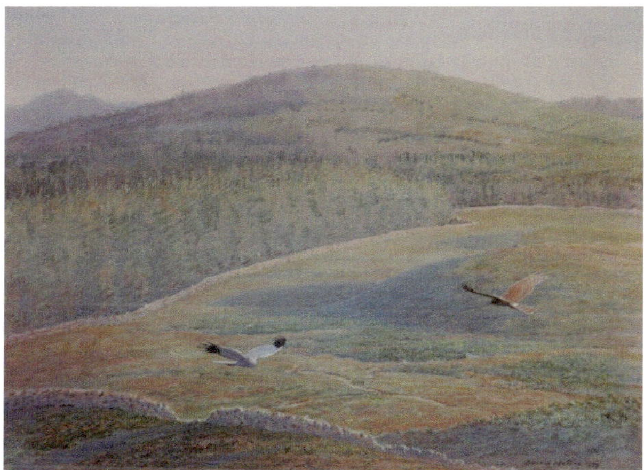

2.16 Donald Watson painting: Hen Harrier pair in flight, 1973

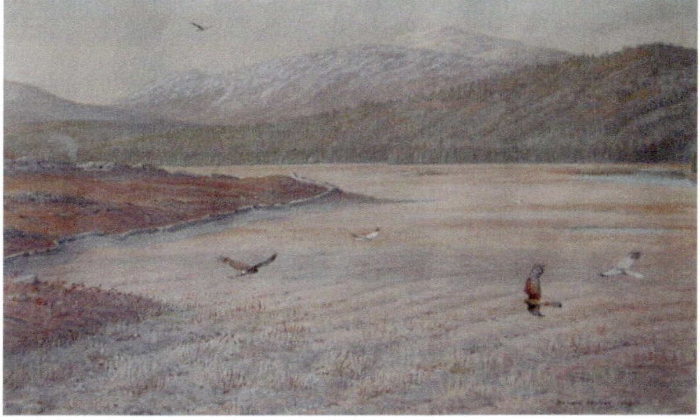

2.17 Donald Watson painting: Hen Harriers pair in flight

Hammond writes of Donald 'capturing the atmosphere of seeing the birds in their environment'.[10] That is a very significant and meaningful phrase to use in describing Donald's evocative paintings. It is that sense of place, the bewitching atmosphere of a precious moment witnessed, and the audacious skill to render that onto paper using a sympathetic medium, a discerning eye for colour, an intuitive gift for composition and all combined with a stringent ornithological accuracy that distinguish Donald's work from that of his peers.

I count myself fortunate to have met with him a number of times, and honoured to have spent time with him in his home and studio, and to have been a recipient of his gentle wisdom and advice. We all, however, have the privilege of being able to view Donald's art today and to enjoy it, savour it, learn from it and appreciate it with its strengths and subtleties, talent and technique, and above all the passion and the depth of feeling within each piece.

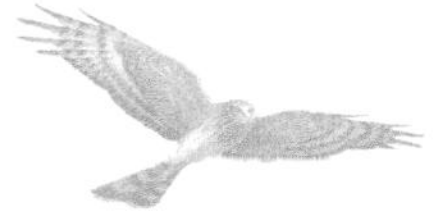

Three

Donald Watson, my father

LOUISE WATSON

> Dad was someone who did not baulk at sitting for hours in the heather waiting for a glimpse of a food pass, or tracking through impenetrable forest to locate a nest, or standing patiently in the chill winter dusk in the merest hope of seeing the birds arrive at their roost.
>
> Louise Watson[1]

Bird artist, ornithologist, writer, family man: I have been asked to write about my father in the context of family, but in truth it is hard to separate out the different aspects of his life and personality. He would work tirelessly on a painting in the barely heated studio at the top

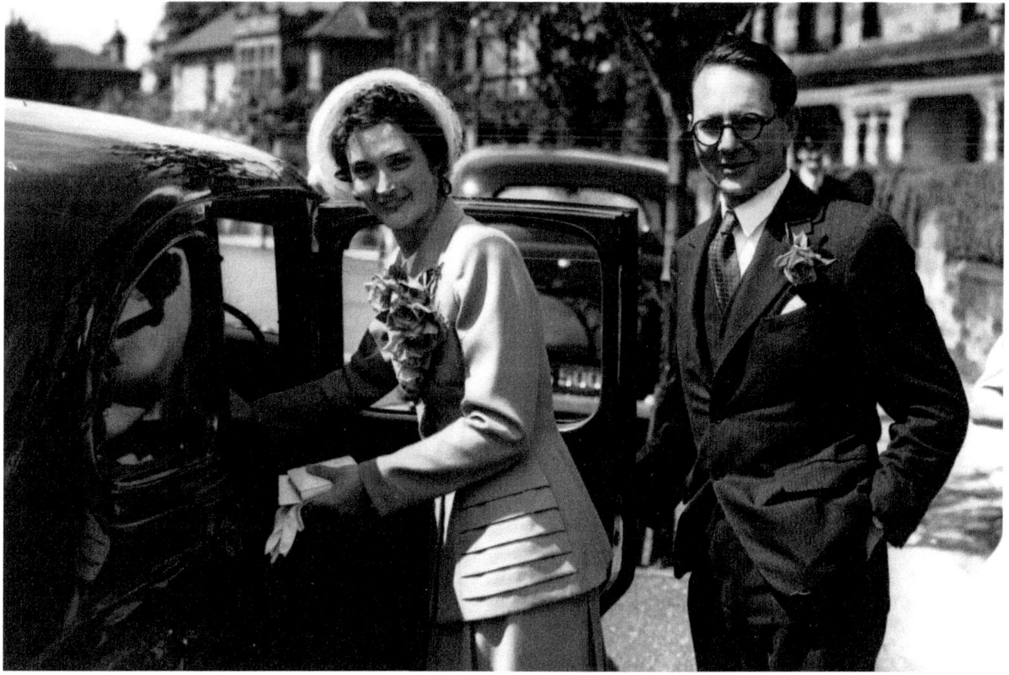

3.1 Mum and Dad on their wedding day in Ayr, June 1950

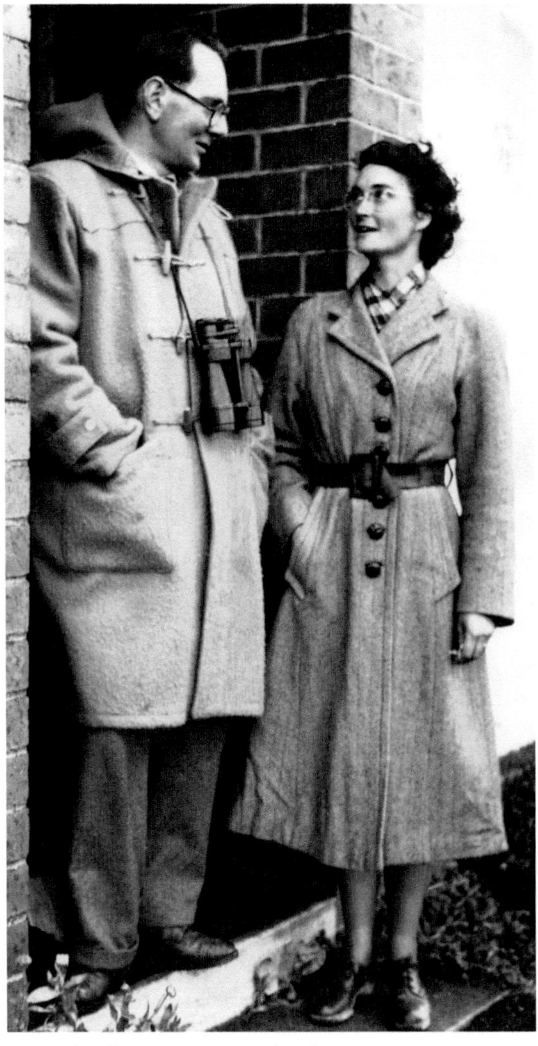

3.2 On their honeymoon on Benbecula

of the house, determined to resolve the challenges of light, perspective and the relative positioning of birds. Often at the end of the day, when there was just enough light in the downstairs sitting room, he would come down with the picture he'd been busy with and ask us for comments. On family walks, he would bring up the rear as he scanned the horizon for moorland birds or stopped to make a quick sketch. In the evenings he would sit by the fire with everyone and write: if he wasn't working on a book, he would be writing letters to a host of correspondents about birds, painting or family. In later years, he enjoyed time spent with his grandchildren, sketching with Ronan or talking to Julian and Alastair about a great spotted woodpecker feasting on the peanuts by the window.

We grew up at Barone, the family home in the middle of Main Street, St John's Town of Dalry; in our day it was known simply as Dalry. For myself and my three siblings – Pam, Jeff and Kate – it was a home of great warmth, support and love engendered by our parents. It is hard to believe that they had not been settled there for decades, but this was not at all the case. Dad first visited south-west Scotland shortly after the Second World War. He had returned home after serving in India and Burma, and was staying in Edinburgh at the family home. It was George Waterston who introduced Donald to Sir Arthur Duncan and the Reverend J.M. McWilliam, those two great Dumfriesshire naturalists. Sir Arthur invited Dad to visit him at Tynron, Dumfriesshire, where the plan was that Donald would paint a series of illustrations of birds in their habitats for a book that Sir Arthur was planning.

Donald and Joan married in 1950, and it was no surprise that after spending their honeymoon in the Outer Hebrides they were drawn to Galloway as a place to settle. In his book *A Bird Artist in Scotland*, Dad wrote,

> We spent that winter in Galloway, on the Solway coast, at first in a bungalow lent by a friend who was abroad, and later in a wooden chalet which was flimsy and cold and could only be reached through a field with an Ayrshire bull in it. The local GP, Dr Milne

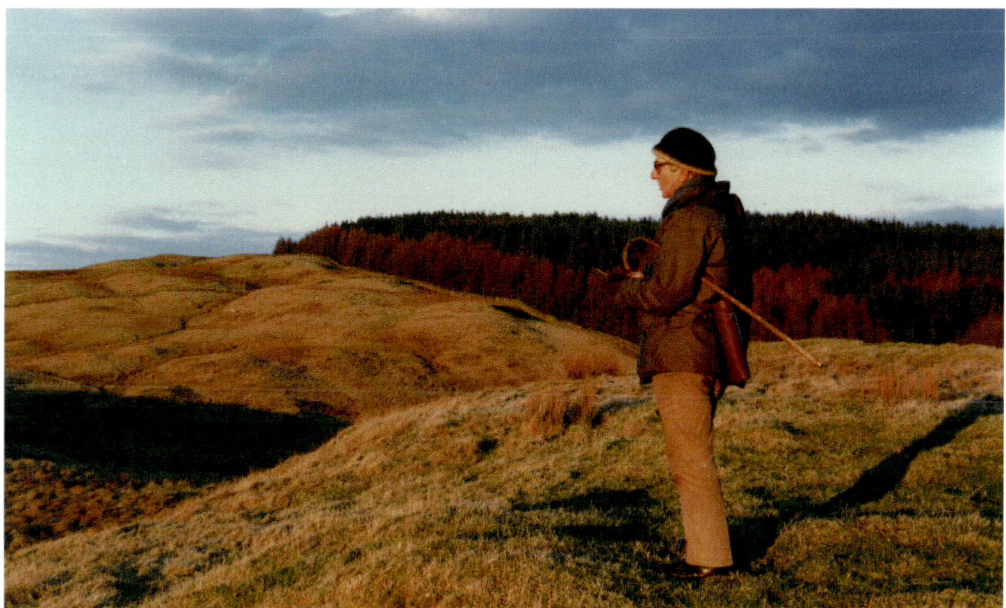

3.3: The Galloway landscape inspired Dad throughout his life

> Redhead, was an expert botanist and enjoyed looking for plants on his way to visit us, when he confirmed that Joan was pregnant. We had no car and travelled on bus or train in search of a more permanent home … There was a house on the market at Dalry in The Glenkens and the owner, a doctor, was becoming desperate to sell … The house was much too big and rambling, but at the back it had an irresistible garden, a slope with a grove of aspens and a mass of daffodils, and an outlook to the Rhinns of Kells, a range of mountains with the most beautiful profile in southern Scotland. Selfishly I also had my eyes on the doctor's bedroom with a north light for a studio.[2]

Mum and Dad moved into Barone in May 1951, just a few weeks before their first child was born. When they acquired a car the following year, they had greater freedom to move around Galloway and explore more fully its varied landscape: the Solway coast, the Loch Ken valley, the Wood of Cree and Grobdale Moor. All proved inspiring to both the naturalist and the artist in Dad.

By the mid-1950s Pam, Jeff, Kate and I had all arrived, and perhaps it was just as well that the house in Dalry was a good size! For us, it was a magical place to grow up, and the garden was a playground full of trees to climb and hidden corners in which to build dens. The house itself was freezing: Mum's family, most of whom lived in South Africa, must have suffered particularly, and I wonder if the bitter Galloway winters were part of the reason that Kate later settled in southern California. As children, we would rush upstairs to Dad's studio when we returned from school each day to view the progress on his latest picture. The sitting room doubled as his study, too, though he would not have described it as such. For us children, this meant the television would have to be turned off when there were visitors in the evening – and there were many such occasions. If this coincided with 'The Man from U.N.C.L.E.' we would be quite distraught!

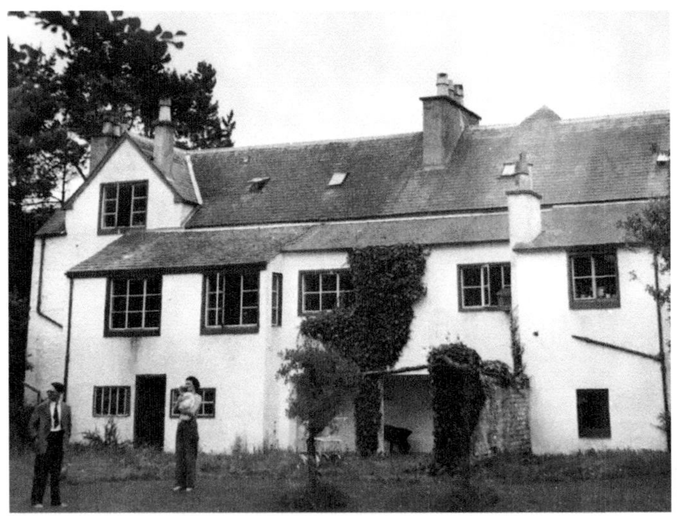

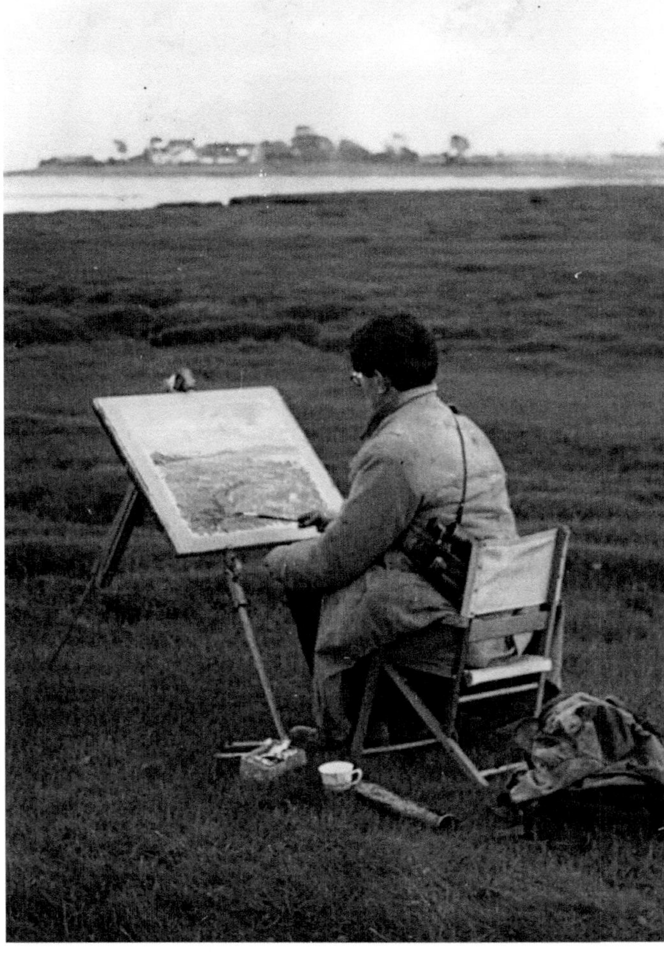

3.4 Top: Early days at Barone – Mum carrying Pam as a baby

3.5 Bottom: Dad would often paint outside in all weathers

We grew up in a house full of paintings. Not all were by my father. Many were by Uncle Harry, a noted artist and illustrator professionally known as H. John Pearson (he was my father's uncle, brother of his mother) and some by Aunt Margaret, my father's aunt on his father's side. A number of delightful watercolours of the Scottish islands and of European mountain scenes were by Uncle Eric, Dad's brother. My sister Pam's atmospheric sepia wash drawings of crowded corners of the house were also on display. And there were many paintings by fellow bird artists whom Donald admired and many of whom he counted as good friends: Robert Gillmor, Chloe Talbot-Kelly, Eric Ennion, John Busby and Ian Willis among others. I recall a recent conversation with my sisters, when we talked about how strange it was to us that many people would go into a house and not look at whatever was on the walls. At a very early age we learned the opposite behaviour from Dad; he would look with an appraising eye at the paintings hanging on the

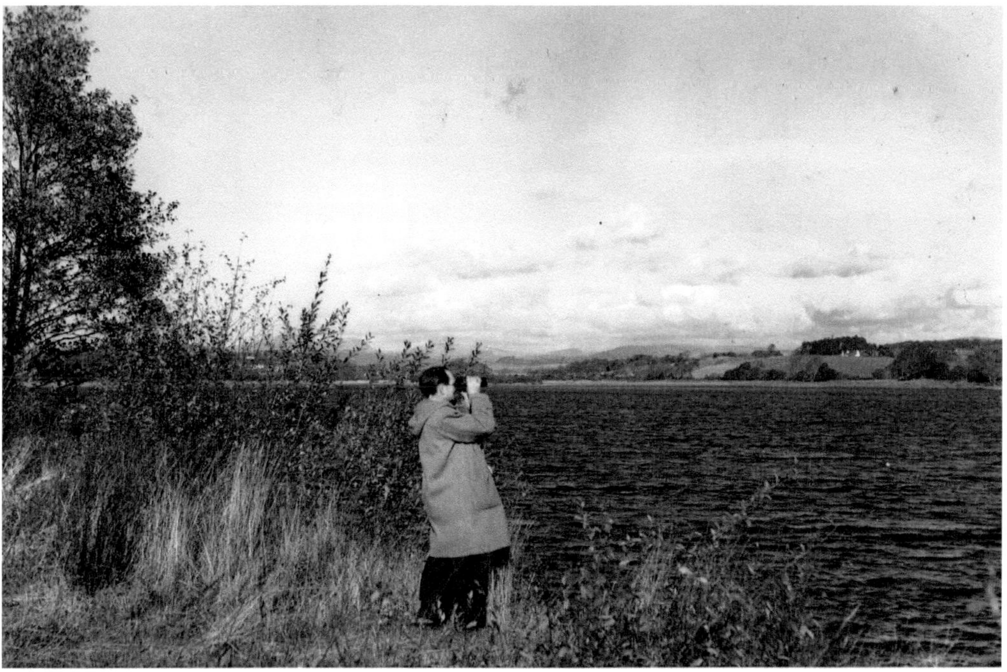

3.6 Dad scanning Loch Ken with binoculars

walls of friends' houses. Not uncommonly, he would comment on a painting of his own, perhaps one that he had not seen for some time, and would continue to debate with himself whether or not he had captured the bird to his complete satisfaction.

In the early 1960s, Dad was commissioned to paint the illustrations for *The Oxford Book of Birds*. This was a huge body of work and had a great impact on his life in terms of raising his profile and also providing financial stability; even though we were all very young at the time, I'm sure we all felt it. As a young boy, Jeff had started school in Edinburgh, and his letters home were often short, but he would regularly ask how the latest book plate was progressing. Kate particularly remembers how intensely Dad worked in those years, as he strove to meet the demanding pace of production without sacrificing quality.

The change in financial circumstances was made clearer to us when we came across a cache of letters while clearing out the family home after both our parents had passed on. They were written by Dad to Mum in the early 1950s, while Dad was travelling round the country exhibiting his paintings in a number of galleries, including in Bristol, London and Oxford. I don't think any of us realised how much time he had spent away from Dalry during that period. These letters brought home to me just how precarious his living was. Although he had been greatly encouraged by several eminent bird artists, he was not yet well known. And every sale of a painting was crucial.

The letters also opened my eyes to the challenges my mother must have faced at home, often alone, with a growing family. She had no relations nearby – her own family lived overseas, and my father's brothers and their families in the south of England. Later, she was to teach at the local schools and help lead the Girl Guides, and she managed to combine these pursuits with

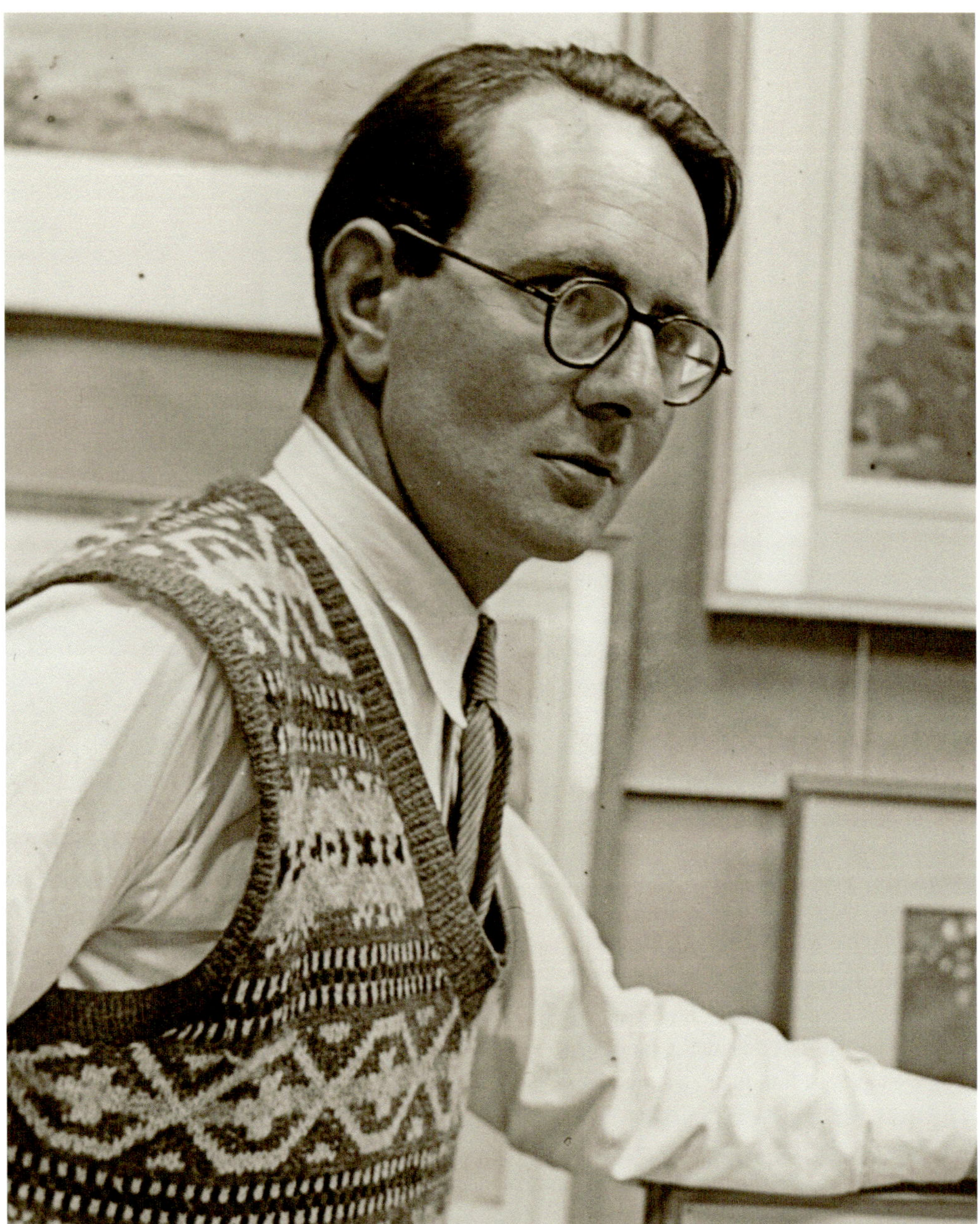

3.7 Dad at one of his early exhibitions in Galloway

supporting Dad in many ways that allowed him to devote himself to his painting. Often, he would arrive home late on a summer day, at the time of year when light evenings offer so much opportunity to birdwatcher and artist – and Mum would be waiting with a meal kept warm in the oven and without a hint of impatience. Of course, she often joined him on his excursions – she had a keen eye and would frequently spot birds before Dad, especially when his vision was compromised in later life. After retiring, she took up her own interest, tracking down and photographing butterflies.

Over the years, family outings were always combined with visits to places where Dad was keen to catch sight of a bird he was trying to paint or write about. Favourite destinations close to home included the Lorg Glen, the Mull of Galloway and the west side of Loch Ken, where the annual arrival of skeins of geese would be eagerly awaited. On days out, the whole family would pile into the old Bedford van, COS 103, which had seats running lengthways and no seatbelts. The boxer dog would come, too – beautiful Judy with her striking red coat, and, later, playful honey-coloured Topsy. While often we would enjoy a walk and a picnic in fine weather, it was not unusual for Dad to watch or sketch birds from the car, using it as a hide. We learned to stay quiet and still when this was necessary. Our memories of these times are happy: my sister Kate recorded in her diary, at age 13:

> Leaders are gathering to discuss the Gold Crisis. The newspapers say that this may be the most critical weekend many of us have lived through – but I'm afraid we spent it duck counting. Dad explained the crisis to me in the car 'cos I couldn't understand it. Dad says even he doesn't fully understand it. Anyway, we had a fabulous time.

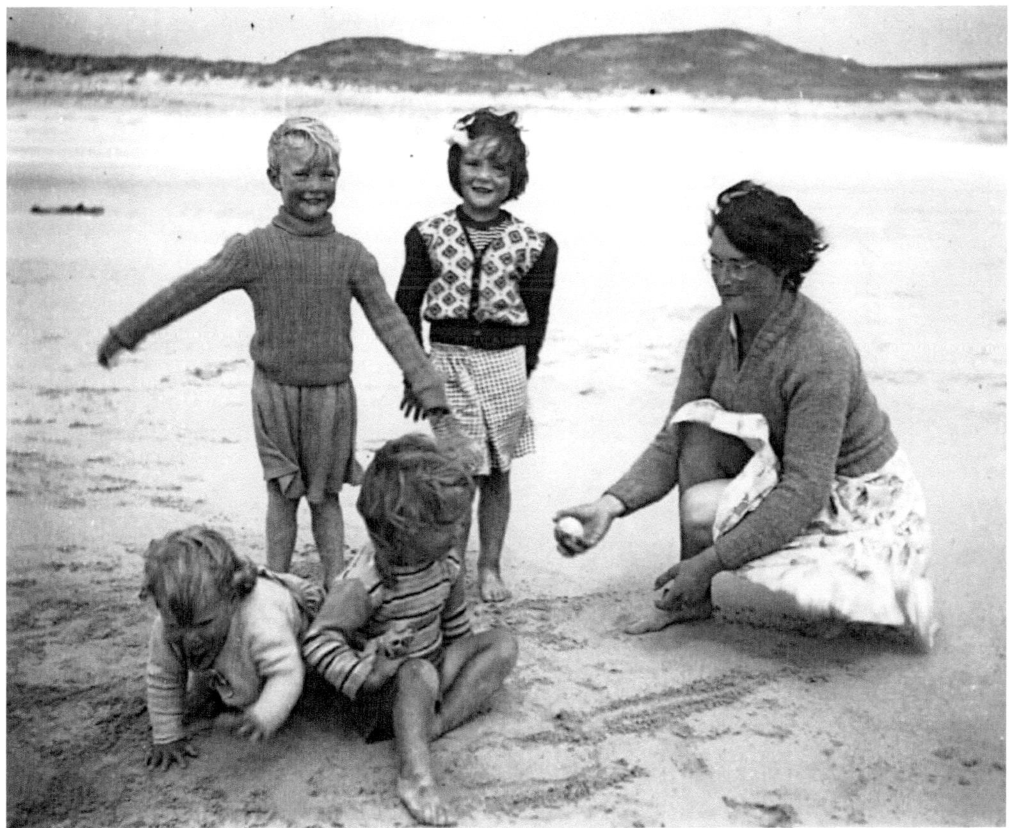

3.8 On the sands, Tiree, summer 1957 – Mum with Jeff and Pam, standing, and me and Kate

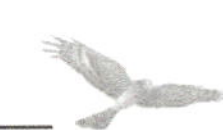

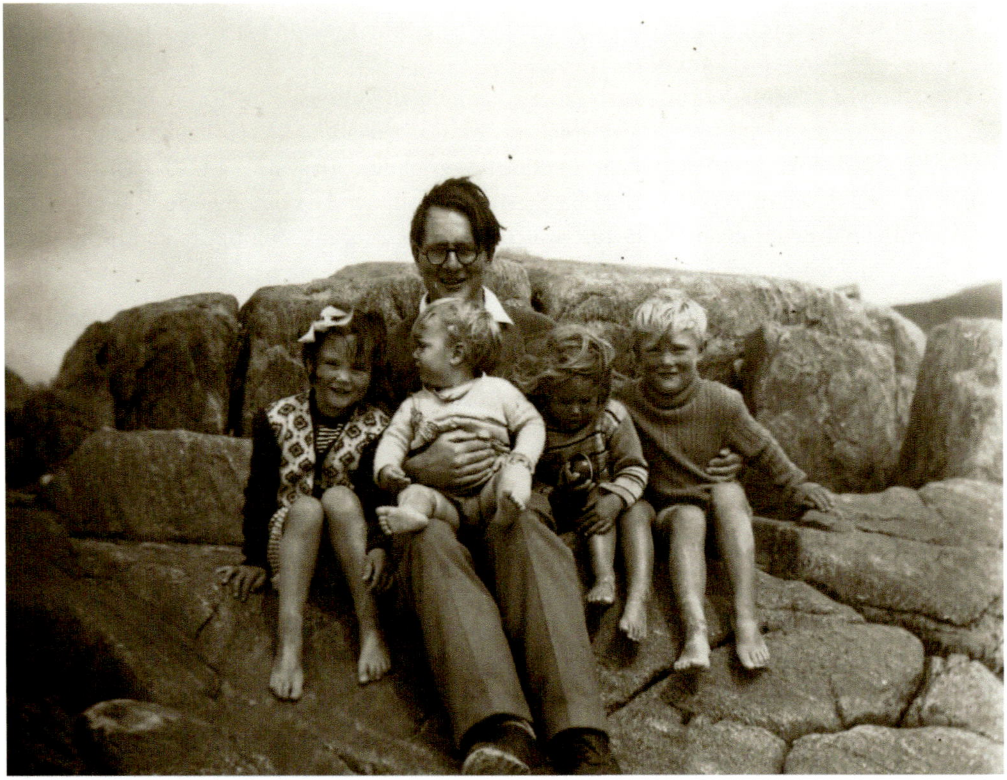

3.9 Dad and the children on the rocks, Tiree, summer 1957

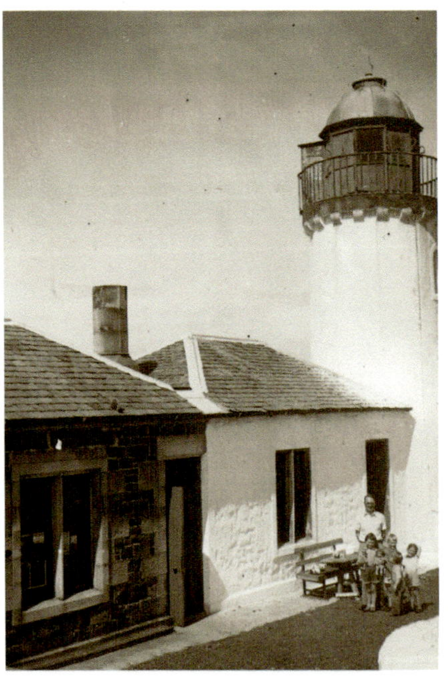

3.10 At the Low Light, Isle of May, July 1958

On family holidays, we would venture further afield, but usually still within Scotland and most commonly to the Inner Hebrides. We visited Tiree, Coll, Islay and Skye – wherever the birdlife and landscapes attracted Dad. For us, they were wonderful places to explore and, if we were lucky and the weather was good, to swim in the Atlantic. In *A Bird Artist in Scotland* Dad wrote

> When we were [on Coll], in 1964, there was no pier and J.'s 75-year-old mother had some hair-raising moments being transferred from a little boat to the island steamer in a heaving sea. With her and my brother Eric we made a party of eight in the old school house at Arinagour. [3]

We only occasionally travelled beyond Scotland, with a trip to the Aran Islands off the west coast of Ireland a memorable exception.

Dad's association with the Isle of May in the Firth of Forth went back to his teenage days growing up in Edinburgh, when he would go with his brother and a group of friends who set up the bird observatory on the island. We first visited as a family in 1958. Later, Jeff, already being encouraged in his interest in birds, was allowed to join the serious birdwatchers. And in the late 1960s Mum, Kate and I joined the party on a couple of occasions; we loved the wild romanticism of living in the old lighthouse, lit only by hissing gas lamps, and writing up the 'chatty log', though I'm not sure my mother was quite so keen when presented with a live crab to cook. Mum was such a calming presence in our lives that it was somewhat unusual to see her quite so uncomfortable!

I recall Dad saying that when Sir Peter Scott visited in the 1950s he remarked that our garden would be a great spot for wildfowl. However, Dad felt that a garden was for garden birds. Watching birds from the house was a constant throughout our lives, and often the first stop when we returned home from university or from our disparate lives was to gather at the window overlooking the lawn to see what could be seen. Dad wrote about the early years at Barone, when over the dyke at the back of the garden he would hear lapwing and curlew, snipe and redshank.

> On soft spring nights when the big wych-elm, laden with flowers, was etched in black against the sky, snipe came bleating over the garden and a woodcock crossed on its roding patrol... In the early years, too, the rasping cry of the corncrake could be heard from the house.[4]

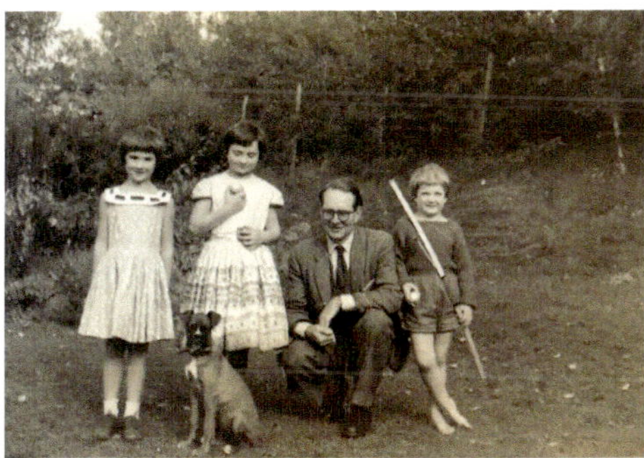

3.11 In Barone garden in the 1960s, Dad with Kate, Pam, me and Judy, the boxer dog

In later years most of these species were long gone, but we still had special favourites among the garden birds: the bramblings and yellowhammers attracted to the seed mixture that Dad put out on the lawn; the swallows, which for years nested in the garage or the garden room and which – after several years when they appeared to have deserted us – returned to nest in the porch immediately above the front door and more than once flew into the house; and perhaps most evocative of all for me, the spotted flycatchers, which took up residence in a nest box visible from the front hall. Dad made sketches of the young birds perching on the washing line and the playpen in the garden when we were small; and in his very last diary he faithfully recorded the progress of the flycatcher's brood.

The bird with which Dad is most associated, both as a bird artist and as an ornithologist, is of course the hen harrier. Dad wrote that for several years he had hoped to find a pair nesting in Galloway, and he was finally successful in 1959.

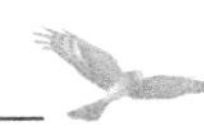

> These elegant but sadly persecuted hawks cast their spell on me that exceptionally fine summer ... They turned me into a more specialized kind of birdwatcher and did much to freshen my eye as an artist for the hill country and its wildlife.[5]

Looking back, I feel a certain sadness that I for one shared less of his time looking for harriers than I now wish I had done. Perhaps it is true to say that this enigmatic bird, one of our most elusive birds of prey, requires a person with particular attributes to track it down – someone who does not baulk at sitting for hours in the heather waiting for a glimpse of a food pass, or tracking through impenetrable forest to locate a nest, or standing patiently in the chill winter dusk in the merest hope of seeing the birds arrive at their roost. My own interest in birds and, indeed, butterflies has grown in later years. When we moved to the country in the mid-1990s and soon realised that on our doorstep we could spot butterflies we had never seen before (white admiral, silver-washed fritillary and green hairstreak, to name a few), it was hugely exciting to share this news with Mum and Dad. Even now, my first thought on spotting a nightjar on the nature reserve just behind our house is to tell Dad and hear the excitement in his voice.

It was part of Dad's character that he was always interested to hear what others had seen and to ask about their experiences. Though he had great knowledge and near-faultless recall, and was always happy to share what he knew (unless it would put birds at risk), he was also keen to seek the views of fellow ornithologists, local farmers and other enthusiasts. I would describe this as a rare and valuable attribute of character.

Many people will tell you that family members rarely mention their experiences in the war, but Dad often recounted his, especially after a glass or two of whisky at Hogmanay. When we were children, he was very selective about what he said in front of us, but as we grew older he told us more. After finishing his degree in history at St John's College, Oxford, he was called up and spent time in the Royal Army Medical Corps and the Army Education Corps. Finally, after deciding that he ought to take a more active part in the war effort, he joined the Royal Artillery and was sent to the Far East. Whatever free time he had was spent trying to identify the bird species around him, and he was supported in this by the GOC, General Sir Philip Christison, an expert ornithologist: 'When he came down to have a look at our regiment the CO dragged me out to talk to him.'[6] To his family back home, Dad sent beautifully painted postcards of the birds and landscapes of Burma, while his friends would receive long lists of the bird species he had seen. In his final months in the army, his 'happiest times were early mornings spent painting evocations of home scenes in poster colours on poplin for the mess hut.'[7]

Dad often told us that he was mocked for showing his distress when one of his fellow soldiers shot dead a pallid harrier for sport. This sensibility was completely in character. His compassion extended to all living creatures, including those that found their way into our home uninvited. Kate recalls the gentleness with which he scooped up a thick black spider from the sink in his palm, saying, as he placed it outside, 'You'll be happier there.' And I remember when a little field mouse appeared one evening in the dining-room fireplace. Dad remarked that it was just looking for a place to spend the winter, and we shouldn't be alarmed about sharing our space with it.

We did share our home with a number of owls, though they were housed in the cellar. Over a number of years, the owls had suffered broken wings when failing to avoid traffic on the roads of Galloway. At one point, we had a short-eared owl as well as a barn owl and a couple of tawny owls. There was little that could be done to get them fit enough to hunt for themselves and return to the wild, so Dad kept them in the cellar and fed them roadkill or pieces of liver with feathers attached. When we were out in the car there would be a regular chorus of 'rabbit!' – a sign that we had spotted a poor, freshly killed bunny that would make a good meal for the owls.

In terms of his professional influence on his family, the most direct impact was on Jeff, who as a youngster inherited Dad's interest in birds before making it his lifelong passion and going on to write his world-renowned book on the golden eagle. Dad showed Jeff his first eagle nest, in Galloway. It is also true that Dad's influence can be seen in all his children in terms of career choice. Pam studied art at Edinburgh and Aberdeen, and of his children's opinions about his paintings, it was hers that Dad valued most highly. Kate and I studied literature at university, and we both went on to make a living as editors, testament to our appreciation of language and its use that was passed on in no small measure by Dad. Kate also became a published poet. After leaving

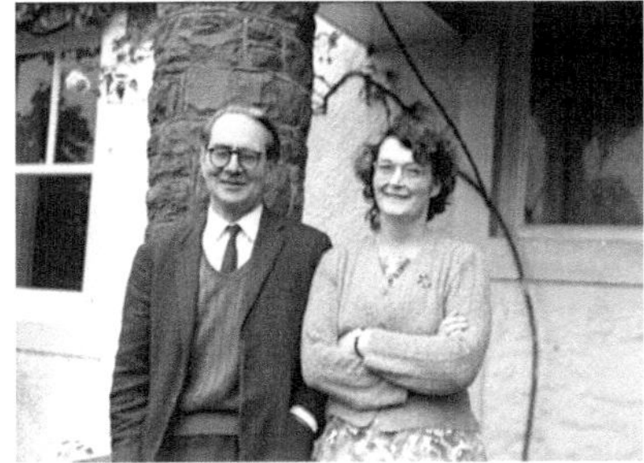

3.12 Left: In the porch at Barone, where many photos were taken over the years

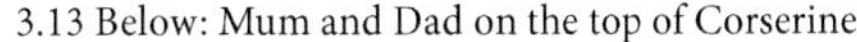

3.13 Below: Mum and Dad on the top of Corserine

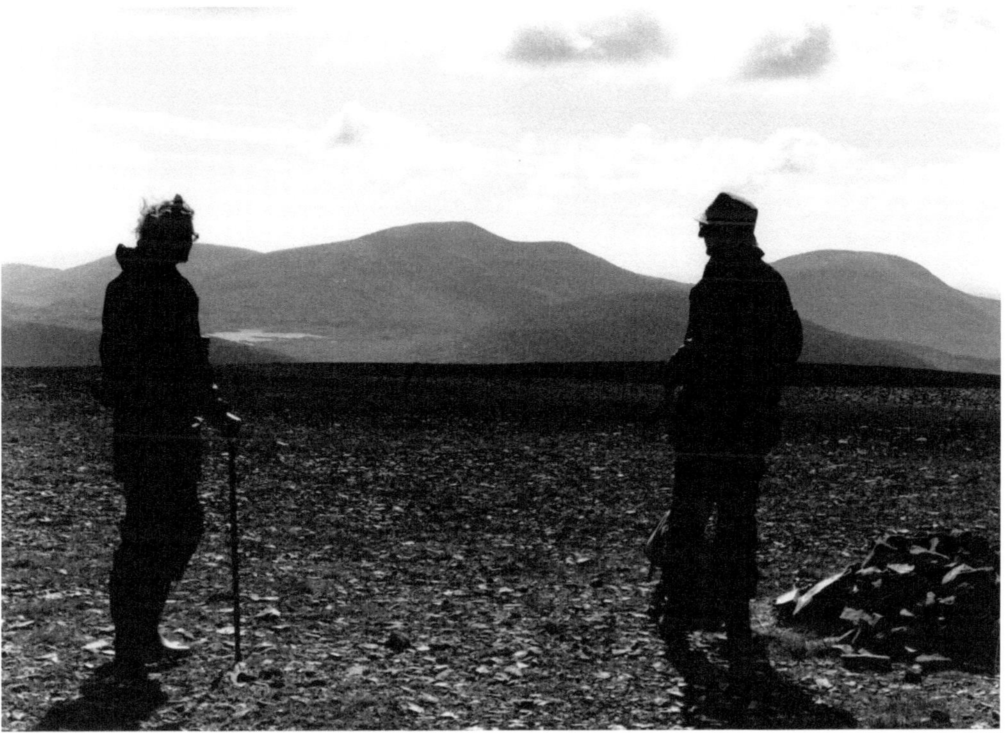

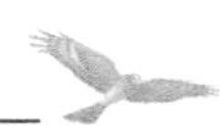

my editing job, I worked in a bookshop for many years. A love of books and reading is another part of the legacy we received from both our parents.

Donald instilled in all his children an abiding love of the natural world, a keen enjoyment of the arts, and an appreciation for silence and simplicity. He had a wonderful ability to keep meeting us at every step of our growth, from youth to middle age, and was willing to be vulnerable and open with us as he grew older. Our mother – his beloved companion for more than half a century – was his rock, and if at times Dad doubted his gifts, she unwaveringly bolstered him with a love rooted in her own inner strength, warmed by her Irish humour, and effectively demonstrated through a range of practical and creative skills. In later years, as her health declined, Dad became the caregiver in the partnership and was devoted to her in that role. Both Donald and Joan were able to stay at Barone until very shortly before they died.

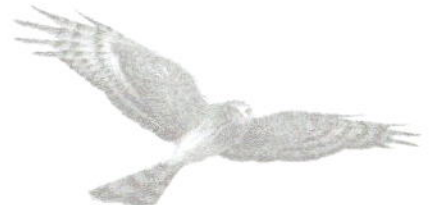

Four
Donald and Jeff

VANESSA WATSON

My father's enthusiasm for birds, both as a painter and as a studiously careful observer of bird behaviour, was an ever-present influence.

Jeff Watson 1997.

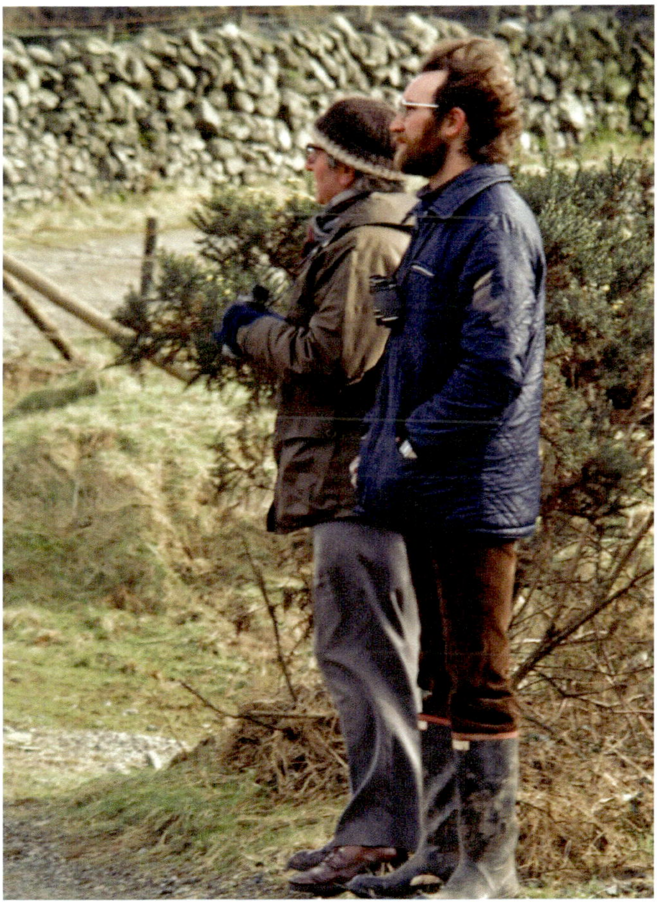

4.1 Donald and Jeff in the field

Donald and Jeff were very close in their shared love of birds and their desire to understand them. For Jeff, this bond formed at a very early age. In his classic monograph, *The Golden Eagle*,[1] he wrote:

> My interest in birds began more than 30 years ago as a young boy raised in the heart of Galloway in southwest Scotland ... My father's enthusiasm for birds, both as a painter and as a studiously careful observer of bird behaviour, was an ever-present influence. Add to this the steady flow of ornithologists through our home and it was perhaps inevitable that birds would figure large in my later life.[2]

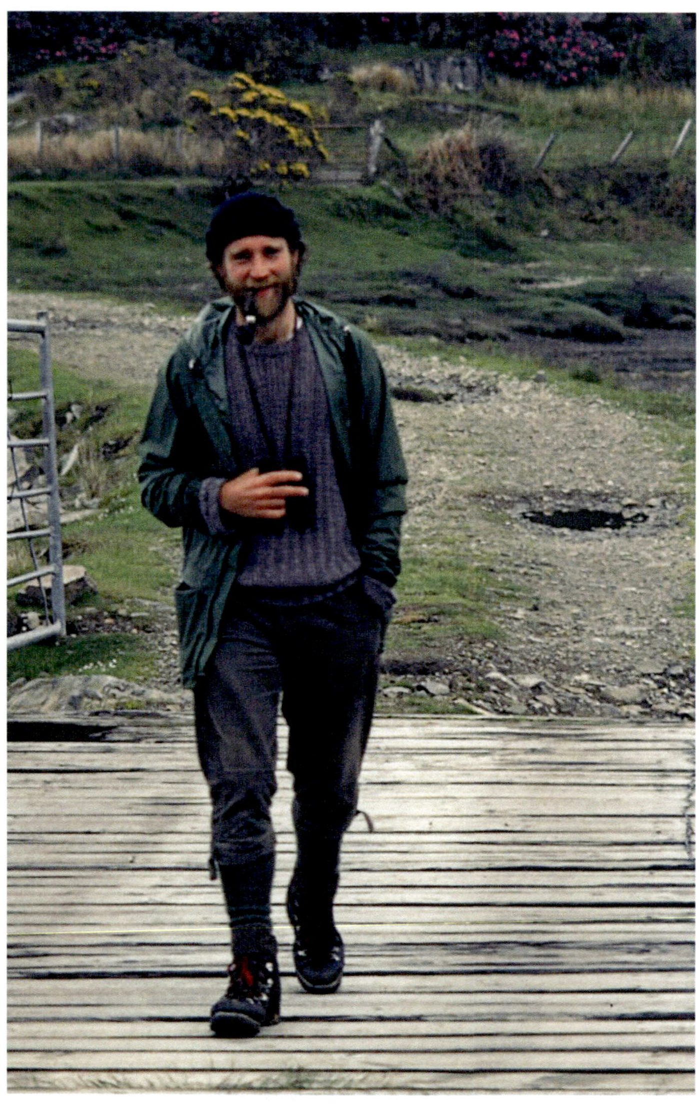

4.2 Jeff on fieldwork

Donald was a respected friend and colleague of many contemporary experts on birds, raptors and conservation. Jeff met many of them in the family home, both as a boy and in later visits. Key among these was Professor Ian Newton, whom Jeff referred to as his mentor, and who presented Jeff with the RSPB Medal for Services to Raptor Conservation in 2007, at the end of his life.

During Jeff's childhood, Donald worked from home and often took his family on bird watching and painting expeditions. Through this, Jeff absorbed Donald's love and enthusiasm for birds, and later he often mentioned memorable incidents from this period. One of special importance was when Donald took him to check a local golden eagle eyrie. 'My earliest memory of Golden Eagles is with my father,' Jeff wrote, 'watching a pair as they soared effortlessly high over a nest site not far from the well-known landmark of Murray's Monument.'[3]

This had a lifelong impact on him. At the start of 2004, *In the Company of Eagles*, an ITV Granada film featuring Jeff,[4] documented his by then world-renowned eagle work, in which he describes it as the first awakening of his future passion for that wonderful bird.

When Jeff became a professional ornithologist, his connection with Donald through birds grew even stronger, and they maintained a frequent dialogue about their respective work and their passions within it. Careful watching in the field and their abiding fascination for the Scottish uplands, birds of prey, and the Isle of May were important aspects of work and leisure for both father and son.

Having been involved in the Isle of May Bird Observatory since the 1930s, Donald also took Jeff there many times in the 1960s to ring migrant birds. Jeff relished these expeditions, and when he went on to the Edinburgh Academy (also Donald's school) he started a small group with his friends the Osbornes, and continued to visit the island whenever possible during the rest of his life.

Conversations between Jeff and Donald about their work came from both shared experience and differences. Donald was self-taught as both a naturalist and an artist. Jeff had studied zoology at Aberdeen University, followed by a PhD for his research on the Seychelles kestrel.[5] From then onward, Donald would often seek out Jeff's knowledge from his scientific work and connections. Similarly, Jeff continued to value Donald's depth of field experience and breadth of contacts.

Jeff's qualifications were the foundations for his initial contract with the Nature Conservancy Council, to research the impact of land use on golden eagles. He worked with Dr Derek Langslow (later CEO of English Nature) as his boss, and with Dr Stuart Rae as field researcher.

The several years of trekking the Scottish hills were followed by many more years of monitoring eyries and analysing and reporting the data collected and developing the Conservation Framework for the Golden Eagle,[6] published in 2008, when he worked for Scottish Natural Heritage. For initial work on this, Jeff worked closely with Dr Phil Whitfield, and they produced a key foundation paper on this in 2002,[7] and a scientific paper in 2006 with several co-authors.[8] Shortly before he passed away, Jeff wrote the foreword to the Golden Eagle Conservation Framework, commenting:

> Undoubtedly the highest priority of all is the need to address the illegal persecution which continues to affect golden eagle populations in the eastern and southern parts of the species' Scottish range. There can be no more urgent task than to eliminate this blight on the population of this majestic bird which, perhaps more than any other creature, is valued as a symbol of wild Scotland.

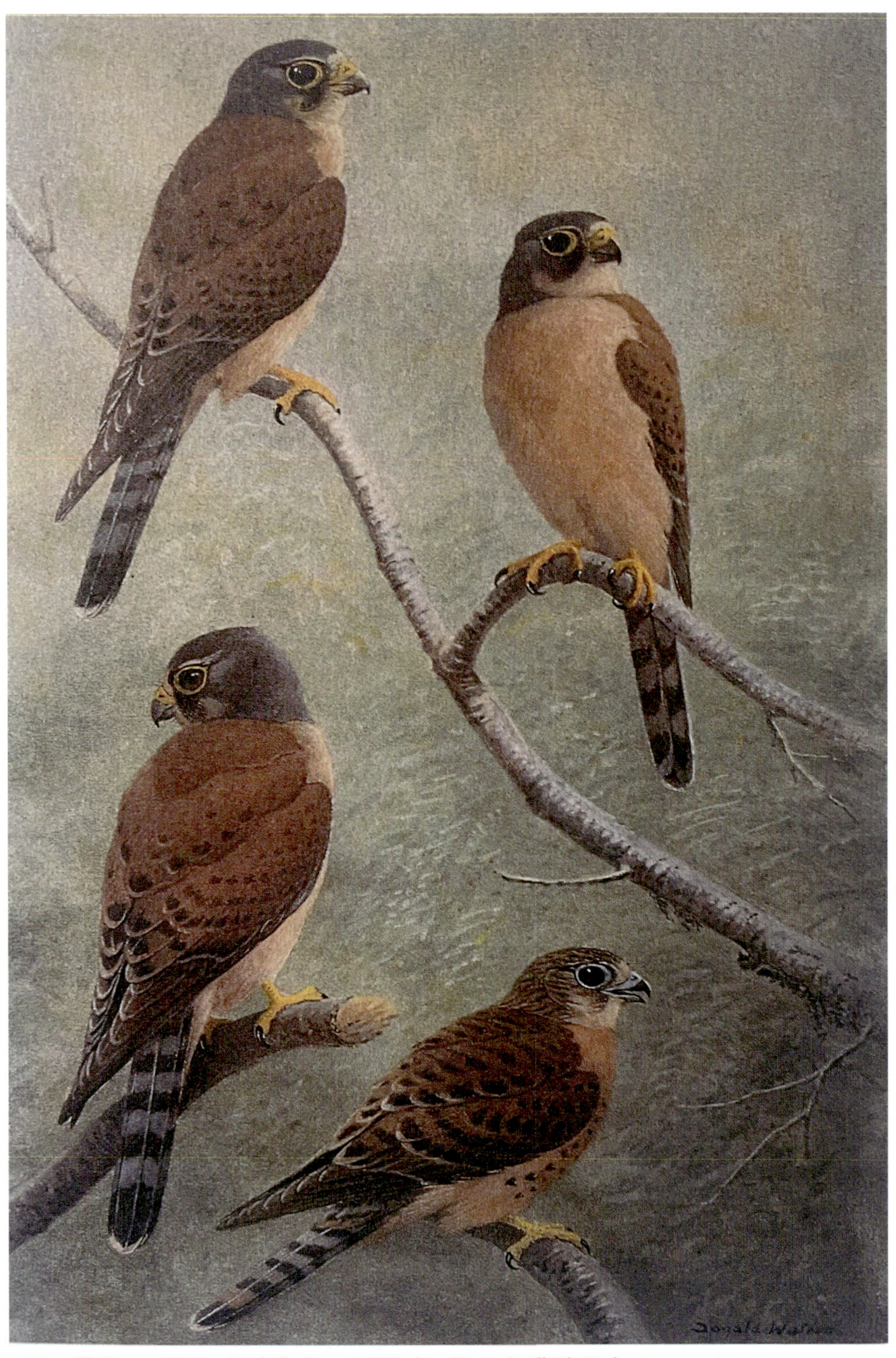

4.3 Donald Watson painting: Seychelles kestrel, 1978, the subject of Jeff's Ph. D. thesis

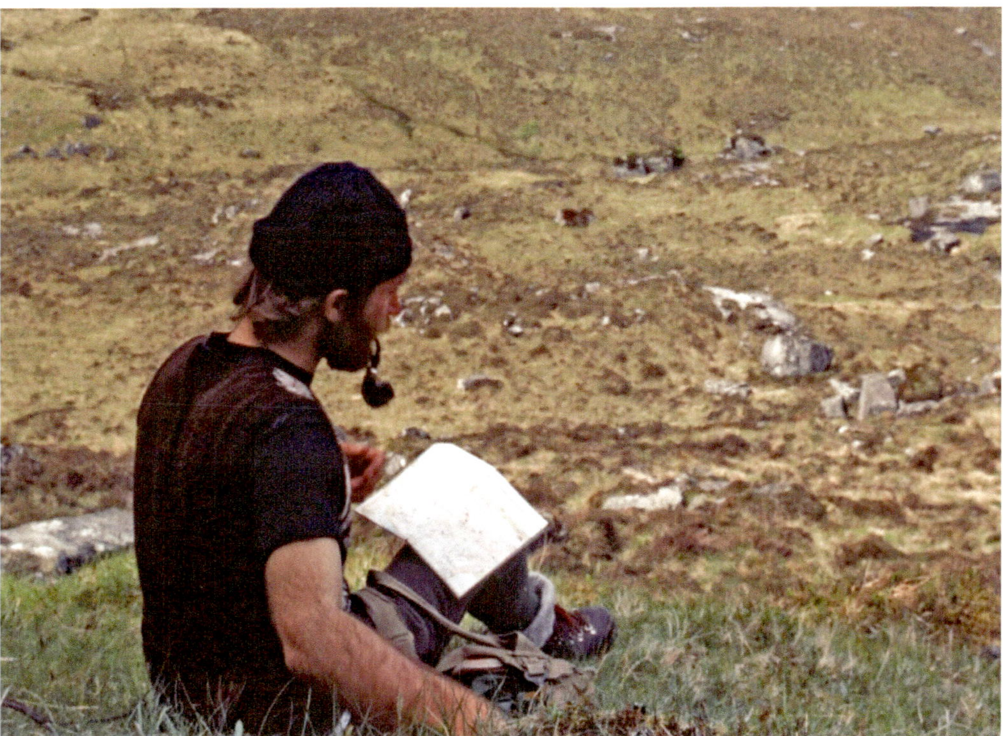

4.4 Jeff on fieldwork

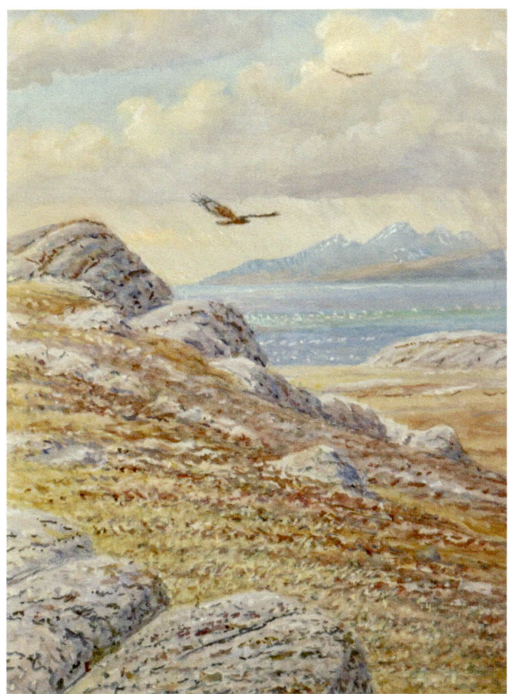

4.5 Donald Watson painting for Jeff's golden eagle book

When Jeff wrote his *magnum opus*, it meant that both father and son had created what remain the definitive monographs on two raptor species – the golden eagle and the hen harrier. Until his untimely death in 2007, Jeff remained the recognised international expert on the golden eagle. His father was very proud of his achievements, and both were strong in their condemnation of the persecution of raptors.

Jeff and his family made frequent visits to Barone, as did Donald to Jeff's home in the Highlands, and Jeff took occasional holidays with Donald and Joan. These were opportunities to explore the local birds, and have long discussions about the issues affecting them, and what was being done to address them.

Donald also had a close relationship with Jeff's son Ronan, who was very proud of his talented and famous grandfather. Donald

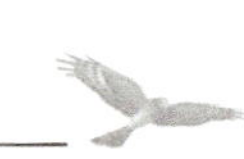

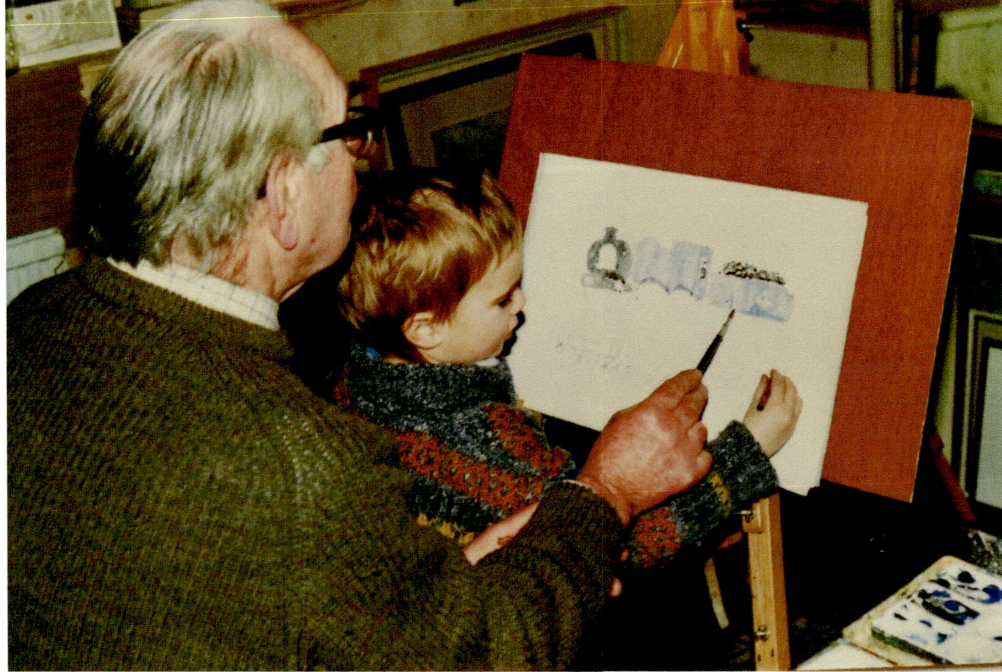

4.6 Donald and Ronan

used to show the young Ronan how to paint. Jeff also had an eye for composition, shown in his talent for landscape photography, described by Ian Newton as comparing favourably with his father's hill and raptor paintings. Jeff would sometimes insert an eagle or other bird to complete the image, just as his father had done, to show the bird in its habitat, as he would have seen it in the field. Ronan has also inherited Donald's artistic talent, as displayed in his skills as a landscape architect and designer, and is now a golden eagle monitor himself. Donald and Jeff live on through the generations.

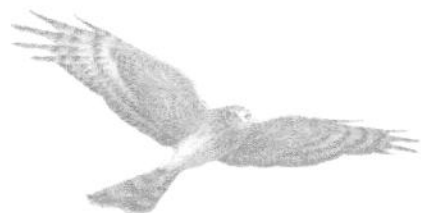

Five

Donald Watson

CHRIS ROLLIE

> When the Hen Harriers on their roost had settled for the night and our twinkling eyes met, words were superfluous, and wonder was all.
>
> Chris Rollie[1]

I first met Donald in the mid-1980s, but I already knew his evocative illustrations in *The Oxford Book of Birds*.[2] These fired my imagination and provided a sort of reference backcloth to my interest in birds as a boy in Ayrshire through the 1960s. Graduation from Stirling University in 1980 was followed by a year at Jordanhill College in Glasgow for teacher training. There I shared a flat with friend Eric, son of Dick Roxburgh, a retired miner and founding father of raptor fieldwork and recording in south-west Scotland. I soon fell under Dick's spell. He became a huge influence on the rest of my life as I became immersed in watching and surveying raptors in the region. Dick gave me a copy of his friend Donald Watson's *The Hen Harrier*. This further encouraged me and others to find the nests and roosts of these birds, so accurately and lovingly described and illustrated in this wonderful book.

Dick had been a friend and correspondent of Donald's for many years, and occasionally dropped into the latter's home at Barone with bird news following a day with eagles and peregrines in Galloway. However, I first met Donald with Dick, Charlie Park and Ricky Gladwell in Carsphairn in the mid-1980s in the Salutation Inn (since converted into private residences). I knew the Salutation from my days (and nights) in the Royal Observers' Corps (ROC) in the early 1970s. Like my home village of New Cumnock, and indeed St John's Town of Dalry, Carsphairn had an underground post (bunker) to which I was assigned on joining the corps as a teenager. The Salutation was a grand old country inn, notable for Charlie Palmar's superb black-and-white photographs of eagles at their Galloway eyrie in 1947, and a very fitting location for my first meeting with the artist and author. He seemed very kind and interested in all we had to tell him about our findings, and particularly regarding hen harriers which at that time were increasingly settling to breed on mosses (moors) near our respective homes in Ayrshire.

Our next meeting was in the Clachan Inn, St John's Town of Dalry, where in the space of 20 seconds or so Donald signed my copy of *The Hen Harrier* and brilliantly sketched a flying male on the title page with just a few strokes of his pen. Naturally, this book remains one of my most treasured possessions. Thereafter, I became a fairly regular visitor to Barone. Indeed in December 1991 my family and I moved to Dalry, and we became firm friends and neighbours on Main Street.

Following the end of the war with Japan in 1946, Donald returned from Burma to his home in Edinburgh, and that year was introduced by his old Midlothian Ornithological Club and Edinburgh Academy friend, George Waterston, to Rev. J.M. McWilliam and Arthur Duncan (later Sir Arthur, Chairman of the Nature Conservancy and Lord Lieutenant of Dumfriesshire). Both men were keen ornithologists and near neighbours at Tynron in Dumfriesshire. Moreover, both were instantly taken by Donald's paintings. Arthur Duncan invited the young artist to stay with him at Tynron to undertake an ambitious series of paintings of birds in their habitats, with a view to illustrating his own proposed, but never completed, book on birds of the Stewartry of Kirkcudbright. In this tranquil and supportive setting, Donald began honing his skill as a professional artist, trying various techniques and methods, and attempting to emulate his favourite bird artists, such as Crawhall, Seaby, Ennion and Thorburn, but always with an eye on the French Impressionists, especially Monet, and other landscape masters. Over three years largely spent in Nithsdale, he became great friends with his host Duncan and McWilliam, or 'The Minister' as he was known by everyone. He also visited Galloway and became immediately impressed as an artist

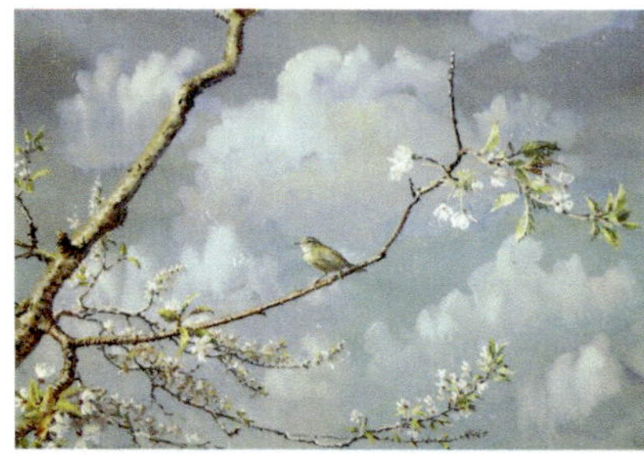

5.1 Left: Donald Watson painting: Willow Warbler in cherry trees
5.2 Below: Donald Watson painting: Curlew over the Mulloch, Dalry 1951

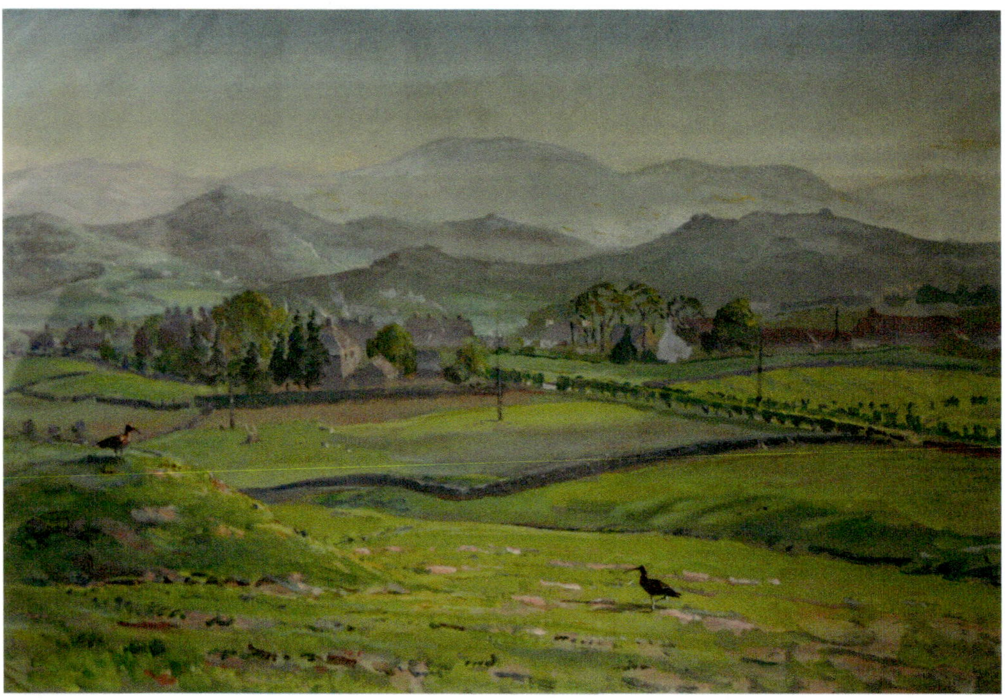

by its quality of light. He and his childhood friend Joan Moore were married in Ayr in June 1950, and enjoyed a three-month honeymoon on Benbecula, where Donald painted for an exhibition in Glasgow that autumn. They spent the succeeding winter on the Solway coast before buying Barone, on Main Street, Dalry. The owner was one Dr Carmichael, who was intent on emigrating to Australia and therefore very keen to sell. Carmichael had been born in Tynron, and Donald always reckoned he dropped the price on hearing tales of his birthplace from Donald's time with Sir Arthur and The Minister.

On moving to Barone in 1951 Donald immediately commenced painting, including a wonderful picture of a willow warbler on a blossoming cherry branch[3] and a pair of curlew overlooking the village from near Mulloch Hill. His preferred method in those days, as described in several of his books, was very much *en plein air*, and his loose impressionistic style is as distinctive as it is compelling. He had several favourite places locally where he set up his easel, including Moss Roddock, Mackilston, Forrest Glen, Grennan, Dalarran and other places that now comprise the Donald Watson Art Trail,[4] and more on which later. His illustrations of birds in their landscapes for *The Oxford Book of Birds*, which made such an impact on my boyhood birdwatching, involved him producing 96 plates at the rate of one per week over two years, whilst his *Birds of Moor and Mountain* combined for the first time his skills as an artist, writer and ornithologist.

Donald the ornithologist

As a founding member of the Society of Wildlife Artists in 1964, and their first honorary member in 1992, Donald's legacy as an artist is secure. But apart from his hen harrier monograph and a couple of papers on roosting hen harriers, his status and contribution as an ornithologist is perhaps less well known to non-birders. As a teenager in the 1930s, he was the youngest member of the Midlothian Ornithological Club, and indeed became their latest surviving member.

He first visited the Isle of May with his older brother Eric in 1933. On arrival they met the 'good ladies', Misses Baxter and Rintoul (joint authors of *The Birds of Scotland*[5]), who were departing the May for the last time after nearly 30 years of ground-breaking migration studies there. Under the guidance of George Waterston, the following year Donald became part of the team who established the Isle of May Bird Observatory in the old coastguard lookout, by kind permission of the Northern Lighthouse Board. A Heligoland trap was built that autumn by his brother Eric, Frank Elder, W.B. Alexander and Ronald Lockley, who had recently set up the first British bird observatory at Skokholm Island. The Isle of May became a very special, almost spiritual, place for Donald, who returned to the island at least once every year for 49 out of the next 50 years.

Encouraged by the writings of E.M. (Max) Nicholson,[6] Donald and his friends had begun to make bird censuses in the 1930s, which he picked up again on settling in Galloway. He had a methodical approach to bird recording, and in partnership with John Young from Sanquhar, who covered Dumfriesshire, he built on earlier work by such as Sir William Jardine, Robert Service, O.J. Pullen, Jack G. Gordon, Hugh Gladstone, Rev. John Morrel McWilliam (The Minister) and Sir Arthur Duncan, to bring Dumfries and Galloway bird recording into the modern age. Indeed, Donald was regional bird recorder for over 30 years, producing annual bird reports from the early 1980s, following earlier sporadic reports with John Young in the 1960s and 70s.

Donald was an assiduous diarist and correspondent, receiving and replying to letters from all over the UK and overseas. He kept most if not all of these, and meticulously collated the annual reports of bird sightings that came to him as local recorder. He was also a great archivist and heir to some of Sir Arthur Duncan's important manuscripts, including the notebooks of T.B. Hough of New Galloway (d.1916) and the near-complete 1930s draft manuscript of Jack G. Gordon's *Birds of Wigtownshire.*[7] Sadly, Sir Arthur's ambition of publishing a book on birds of the Stewartry of Kirkcudbright was never fulfilled, though he did publish a list.[8]

Donald had arrived in Galloway at a very exciting time for birds. The widespread removal of grazing animals, particularly sheep, which accompanied the huge increases in afforestation from the 1950s encouraged a flush of vegetation growth that saw numbers of voles, pipits and larks multiply to levels unprecedented in recent history. Black grouse also flourished, and their numbers returned to, and perhaps even exceeded, levels not seen since Edwardian times. There were corresponding increases in predators, including short-eared owls, kestrels, hen harriers and even golden eagles, in turn facilitated by a sustained reduction in gamekeeping. Donald set to work painting these beautiful birds in their habitats in a captivating way that showcased Galloway's countryside to a wide audience. However, one species particularly drew his attention on the moors of Grobdale on the road between Laurieston and Gatehouse of Fleet. Hen harriers had been virtually extinct as a breeding species on the UK mainland since Victorian times, and when Donald found a nest on Craig of Grobdale in 1959 it was the first definite report of breeding in the south of Scotland in the 20th century, although from the reports of local shepherds he felt sure there had been earlier attempts. Four young fledged that year, and so began an artistic and ornithological association with hen harriers that endured for the rest of Donald's life. Together with Bert Dickson in Wigtownshire in a pioneering study, he recorded communal roosting of hen harriers on a scale unheard of hitherto in the UK. He must have painted hundreds of pictures of hen harriers in all situations: foraging, displaying, nesting, food-passing and roosting. He made

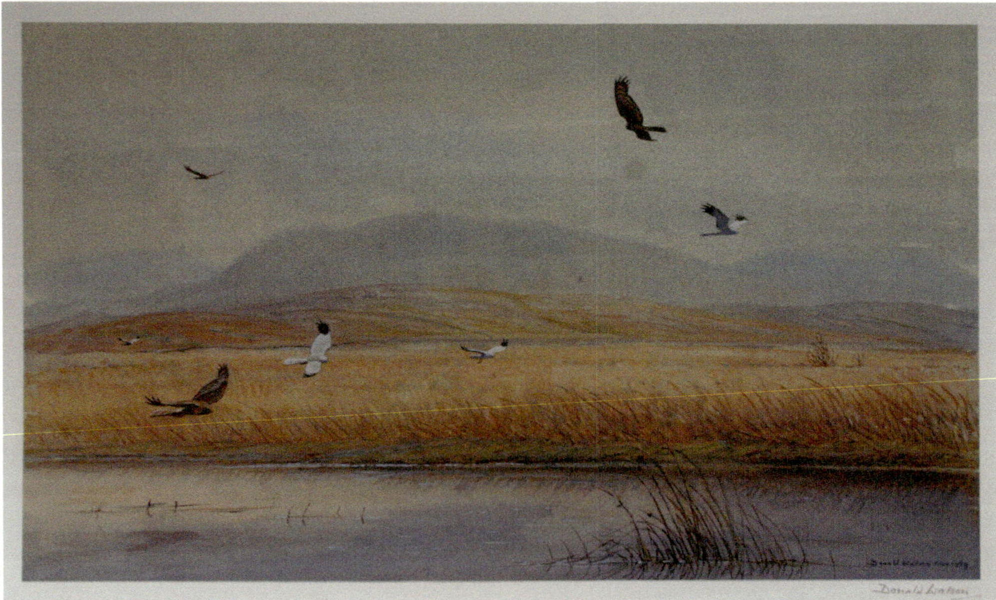

5.3 Donald Watson painting: Hen Harrier winter roost, 1969

the species his own with his celebrated monograph, *The Hen Harrier*, which is a classic marriage of ornithology, art and evocative writing bordering on poetry at times. Unsurprisingly, it is one of the most acclaimed books in Poyser's prestigious ornithological catalogue.

In 1983, Donald and fellow hen harrier enthusiast Roger Clarke commenced the Hen Harrier Winter Roost Investigation, which involved encouraging a bunch of dedicated volunteers to monitor their local hen harrier roosts on the third Sunday of each month in October to March inclusive. Donald collated the Scottish results, with Roger covering roosts in England and Wales. I became involved from 1984 and assisted Donald with co-ordinating and collating results from the mid-1990s. The BTO took over co-ordination of the investigation in England following Roger's death in 2007, and I believe it is now the longest running non-breeding raptor survey in the world. In this way, Donald encouraged very many people over a wide area to become interested in and to watch hen harriers. Encouraged by the local council, he also ran several night classes in birdwatching in Castle Douglas and Newton Stewart, and gave various illustrated talks to ornithological and other community groups in Dumfries and Galloway and beyond.

Donald and nature conservation

The Galloway countryside was and still is under great threat from conifer afforestation, with the consequent loss of open country and associated habitats and species. What began as a great boon for wildlife in the late 1950s and 60s became increasingly oppressive and destructive as the conifer canopy closed, moorlands disappeared and predators such a foxes and crows increased with resultant huge losses of ground-nesting birds like curlew, lapwing, skylark, black and red grouse, hen harriers and merlins. The initial increase in breeding golden eagles reversed, and four pairs became two by 1990. His pioneering study of breeding hen harriers, so important to their recolonisation of mainland Britain as a breeding species, was already waning as the initially productive open ground habitat was succeeded by blanket Sitka spruce. Breeding locations became deserted as the conifer thickets closed; the harriers moved on to more open areas and essentially followed the new planting until there was insufficient ground to hold them. Increasingly, the nests of the reducing population were predated, with foxes being the culprits when these could be identified. Charlie Park and I found the last nest in the area near Loch Grannoch in 1992, which fledged three young. The female at this nest was a first-year female, wing-tagged as a chick the year before in Argyll. Donald documented this decline in various publications, especially in *In Search of Harriers*.

Like most ornithologists and wildlife watchers of the time, he was very concerned about the seemingly inexorable march of afforestation over his beloved moorlands in Galloway, together with the more widely known and criticised planting of the blanket bogs of the Caithness and Sutherland Flow Country, encouraged by the lucrative tax incentives to the super-rich and pension funds etc. He had been a close friend for many years of Derek Ratcliffe, then chief scientist of the Nature Conservancy Council, who was in the thick of the battle between wildlife conservation and state-funded forestry. Thankfully, before he retired Derek was instrumental in the designation and thereby protection of several of the last remaining extensive quality moorland habitats in Galloway, including Cairnsmore of Fleet National Nature Reserve and Merrick-Kells SSSI, including the Silver Flowe bog system with pools, the only extensive area of such habitat south of the Flow Country, and where he discovered azure hawker dragonfly, a species more associated with more northern bogs. Of course, Donald had illustrated Derek's monograph, *The Peregrine Falcon*, and often had days in the field with him on his annual spring pilgrimages to the Galloway Hills.

Donald played his own part in trying to halt the afforestation madness through reasoned letters to various politicians and people of influence, including senior foresters (see Chapter 8 for more detailed discussion). As a published authority on moorland birds and honorary president of SOC, he was highly respected by the local Forestry Commission (FC) and engaged with them and their head wildlife ranger, his friend Geoff Shaw, in documenting the important remaining birds and locations in Galloway Forest Park, and what could be done for them. This included various initiatives including the regional Indicative Forestry Strategy, the Forest Birds of Galloway Project, and of course involved RSPB, Nature Conservancy Council (Scotland), Dumfries and Galloway Raptor Study Group, and individual ornithologists and entomologists etc. However, it is fair to say that for all the hopes and good intentions of wildlife enthusiasts and sympathetic FC staff like Geoff, none of these initiatives ever really progressed beyond liaison box-ticking.

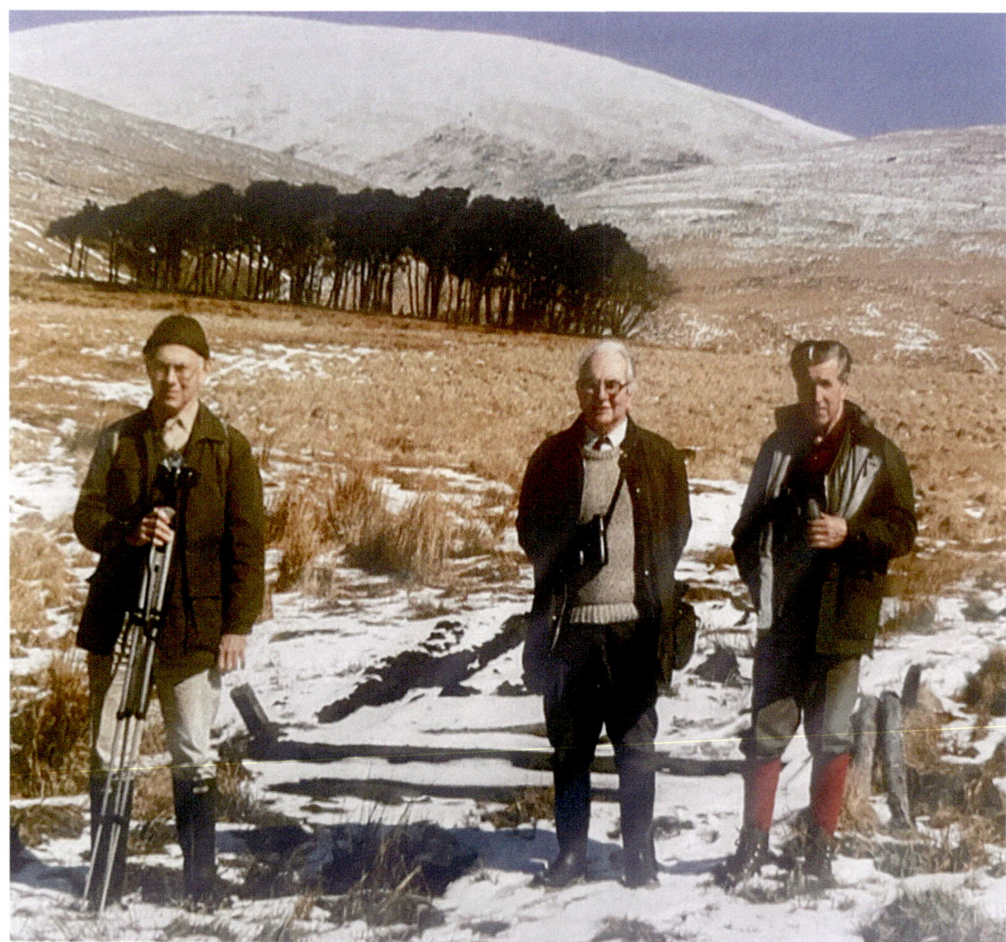

5.4 Donald with Dick Roxburgh (right) and Derek Ratcliffe (left) in the hills near Carsphairn

Economics and production foresters held sway, in Dumfries and Galloway at least, and even after 1988 when then Chancellor Nigel Lawson announced the end of the 'absurdity' of the forestry tax shelter, state forests continued to expand and increased grants for private forestry resulted in the loss of yet more open ground, albeit at a greatly reduced rate. Cheap imports and other market forces caused new planting to dry up for a while, but sadly the pressure is now back on with targeted financial encouragement from the Scottish Government and foresters audaciously claiming carbon sequestration as a key driver despite significant evidence to the contrary. Sadly, in Dumfries and Galloway this means yet more Sitka spruce planting with further pressure on the fast-declining curlew population and threatening the prospects of an increased population of breeding golden eagles.

Of course, Donald also witnessed the switch from hay to silage, the loss of mixed arable farms, increased drainage and stocking rates and other agricultural improvements, with all their corresponding impacts on farmland birds. He documented these in his various writings, particularly *A Bird Artist in Scotland* and *One Pair of Eyes*, and including the loss of calling corncrakes, roding woodcock and displaying snipe from around his home in Dalry. However, whilst deeply saddened by this, to some extent he saw some inevitability in these changes, driven as they were by the need for food and the EU Common Agricultural Policy. He felt very different when it came to game preservation and the senseless illegal slaughter of birds of prey by gamekeepers on grouse moors and pheasant shoots. In the latter decades of the 20th century poison baits were commonplace in the UK countryside and had a huge negative impact on populations of common buzzards and ravens, restricting their breeding ranges, and to a large extent confining red kites to a few pairs in mid-Wales. Thankfully, this practice became increasingly illegal and socially unacceptable, and the hugely expanded populations of these species now are testament to this.

However, the persecution of raptors by trapping and shooting continued largely unabated, and chief amongst the victims were his beloved hen harriers. Driven grouse shooting had greatly declined in Galloway and by the time of his arrival in 1951 had virtually disappeared around Dalry. There was still good heather cover and impressive shooting butts on recently abandoned grouse moors at nearby Mackilston and Marskaig, for example, and indeed grouse and golden plover prevailed in these areas up to my arrival in 1991. I remember Robbie Dalziel, brother of Donald's good friend, Frank, telling me that he used to drive grouse onto the guns on these places before and just after the Second World War. Other active grouse moors in those days were at Corriedoo, Blackcraig, Troquhain and Laggan (Loch Howie), where Robbie and George Wood, both village acquaintances of 'the artist', also beat grouse.

It was at Corriedoo in 1953 that a gamekeeper, then working part-time for the Forestry Commission, trapped and killed a female Montagu's harrier at her nest. She had been ringed as a chick on Anglesey, and Donald recounted the incident in his posthumous book *In Search of Harriers*. Back then such trapping was commonplace, but Donald was appalled many years later in finding and reporting to the police a trapped sparrowhawk on a moorland fencepost near Stranraer, and, whilst respecting people's legal right and desire to shoot, he increasingly engaged in deploring the criminal actions of gamekeepers and questioned the lack of action by their employers. However, despite all this he generally always enjoyed good relations with local farmers and estate owners in Galloway, and indeed several even kindly lent him their shooting and vermin logs, going back to Victorian and Edwardian times. These showed both the extent of gamekeeping in the area – there were at least six gamekeepers living in and around Dalry when he arrived in 1951 – and the numbers of grouse, partridge, pheasant and wildfowl being shot annually. Almost invariably there is an exception, the proof to every rule, and one old farmer, well known for his anti-raptor attitudes, hated raptors and their followers with a passion. In fact, Donald said that he was the only landowner he was aware of who had taken a dislike to him since he arrived in the region, but this animosity was immediate, serious and sustained. So much so, in fact, that I remember we were obliged to clamber into the back of Geoff Shaw's FC van to conceal ourselves from detection as we crossed that farmer's land on a shared access to reach the site of a breeding marsh harrier, an extremely rare breeding bird in southern Scotland.

Donald Watson, raptor recovery and 'the raptor men'

Donald's book *The Hen Harrier*, Derek Ratcliffe's *The Peregrine Falcon* and Ian Newton's *Population Ecology of Raptors*[9] arrived on a wave of raptor recovery from the pesticide-induced population crashes of the late 1950s and 1960s. Peregrines, sparrowhawks, kestrels and buzzards were all on the increase, and 1980 saw the birth of the raptor study group movement in Scotland, to whom Donald Watson, Derek Ratcliffe and Ian Newton were revered heroes – and still are today. In fact, Donald was a founding member of both the South West Scotland Raptor Study Group in 1983 and the Dumfries and Galloway Raptor Study Group in 1990.

Inspired and mentored by Dick Roxburgh, I was an early convert. On first seeing Donald's paintings of birds in their landscapes, particularly peregrines, short-eared owls, hen harriers and merlins, I was struck by how much other artists had missed. Here was someone who was

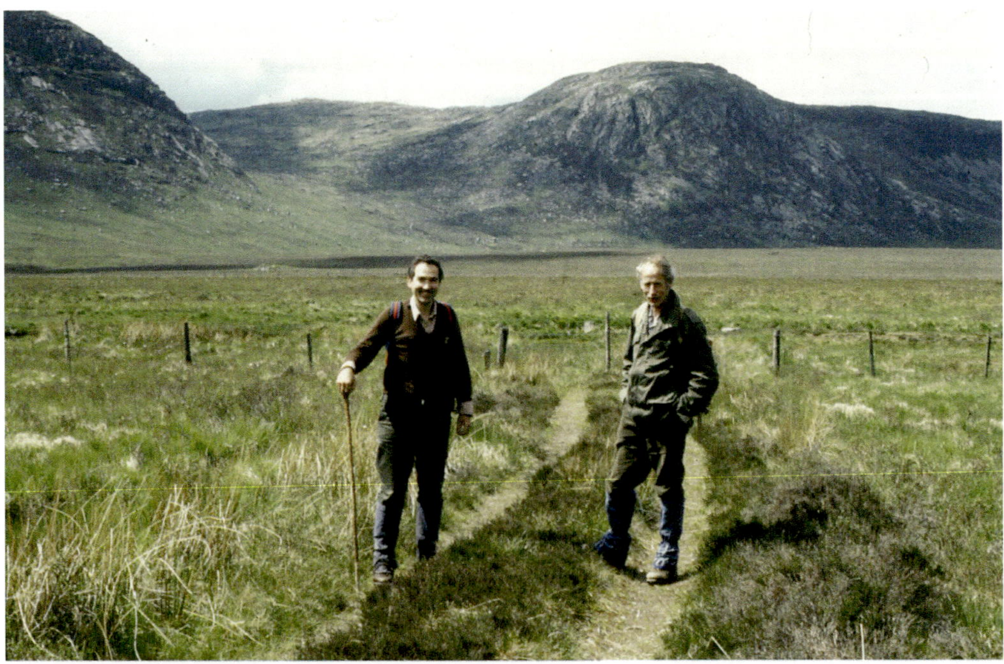

5.5 The 'raptor men', (l-r) Ricky Gladwell and Charlie Park by the Silver Flowe

somehow able to capture more of the essence of my interest and the reality of the scenes before me than any other bird artist I had encountered, yet I could not put my finger on just what it was. I was not alone in this, and many hours were spent with enthusiast friends like Dick, Charlie Park, Ricky Gladwell, Bob Stakim, Ian Miller, Dave Dick, Geoff Shaw, Gordon Riddle, Ray Hawley, Brian Etheridge and Roger Clarke – real raptor men all – marvelling at and trying to define just what made Donald's work so special. Perhaps part of the answer lay in the fact that not everyone could see the beauty in a gathering of hen harriers to roost in the darkness at the onset of rain, the high lurking peregrine in the distance from swirling coastal birds before their nests on sea cliffs, or the down and dropping bespattered brood of young merlins in a heathery forest at close quarters on the ground. But we did. Donald knew this, of course, and he always eagerly awaited all the comments on opening nights of his exhibitions through the 1980s and 90s – but none more so perhaps than those of the 'raptor men', as he called us. Even better for him was when he was able to draw some rare suggestion or even criticism on a work in progress; then he noted every word and inference with remarkably keen inspection.

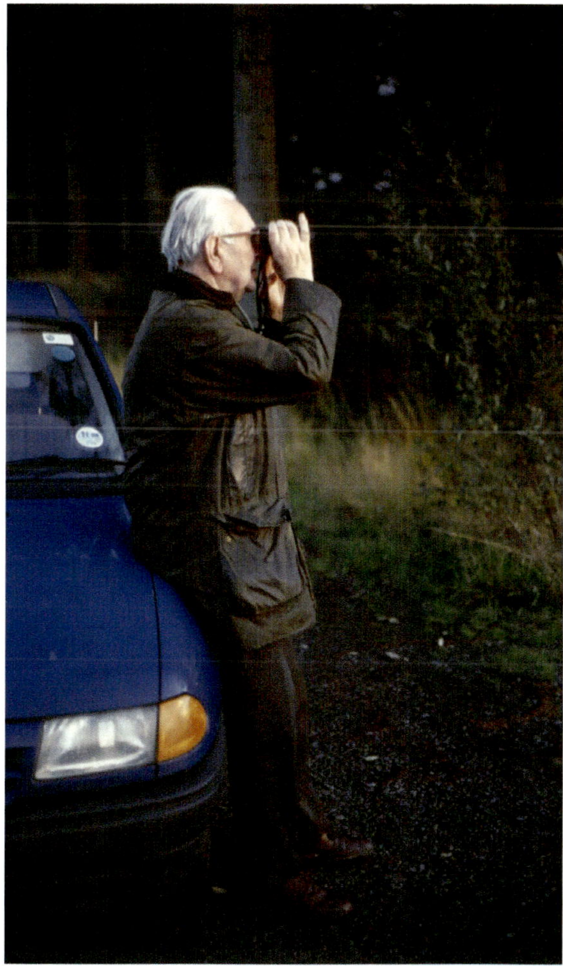

5.6 Donald at Hen Harrier roost

Donald Watson and village life in St John's Town of Dalry

When the couple moved to Dalry in 1951, Joan was pregnant with their eldest daughter, Pam, and Jeff, Kate and Louise followed through the 1950s. The young couple settled quickly, and their children were soon engaged in local school activities. Joan later became a popular home economics teacher for some years and got to know virtually every family in the parish. Early friends in the village included Frank Dalziel, General Jock Holden, Pamela Young and, especially, Louis A. Urquhart. Louis was a Glasgow man who worked for the Royal Bank of Scotland there. He and his wife Kathleen often spent holidays in Dalry soon after the war, and it was there that Donald and Joan met them in 1953, and they instantly became friends.

By that time, Louis was already a keen ornithologist and had published a few short notes on birds of the Clyde area. He also found and reported Scotland's first buff-breasted sandpiper. Louis was a quiet and reserved man, with a dry wit and keen sense of humour, which, allied to his sharp observational skills and love of the outdoors, made him the perfect field companion for Donald. Over many years the pair watched nesting and roosting hen harriers and merlins, and they even found breeding dotterel together on the Galloway tops. On retirement in 1970, Louis and Kathleen came to live in a bungalow just across the street from Barone, but sadly Kathleen died in 1978, whereupon Louis resourcefully looked after himself and vigorously pursued his outdoor passions. Though a keen trout fisherman, Louis' favourite bird was the goosander, and each spring he had great fun checking out and recording the happenings at various traditional nesting sites, often in holes in deciduous trees by burns. He accompanied Donald and Joan on holidays to Andalusia in 1980 and to Mallorca in1982, and was twice on the Isle of May with Donald. Louis' friendly smile, beneath a thin horizontal moustache much favoured by military men of his day – he was in the RAOC during the war – was a familiar sight on Dalry's Main Street, and he always had interesting observations to share on his beloved goosanders. Following his death in 2001, his meticulous diaries were lodged in SOC headquarters at Waterston House, Aberlady.

The Watsons were a popular family in the village and fully integrated into village life, with the children attending school there, though Jeff later boarded in Edinburgh. Donald was a frequent attender of SOC meetings in New Galloway, and Joan sometimes attended, too. Then there were the celebrated goose weekends each winter in the 1960s and 70s, when SOC members from all over Scotland and beyond descended on the Nith Hotel in Glencaple for a weekend of 'goosing' and socialising on the Solway. Donald was also a regular attender of RSPB's Galloway Local Members Group meetings from 1985, and with friend Ray Hawley helped illustrate the group's highly successful *Bird Walks in Dumfries and Galloway*, produced to celebrate RSPB's centenary. It is fair to say that Donald had a huge circle of friends and admirers throughout Scotland, and especially locally, including Fraser Paterson, Jim Barclay, Derek and John

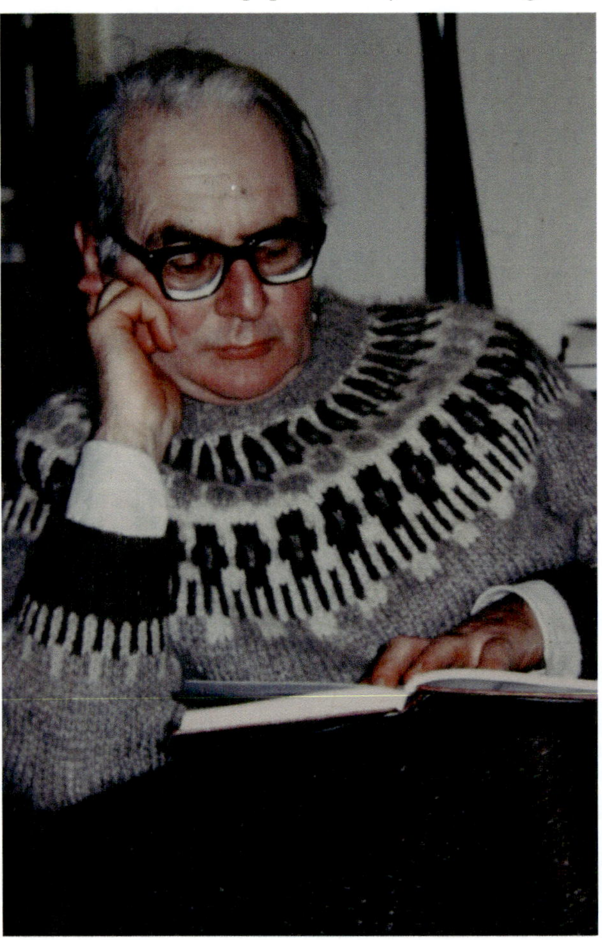

5.7 Donald in Barone sitting room

Skilling, Edmund Fellowes, Richard and Barbara Mearns, Geoff Shaw, Willie Brotherston, Bobby Smith, Pamela Pumphrey, Ian Balfour-Paul, Joan Howie, Kenneth and Helen Halliday, Bryan Nelson and Sir Nigel and Lady Catherine Henderson, in addition to the 'raptor men' mentioned above.

His house in Dalry had been a place of pilgrimage for friends and followers of his art for several decades before I knew him. Visitors included people from all over the country and oversees, including well-known wildlife artists such as Sir Peter Scott, John Busby, Ian Willis, Keith Brockie and John Threlfall, plus ornithological luminaries like Hugh Boyd, David Bannerman, Derek Ratcliffe, Lars Svensson, George Waterston, Frank Hamilton, Adam Watson and Roy Dennis – to name only a few.

Although I had corresponded with Donald and visited him at home occasionally for several years beforehand, it was not until my appointment as RSPB conservation officer for Dumfries and Galloway in February 1991, and subsequent relocation to Dalry from Ayrshire in December, that I began to get to know him as a close friend and near neighbour in Main Street. This was fairly gradual to begin with, as I was extremely busy ensuring that my major change in career – leaving teaching, to join the RSPB with corresponding drop in salary – was going to be a success. Consequently, I was completely immersed in work when not away on holiday. Of course, at that time, he was still very much a professional artist, painting, preparing for exhibitions and continuing to attract prospective buyers to Dalry. I was already aware that the list of past visitors to Barone would form a virtual *Who's who* of the wildlife art and ornithological worlds, but it was only now that I realised just how busy he was and how many people dropped in to see him. There were regular collectors who had cyclical urges to buy more of his pictures and who were not prepared to wait until the next exhibition if they could persuade him to offer a private viewing. Of course, as a great admirer of Donald's art myself, I developed a special insight into this behaviour. In the course of my work for RSPB in the region, I came to realise just how well known his paintings and indeed his style were – his trademark skies were so attractive and evocative of the Galloway countryside, as were the shining wet sands of the Solway with their waterfowl. His paintings were a great advertisement for the area, and many people visited Galloway on the strength of them.

He had favourite places around The Glenkens – several of them now forming the Donald Watson Art Trail – where he would often sketch in the car, and now and then have an easel outside. In his early days he liked to paint outdoors mostly, and several of his pictures from that time bear the telltale raindrop smears as evidence, which he would sometimes leave on the picture as it suited him. Later, he was more likely to make sketches in the field and complete the works in his studio. Although he was normally a very approachable and affable person, one quickly learned to be careful in disturbing him at work, especially if in his view he was making either very good or very bad progress. If it was going very well, he wanted to make the most of this and continue at all costs, whereas if it was going rather badly, he was determined to break on through into a more productive and satisfying phase. Somewhere between the two was when to catch him, when he was open to indifferent achievement being improved by a break. This carried through into his studio, and early in our friendship I always waited for his invitation to view what he was working on. It was always exciting and a special privilege to be taken upstairs past paintings by his uncle Harry (Pearson), Eric Ennion, Bruno Liljefors and others to see his own works in progress, with others long completed

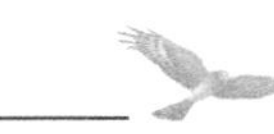

lying around and sometimes framed and ready for exhibition. Of course, approaching the time of a new exhibition there was always a whole batch waiting to be carted off to be framed.

Barone

In the 1990s, I became an increasingly frequent visitor to Barone, often with my own toddlers, who Donald and Joan adored. At that time – and indeed until 2002, when I established the first local RSPB office at Crossmichael – I worked from a room in my home, and Donald would sometimes drop in with bird or other news on his way back up on foot from the local shop/newsagent to Barone. On other days, I remember the peculiarly distinctive sound of his engine from his unique approach to clutch control as he took the brae in his car on an 'altogether too foul' day, as he would say in quoting his old birding friend M.F. Maury Meiklejohn, professor of Italian at Glasgow University and long-time weekend columnist in the *Glasgow Herald*. Donald and Louis were big fans.

Family Christmas and New Year festivities were always a feature at Barone, and cemented early and firm friendships in Dalry. Hogmanay and 'the bells' were keenly celebrated in the Watson home, with home-baking, lumps of coal, first-footing, whisky and other refreshments all on hand. Both Donald and Joan had lovely tales of past visits by friends and neighbours through the early hours and into New Year's Day and beyond. In later years, I was a regular first foot, perhaps most memorably at the Millennium, when I took my family up to the mast at the top of Benniguinea, a prominent hill just south of Clatteringshaws in the heart of what is now the Galloway Dark Sky Park. With so many bonfires and fireworks displays advertised, we were keen to do something different and memorable, and I will never forget the flashes that lit up the horizon in virtually every direction as Big Ben sounded out across the air waves and heralded the new millennium. Then it was back *en famille* to Barone to celebrate with Donald and Joan, who were delighted to hear of our experience. Both had a wonderful sense of humour, and we always had great fun discussing all manner of things, including various local happenings.

Donald was one of our last living links with the Edwardian and even late Victorian eras, having met and conversed with various ornithologists, landowners and workers on the land who had lived during these periods. I loved to hear of his visit as a boy of 12 in 1930 to have tea with the renowned wildlife artist Archibald Thorburn, then in his sixties and a near neighbour in Surrey. I have already mentioned 'the good ladies', Rintoul and Baxter, Maury Meiklejohn, George Waterston and Ronald Lockley, but Donald also became a friend of Desmond and Maimie Nethersole-Thompson and indeed illustrated their *Greenshanks* and *Waders* books. Desmond Nethersole-Thompson, of course, was a great character, well-known ornithologist and pre-war egg collector, who was involved in finding the early celebrated breeding attempts by ospreys in Speyside in the 1950s. Donald first contacted him in 1967 upon confirming breeding dotterel in Galloway following a tip-off from local shepherd W. Russell. Nethersole-Thompson and Derek Ratcliffe both reckoned this was the first fully documented and confirmed breeding by dotterel in southern Scotland. However, my own favourite story is of Donald's meeting in 1964 with then retired keeper, Jimmy Nicholson of Cairnsmore Estate, when the latter told him of how as a boy, he had the duty of feeding an aged, blind white-tailed eagle which had been taken as a chick from an eyrie on Cairnsmore in 1852. As I sat listening to this story in Donald's sitting room, there before me was a living link to the days when these great birds were breeding in southern

Scotland. I can scarcely put into words the thrill this gave me – and does still today in recounting it, especially in the realisation that it will not be too long before white-tailed eagles are nesting here again.

Derek Ratcliffe first visited Galloway as a 16-year-old boy in 1946, when living in Carlisle. Thereafter, he visited Galloway annually, missing only his graduation year in the next 59 years. He first met Donald in the early 1960s during his peregrine work that led to the elucidation of the organochlorine pesticide-induced crashes in the populations of some raptors. He encouraged Donald to look for dotterel in 1964 and together they found a pair breeding on a Galloway top in 1975.[10] Derek always visited Barone during his spring visits and indeed stayed there overnight

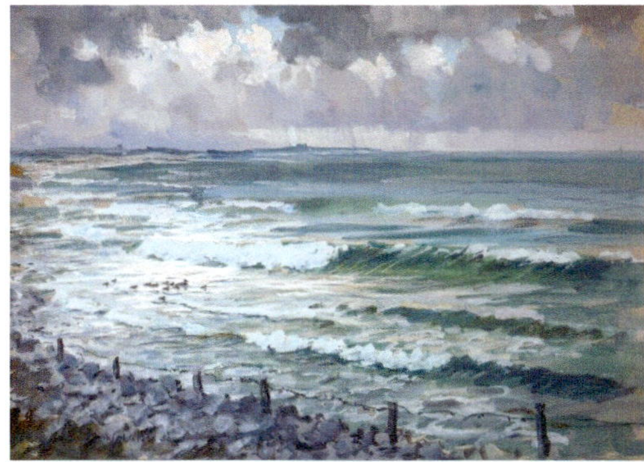

5.8 Left: Donald Watson painting: Eiders in an Atlantic gale

5.9 Below: Donald Watson painting: Cock Hen Harrier, South Uist, 1974

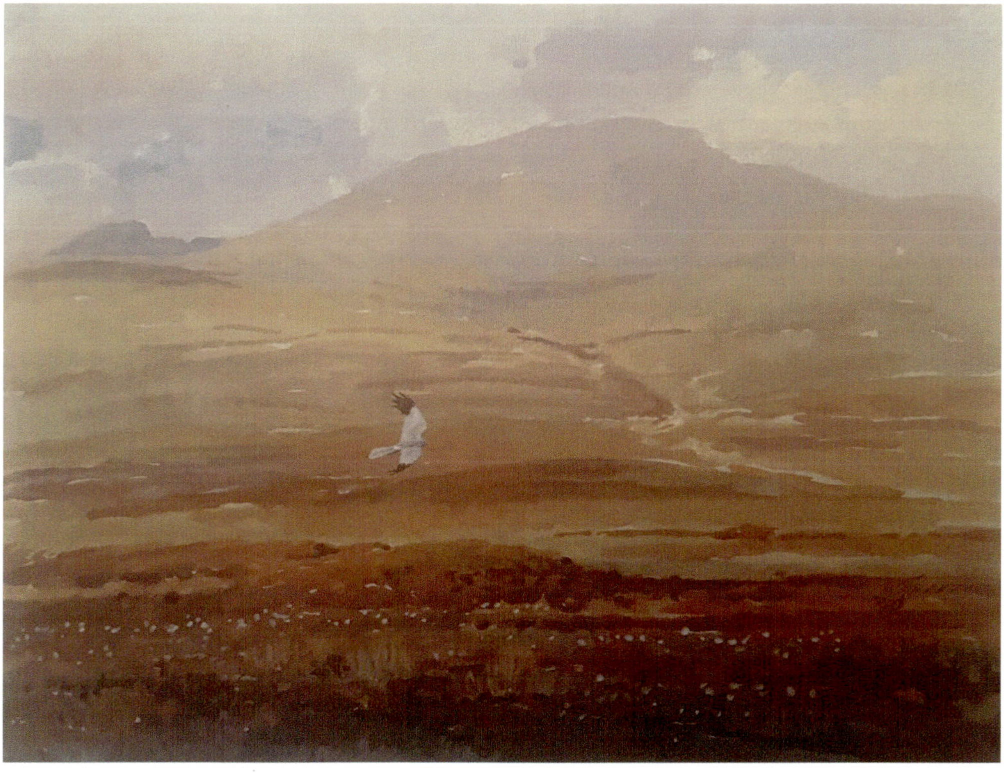

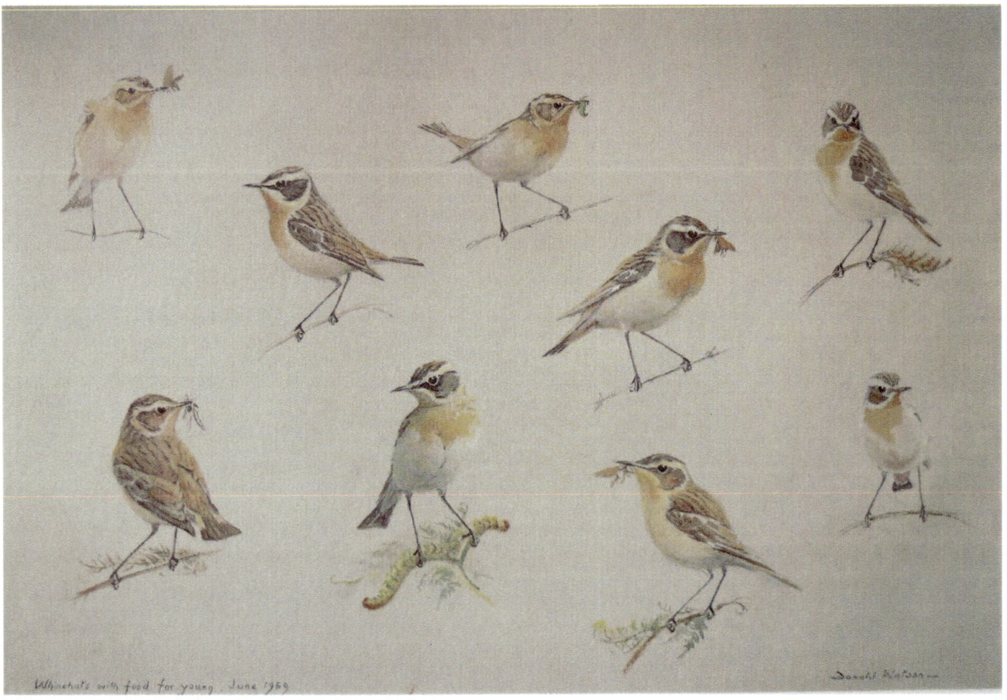

5.10 Donald Watson painting: Whinchats, 1959

sometimes. I had first met Derek with Dick Roxburgh in Galloway in the mid-1980s, but really got to know him as a close friend and field companion in the 1990s, when we would often visit Derek's favourite peregrine, curlew and botanical sites. In the evenings, we often sat in the sitting room at Barone and talked about hill birds and their followers over a Highland Park single malt, Donald's favourite.

Many an evening was spent in this way, listening to wonderful tales of yesteryear and talking through the conservation issues of the day, but it was not only the shared appreciation and love of hen harriers, their beauty and mystique, that bonded Donald and myself. We also shared a passion for poetry. I had known and loved John Clare since my schooldays, especially his *Shepherd's Calendar* and *Midsummer Cushion*[11] with its sublime nature poems. Indeed, I have always regarded him as the greatest nature poet I have read. Donald, a fellow admirer, introduced me to Clare's little-known prose writings, but also to the wonderful Jacques Delamain and his *Why Birds Sing*.[12] Edward Lear and Lewis Carroll were also firm favourites of Donald. This love of poetry was shared by our mutual friend and hen harrier expert, the late Ricky Gladwell from Galston in Ayrshire, who often visited with me and indeed occasionally stayed over at Barone in earlier years. Ricky was more of a Burns and Norman MacCaig fan, amongst others. Moreover, Ricky was a keen follower of nesting and roosting hen harriers, and developed a perhaps unrivalled knowledge of their behaviour through several decades of intensive study. He was also a lovely, spirited man, a free-thinker with a great sense of humour and excellent company in the field, bar or Donald's pipe-smoke filled sitting room at Barone, surrounded by pictures to remind us of our shared passion. The harrier pictures in the sitting room I remember were 'Cock Hen Harrier over South Uist Moorland',[13] which at once captures the wonderful movement and method of a harrier hunting into the wind; the other is 'Hen Harriers over a Winter Roost, Galloway'[14] one of Donald's best known roost pictures. On the chimney breast was his large honeymoon painting 'Eiders in an Atlantic gale, Benbecula',[15] while on the front wall hung a fine portrait of Joan in a blue cardigan, knitting contentedly.

I had known Joan for many years and she took a great interest in my own family and our travels. A keen and empathetic listener, she had a great store of funny tales of family and village life in Dalry. From an Anglo-Irish family, she had grown up in South Africa and, aged eight, gone to boarding school at a convent in Belgium, where her elder sister was already established. They would go home one Christmas, and their parents would visit them the next, and of course there were various visits to Surrey, where she first met Donald as a child. Joan was a nurse during the war and followed the Allied advance north through Italy, just behind the fighting, where she witnessed incredible courage, suffering and death, which naturally affected her deeply. Of course, in Louis Urquhart she had a friend and neighbour with a shared Italian wartime experience and his own story to tell. I felt privileged to hear Joan's recollections and I miss her kindness. I will never forget the thrill and life-giving energy that both she and Donald derived from conversations around the hearth. The nearest I can get to describing this is that it was like plugging into an energy source. Passion is infectious.

Joan was a very fond and skilled observer of butterflies. In spring and summer months she and Donald had special places to visit for different species, including Mabie for pearl-bordered fritillaries and the Tarberts on the Wigtownshire Rhins coast for graylings and late summer clouded yellows, painted ladies and others. Donald describes these visits in his books, and there is no need to dwell on them here. He loved butterflies, too, and would often call for a quick stop at favourite roadside verges for small pearl-bordered fritillaries as we motored on outings to our moorland destinations to look for nesting hen harriers and other birds. Like everyone, he was a creature of habit and had time-honoured places to visit locally throughout the year. In March we drove up annually to Mackilston and past Corseglass School towards Lochinvar on the hunt for early wheatears, and he became animated, and in some way rejuvenated, to see his first handsome male of the year. The chats always held a special place in his heart, and he painted very many pictures and illustrations of them, which now look out from many pages of his books. The roadside by Mossdale was the place for whinchats, and of course whaups had bred there before

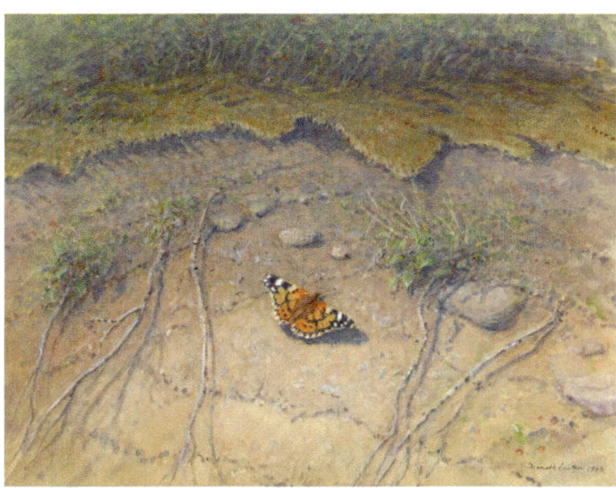

5.11 Donald Watson painting: Painted Lady Butterfly, 1983

the forestry encroached too far. Donald's birthday fell on 28 June, and a regular birthday jaunt was to hear nightjars at Bennan, near Mossdale. From memory, we were always successful in this, and to his delight he was able to hear nightjars churring throughout his long life, whereas he had ceased to hear goldcrests, grasshopper warblers and skylarks in his late 70s or even earlier. However, by far his most frequent and favourite place of pilgrimage was in autumn and winter to his beloved Airie Flowe, where he had first discovered roosting hen harriers in the 1960s and saw their numbers increase to over 30 birds as the population reached its peak in the 1970s. I remember seeing around 20 in the early 1980s, but with the cessation of local breeding numbers have decreased greatly since then. However, he was able to return to watch the roost well into his 80s. It was always a pleasure to be with him on such vigils and especially when we picked up a harrier or two in the fading light. When they had settled for the night and our twinkling eyes met, words were superfluous, and wonder was all.

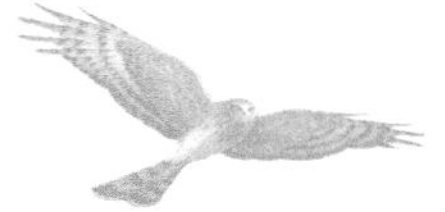

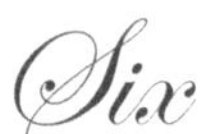

The Hen Harrier from a beginning in the long, fine summer of 1959 – a prescient eye for beauty and danger

DES THOMPSON AND COLIN GALBRAITH

> Before 1939, the disappearance of the Hen Harrier *Circus cyaneus* from most of the British Isles had the same apparent finality as that of the Osprey and the Sea Eagle. There was little chance of seeing a pair of Hen Harriers in the breeding season outside the Orkney islands and some of the Outer Hebrides or, possibly, in Ireland.[1]

Donald Watson's classic monograph on the hen harrier opened with the above lines, giving a vivid sense of the endangerment of this beguiling raptor across the British Isles.

The monograph – first in the Poyser series

Donald's book on the hen harrier was the first monograph in the ground-breaking Poyser series. Writing the monograph was a special challenge, for no detailed scientific treatment on a raptor in Britain or Ireland had been published previously. Seton Gordon provided the closest to it, with his evocative books on golden eagles, notably *The Golden Eagle*. Leslie Brown published *British Birds of Prey* (1976) in the Collins New Naturalist series a year before Donald's tome.

Following an introduction to the harriers of the world, *The Hen Harrier* is divided into two parts. The first explores the history of the bird in Britain and Ireland, before going into detail on its predatory habits, breeding cycle, migration and winter distribution, and the bird as 'an artist's bird'. Donald explains early on his fascination with the plumages of the birds, and the

> startling contrast in appearance between the sexes … No book illustration, even less any museum specimen, had given any idea of the conspicuousness of the light grey male when sunlit against a background of rich colour. This, no doubt, was why a cock Hen Harrier over heather moorland pleased me even more than the slightly darker Montagu's over cornfield, meadow or marsh: the male Hen Harrier was once aptly named the Seagull Hawk.[2]

Donald's watercolours certainly rectified the need for a worthy illustration – just look at the jacket of the book (Figure 6.1).

The second part of the book is devoted to Donald's studies in south-west Scotland. He writes

> This account of the Hen Harrier in my home region begins in the long, fine summer of 1959 and spans 17 years, finishing in the even warmer, sunnier summer of 1976. During this period, I studied Hen Harriers at all seasons.[3]

It is an absorbing account of painstaking observations made on 11 study areas, charting the steady but small rise in numbers. We read about his first nest found, in May 1959, and key observations on harriers nesting and foraging over moorland and forestry, food and hunting behaviour, and communal roosting in winter. The final chapter, an essay entitled 'The Hen Harrier: A Controversial Bird', is in places an agonising read, for it betrays Donald's frustration at the scarcity of the bird because of persecution. Reflecting on the many pressures on birds of prey, the book closes with

> The importance of all these factors varies for different species but it cannot be denied that direct human destruction has been, and regrettably still is, a major hazard as far as harriers are concerned.[4]

Impressions – a quarter-century ago

When the book was published we were very young students; now we recall four standout impressions. First, nesting hen harriers were not just rare back then but scarce, and seemingly impossible to locate. Many days were spent trying to locate potential nesting habitat close to where the male hunted, mindful that he could range up to 10 miles from his incubating mate, whom he visited fleetingly. If you were lucky, you saw and heard the 'food pass', but that was a red-letter day.

Second, Donald's illustrations of the bird and its habitat breathed life into the open moorland landscape and demonstrated the connectivity between bird and ecosystem. In vivid colour, black-and-white watercolours, distinctive scraperboard etchings, and an elegant depiction in words, Donald held you spellbound in his vivid accounts of encounters with the birds. Possibly uniquely for someone writing about a bird, Donald conveyed his passion and expert knowledge in both his art and prose.

Third, unusually for an early monograph, Donald described the bird's ecology and behaviour throughout the year. That in turn helped to broaden the conservation effort for the species into wintering as well as breeding areas. In this case, the winter communal roosts are depicted for their energy, grace, and beauty. Vigils are described and portrayed in exceptional detail. Donald remarks

> Roosts may provide staging posts in an essentially nomadic winter existence, enabling contact to be made between birds which are experienced and those which are inexperienced in utilising the food resources of a region. Additionally, the roosts appear to give opportunities for males and females to associate in winter and probably to form pairs.[5]

These were inspired thoughts; now they are testable hypotheses.

And fourth, there was the relentless undercurrent of persecution. Every form of harassment – trapping, injuring and killing – is described. In Donald's day, seeing a hen harrier nest was a privilege, with secrecy on location the watchword for commenting on breeding success. Now we are aware of the scourge of persecution of hen harriers, but back when Donald published his book it was a different era. Hen harriers had been virtually eliminated from our land, and the chances were that many nests found on mainland Britain would suffer failure, with gamekeepers perceived as being responsible for the demise of the species. Back then, it seemed that merely keeping quiet, and not reporting or telling of nesting hen harriers, offered the best prospect for their survival. Yet throughout *The Hen Harrier* Donald rejoiced in the limited and piecemeal recovery of the population in south Scotland.

What of the hen harrier now?

Drawing on the narrative in Donald's monograph, and looking ahead, we have assembled key events and activities connected with hen harriers (Table 6.1). Three themes emerge through this timeline – a growing understanding of the ecology and behaviour of the birds; a deepening and emotional concern for their plight; and the politicisation and polarisation of society's response to what many might view as one of Donald's closing key remarks:

> Whether or not Hen Harriers continue to inhabit this world is a matter of indifference to the great majority of mankind.[6]

Understanding hen harriers

Donald's book laid the foundations for our understanding of the former distribution and punctuated recovery of hen harriers across the uplands. In the early 1900s, the hen harrier in mainland Britain was recorded only in Kintyre, and in Orkney and the southern Western Isles (with the lowest numbers estimated in the 1930s). Upland afforestation from the 1940s through to the 1970s encouraged the colonisation of many upland areas, with Donald estimating the overall British population at around 500 pairs. But it took more than ten years after the publication of Donald's book for there to be a systematic survey, with the first taking place in 1988–89. This was undertaken across the UK and the Isle of Man, and was the first of six surveys that would be undertaken over subsequent years. Figure 6.2 summarises the results of the first five surveys (2023 is the year of the sixth).

The bulk of the population in the UK is in Scotland and, strikingly, over 28 years numbers have oscillated between estimates of 436 and 637 pairs. Given the slow recovery of numbers in the post-war 1950s one might have expected a much larger increase in numbers to the present day, but this has not happened. The underlying reason is betrayed in the trends: 570 pairs in 1988–89, falling to 436 pairs in 1998, then rising to 637 pairs in 2004 before falling back to averages of between 460 and 505 pairs during 2010–16. Furthermore, the 2016 survey in Scotland found that hen harrier numbers on grouse moors declined significantly by 57 per cent between 2010 and 2016, with a marked fall in the proportion of the Scottish population using this habitat from 30 per cent to 14 per cent. Numbers on other heather moors, however, remained stable (Wotton et al 2018).[7]

As revealed by each survey and other research listed in Table 6.1, illegal persecution remains a critical constraint on population size and range, especially in areas with grouse moor management, where hen harriers have been especially harshly persecuted. Since Donald's studies,

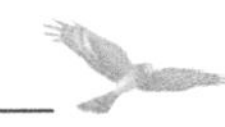

wind farms and forestry (and most recently some natural woodland regeneration) have expanded across the uplands, and research continues to study the impacts of these changes, drawing heavily on data from satellite-tagged birds and detailed field-based studies.

Looking at the current situation, it is clear that Donald's work was highly important not only in describing (and foretelling) the nature of persecution, but also in detailing the bird's complex relationship with the upland landscape, notably with forestry – beneficial in the early stages, but more varied as the forest closes.

Interestingly, some of the recent findings of some hen harriers nesting in open areas in and adjoining mature forestry in Argyll and north Scotland would have astonished and excited Donald. The 2016 national survey found that numbers of hen harriers in young forests declined significantly in Scotland between 2010 and 2016, and the numbers using mature plantations declined significantly between 2004 and 2016.[8] The authors suggested that this arose from density-dependent breeding habitat selection, with open moorland selected first, and young forest later when suitable moorlands are fully occupied. However, Paul Haworth and Alan Fielding suggested that a substantial and possibly increasing proportion of the hen harrier breeding population in Scotland was now found in forest/woodland areas.[9] In the West Highlands extensive areas of forestry have been felled, replanted and restructured in recent years, whilst some areas that were planted or replanted in the 1980s and 1990s are reaching maturity. As Simon Wotton and colleagues point out, this will result in areas becoming more or less suitable for breeding harriers depending on the current state of the forest. More potentially suitable forest habitat for hen harriers is being created under the Scottish Forest Strategy,[10] and this may considerably influence the overall nesting distribution of hen harriers.

The plight

Persecution features more prominently throughout *The Hen Harrier* than any other facet of the hen harrier's ecology and conservation. The subsequent national surveys and related research on the birds pay tribute to this understanding. However, as the timeline in Table 6.1 reveals, it is only in more recent years that we have come to realise the seriousness and long-lasting nature of the impact.

Looking down Table 6.1 at the chronology of events there is a particular narrative which begs closer examination. In 1988–89 the national survey found 570 pairs. Whilst the results were not published until 1993, they were widely discussed, and not least the adverse impacts of persecution reducing harrier numbers and productivity on grouse moors. Following this time, from 1992 to 1997, the Joint Raptor Study took place, quantifying hen harrier ecology in intimate detail, and their potential impacts on the numbers and shooting bags of grouse on Langholm Moor in the south of Scotland (and less intensively on five other moors). On Langholm hen harriers were protected to the extent that there was no observed persecution over the time of the project, and the harrier population rose from two to fourteen breeding females during 1992–96. Redpath and Thirgood (1997)[11] describe the findings in detail, and the upshot was that grouse numbers steadily declined, to the extent that the gamekeeper team was laid off at the end of the study. Subsequent trials of supplementary feeding of harriers on the moor – timed so as not to increase the brood size of each nest – did, however, show that the overall predation pressure from harriers could be significantly reduced and that wider habitat quality and species interactions also played a key part in determining the overall productivity and grouse numbers in the area (e.g. Redpath and Thirgood 2009).[12]

Expectations in parts of the grouse moor management community were that the initial study would point to a suppressive impact of hen harriers (and other raptors) on the grouse population, resulting in licences to control raptors. These did not, however, materialise, and the 1998 national survey of harriers finding only 436 pairs (the lowest recorded) may well have been a consequence of heightened persecution following the publication of the Joint Raptor Study report.

Two years later, in 2000, the UK Raptor Working Group Report – produced through consensus by government, agencies and a wide range of stakeholders, including key representatives from the conservation and shooting communities – pointed to wider issues concerning raptor conservation across Britain. Importantly, the relationship between hen harrier conservation and grouse moor management features in the UK Raptor Working Group (Anon, 2000),[13] which gives a definitive overview on both the land management issues and legal issues involved.

In 2002 the Scottish Raptor Monitoring Scheme was set up, and put in place a systematic programme of raptor monitoring in Scotland. A year later, in 2003, research led by Brian Etheridge and Ron Summers[14] presented the first compelling evidence of the impacts of grouse moor-related persecution of hen harriers on their overall population (building on their earlier 1997 paper). In 2008 the Langholm Moor Demonstration Project set about trying to revive grouse numbers whilst protecting hen harriers, and succeeded in significantly reducing the predation pressure on the grouse population; however, the work ceased in 2016.[15] Intensive management for grouse was abandoned and the moor was put up for sale in 2019; it is now being run as part of the Tarras Valley Nature Reserve.

The extent of hen harrier persecution has been detailed by, for example, Redpath et al (2010)[16] who found that there were records of only five successful hen harrier nests on the estimated 3,696 km^2 of driven grouse moors in the UK in 2008, an area of habitat estimated to have the potential to support about 500 pairs. Fielding et al (2011)[17] estimated that on the basis of 10km-square models, the potential national hen harrier population of Scotland was within the range 1467–1790 pairs. This compared with population estimates of 436 and 633 pairs in the 1998 and 2004 surveys respectively. Clearly, from these research investigations, the population is still being held below what might be considered as a more 'natural' population level, given the habitat potentially available to the species.

Seventeen Special Protection Areas (SPAs) have been identified for breeding hen harriers in the UK (ten in Scotland), with thirteen formally classified.[18] Bowland Fells was the first SPA classified (1993), followed by Glen Tanar (1994) and the Rhinns of Islay (1995). Currently the suite of sites holds almost 30 per cent of the GB population. For the non-breeding population, there are twenty SPAs identified (three not classified), with four in Scotland. The first SPA was classified in 1992 (Minsmere–Walberswick) followed by the Ouse Washes (1993). The suite of SPAs holds almost 15 per cent of the non-breeding population in Great Britain, and around 0.5 per cent of the biogeographical population of 46,500 birds.[19]

Society's response and conservation action

As reports of persecuted hen harriers gripped the public imagination, a genuine public movement formed to support the iconic birds. Helped by social media (most notably Raptor Persecution UK)

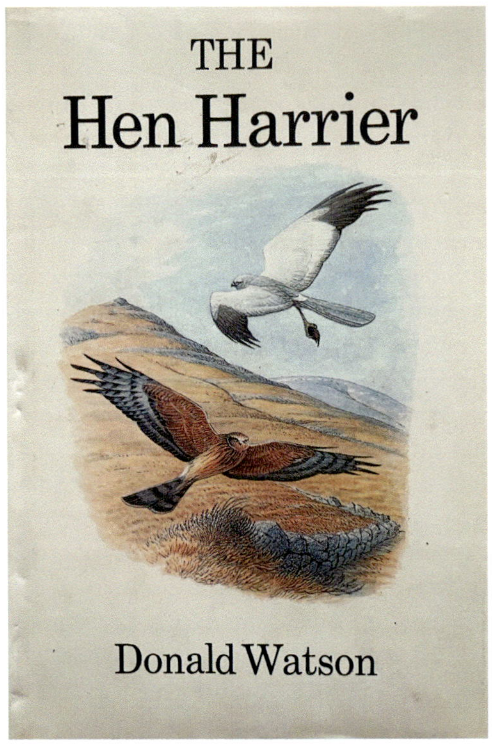

Figure 6.1. The cover of *The Hen Harrier* by Donald Watson (Poyser)

and some prominent advocates for protecting them and banning grouse moor management, the public focus sharpened on protecting them. A conservation framework on hen harriers, published by the JNCC in 2011,[20] showed how much larger their population could be in the absence of persecution. That year saw the launch of the Skydancer Project,[21] promoting hen harrier conservation, and three years later the first national Hen Harrier Day was held (in 2015 in England; a year later it included Scotland). This was a series of public events promoting the importance of hen harriers, and outrage over persistent persecution, especially associated with grouse moor management.

Steadily and inevitably, as the evidence base – started by Donald in his early work – mounted (with key studies drawing on the fates of satellite-tagged golden eagles and hen harriers strongly associated with grouse moor management), legislative proposals

Figure 6.2. Estimates of Hen Harrier breeding populations in Scotland (grey) , and in the UK and Isle of Man as a whole (white) during five national surveys, from 1988-89 to 2016. Vertical lines show 95% Confidence Limits. The early results of the 2023 survey are given in the text. From: Wotton *et al* (2018).22

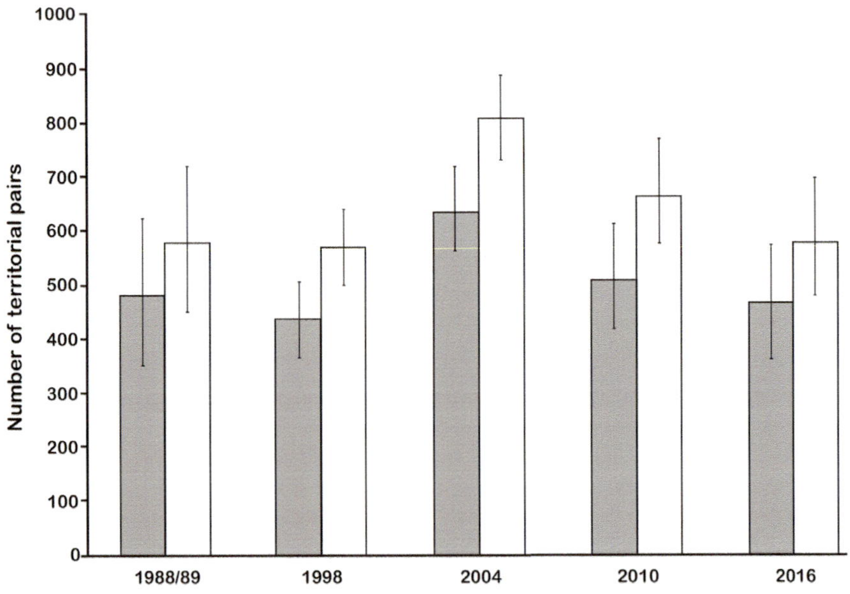

were announced. The Werritty Review of grouse moor management in Scotland reported in 2019,[23] with the chair advising the introduction of licensing of grouse moors (and the group as a whole advising licensing after further evidence was collected). Ministers responded in 2020, indicating that legislation would be introduced to cover a licensing scheme for grouse shooting. In March 2023 the Wildlife Management and Muirburn (Scotland) Bill was introduced to the Scottish Parliament, proposing provisions around licensed predator control and shooting of grouse, and around muirburn (the controlled burning of heather and other plants for land management purposes).[24]

In all of this, what is most telling is the many years, indeed decades, that have elapsed between the timing of findings on the status and plight of hen harriers, and actions proposed to remedy the situation. We are unsure if Donald, on putting down his pen on completing *The Hen Harrier*, really thought it would be around 45 years before legislation was introduced to address the key persecution-related issues he wrote about so passionately. It is clear, however, that Donald's work is still the bedrock for conservation action today, and his evocative writing and art continues to inspire many young, and some now not-so-young conservationists, land managers, artists and hen harrier watchers.

Table 6.1 Some milestones for work on hen harriers in Scotland

Date	Event
1840s	Onset of moorland management for red grouse, with muirburn and predator control, with intensification beginning in the 1840s onwards. Virtual elimination of hen harriers and other raptors.[25]
1900s	Hen harrier in mainland Britain recorded only in Kintyre, and in Orkney and south Western Isles (with lowest numbers estimated in the 1930s).[26]
1950s	Improved fortunes of hen harriers in mainland Britain, following decrease in gamekeeper activity during 1939–45 WW2 (less muirburn and persecution), and spread of afforestation benefitting nesting in early growth phase.
1957	Publication by Eddie Balfour of 'Observations on the Breeding Biology of the Hen Harrier in Orkney', drawing attention to polygyny. This was a pioneering study, giving rise to several publications between 1959 and 1975.[27]
1970s	Spread in range and numbers breeding across mainland Scotland, with southward extension into north England in 1968–72 for first recorded breeding in 20th century. British and Irish population estimated at 500–600 nests (62 known nests in Orkney in 1974).[28]
1977	Publication of *The Hen Harrier* by Donald Watson.[29]
1978	Nick Picozzi's important early publication estimating hen harrier predation on NE Scotland moors may have reduced red grouse available for shooting in August by no more than 7.4%; harrier population mainly monogamous.[30]
1979	Addition of hen harrier to Annex 1 of the EC Birds Directive.[31]
1980s	Detailed estimates of recolonisation in different parts of Scotland provided by Thom (1986) drawing on further work by Donald Watson.

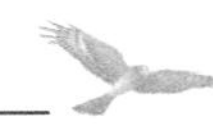

1988–89 First national survey estimated 570 ± 150 pairs in Scotland.[32]

1992–97 The so-called 'Langholm Study', running from 1992 to 1996, with publication in 1997 of *Birds of Prey and Red Grouse* (detailing extensively research on hen harrier and red grouse associations).[33]

First Special Protection Area (SPA) in UK classified for breeding hen harriers: Bowland Fells SPA (December 1993), followed by Glen Tanar (September 1994) and Rhinns of Islay (November 1995).[34] First SPA for non-breeding hen harriers was Minsmere – Walberswick (May 1992).[35]

In 1997 formation of the Moorland Working Group (chaired by Scottish Natural Heritage) to address raptor (especially hen harrier)–human conflicts.

First published scientific evidence on persecution limiting the numbers of hen harriers on grouse moors.[36]

1998 Second national survey estimated 436 pairs in Scotland.[37]

Paper published by Dick Potts estimated the impacts of grouse moor-related persecution of hen harriers on the overall population in the UK.[38]

Moorland Working Group published 'Action for Scotland's moorland: a Statement of Intent'.[39]

2000 Publication of Report of the UK Raptor Working Group, which drew heavily on work on hen harriers on grouse moors.[40]

2001 Publication of research on diversionary feeding of hen harriers to reduce take of red grouse.[41]

2002 Formation of Scottish Raptor Monitoring Scheme involving SNH (now NatureScot) as chair, JNCC, SRSG, BTO, RSPB, RBBP and SOC, with heavy emphasis on survey and monitoring of hen harriers.[42]

Formation of Scotland's Moorland Forum (chaired by Lady Isabel Glasgow), succeeding Moorland Working Group.[43]

2003 Ron Summers and others publish key paper on changes in hen harrier numbers in relation to grouse moor management, building on earlier work by authors.[44]

2004 Third national survey of harriers estimated 637 pairs in Scotland, with increases except in south and east, where numbers decreased.[45]

2008 Langholm Moor Demonstration Project began, ending in 2018. Focused on hen harrier and red grouse associations, giving rise to many publications.[46]

2010 *In Search of Harriers – Over the Hills and Far Away*, by Donald Watson, published, with many watercolours and scraperboard images. Donald had completed writing this before his death in 2005.[47]

Fourth national survey estimated 505 territorial pairs in Scotland, with notable decreases in pairs within plantations and mature forestry.[48]

Publication of 'People and Nature in Conflict: Can We Reconcile Hen Harrier Conservation and Game Management?' setting out five options (Improved enforcement; Financial compensation for losses inflicted by hen harriers; Increasing grouse numbers through rear and release; Reducing predation levels on grouse through diversionary feeding and habitat manipulation; and Reducing hen harrier settling densities through e.g. deterrent and habitat measures, and supporting predators such as golden eagles).[49]

'Raptor Persecution UK' blog began, and to date has received over nine million views and generates wide media interest and coverage. Much of its content concerns illegal persecution of hen harrier incidents and commentary.[50]

2011 Publication of 'A Conservation Framework for Hen Harriers in the United Kingdom'. It complements and extends earlier analyses of national hen harrier datasets by looking for environmental factors that correlate with, or are otherwise associated with, the distribution of breeding hen harriers in the UK, and at a regional scale within Scotland.[51]

Launch of the RSPB Skydancer Project, which ran until 2015, aiming to protect and promote the conservation of hen harriers across their remaining breeding stronghold in northern England (with some birds emanating from Scotland).[52]

2014 Advent of Hen Harrier Day, growing into a large range of virtual and on-site events on moors in north England and in the south Scottish Highlands, concerned with promoting the importance of hen harriers, and action to tackle wildlife crime.[53]

Hen Harrier LIFE Project launched (ran until 2019), aimed to provide the conditions in which the hen harrier's population and range could recover, particularly in areas where the species was most threatened. It satellite-tagged more than 100 birds.[54]

2016 Fifth national survey found 460 (359–473) territorial pairs in Scotland, marking a significant decline by 24% since 2004. Significant decreases were recorded in the number of pairs using grouse moor (−57%) and young forest (−54%).[55]

Guidance published on 'Wind Farm Proposals on Afforested Sites including Advice on Reducing Suitability for H Harrier, Merlin and Short-eared Owl'. Advice on deterring hen harriers and other raptors nesting close to wind farms.[56] Devised to limit increased suitability of wind farm sites to these three species in situations where forestry is being 'opened up'. Crucially, this guidance aims to limit any increase in collision risk to these species.

2017 Second edition of Donald Watson's *The Hen Harrier* published, with a foreword by Mark Avery.[57]

Scottish Government commission the Grouse Moor Management Group (chaired by Professor Alan Werritty) to 'examine the environmental impact of grouse moor management practices such as muirburn, the use of medicated grit and mountain hare culls, and advise on the option of licensing grouse shooting businesses'. This was prompted by the report from NatureScot in May 2017, which found that around a third of satellite-tagged golden eagles in Scotland disappeared in suspicious circumstances, on or around grouse moors.[58]Publication of *Bowland Beth: The Life of an English Hen Harrier*, a vivid portrayal of persecution of hen harriers.[59]

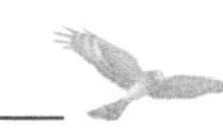

2018 The Grouse Moor Management Group met on 18 occasions between January 2018 and July 2019, mainly at the Royal Society of Edinburgh, but also took evidence in the field from a variety of grouse-shooting estates and one estate managed by a conservation charity.

2019 'Grouse Moor Management Group: Report', the Werritty Review, published in December.[60] Publication in journal *Nature Communications*, using data from 58 satellite-tracked hen harriers. Showed high rates of unexpected tag failure and low first-year survival compared to other harrier populations. The likelihood of harriers dying or disappearing increased as their use of grouse moors increased.[61]

2020 Scottish Government responded to the Werritty Review, indicating that legislation would be introduced to cover a licensing scheme for grouse shooting.[62]

Heads up for Harriers (2015–19) published a report based on the analysis of over two million hen harrier nest camera images, and identified trends that influence survival to fledging. Meadow pipit accounted for 77% of bird prey items.[63]

2022 Publication of *The Hen Harrier's Year*, includes a chapter on 'Conflict on the Grouse Moor'.[64] Several other books published recently with closely related titles, including *Sky Dancer, Sky Dance, Skydancer, Dancers in the Sky* and *Hen Harrier Poems.*

2023 Wildlife Management and Muirburn (Scotland) Bill introduced to Scottish Parliament, which should have significant implications for the conservation and management of hen harriers (and other raptors).[65]

Sixth national survey undertaken.

Major paper in journal *Biological Conservation* analysed movements and fates of 148 hen harriers, satellite-tagged in nests across Britain and Isle of Man between 2014 and 2021. Found annual survival was low, especially among first-year birds, with illegal killing accounting for 27–43% of overall mortality and 75% of mortality in first year and subadult (1–2 years) harriers, respectively. Illegal killing was likely attributable to grouse moor management.[66]

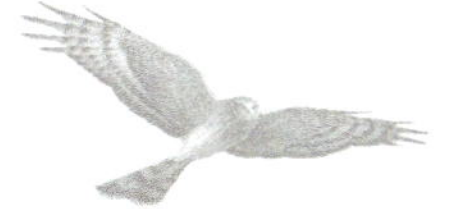

Seven

Donald Watson the writer and illustrator

ROGER CROFTS

It is relatively easy for the modern writer to assess the works of those from recent decades, but the context is often different, and an accurate perspective of the value of the writing at the time of its publication is lost. This chapter therefore focuses on the perspectives of reviewers at the time of books that Donald Watson authored and those that he illustrated. These reviews are from the bird magazines of the official charitable bodies in the ornithological and birdwatching fields. They provide an inside view of his work, his status and standing in the bird art, bird science and bird writing worlds. In addition, there is a reflection on the status of these books over the passage of time since their publication. If you detect a lack of objectivity here, then it is best for you to read the books yourself and come to your own opinion. While none are currently in print, with the exception of *The Hen Harrier*, which was recently reprinted, they can be acquired from booksellers on the internet.

Donald's approach to writing

Donald read widely, as was clear from the shelves of his studio. He was given material through his copious correspondence with leading figures in the bird art and bird conservation world. As others have told in earlier chapters, Donald was a keen-eyed observer in the field, and kept voluminous notes and made hundreds of sketches. He used all of this material in developing his thoughts for an article and more specifically for his books. He set out first an outline of a book with chapter headings and some subheadings. Then began the task of writing. He wrote in freehand, in a very rounded lettering style which is very legible. He always used a fountain pen filled with mid-blue ink. Once a manuscript had been drafted, Joan took over and typed it as a draft, and returned it to Donald. He went through, correcting it again with his fountain pen

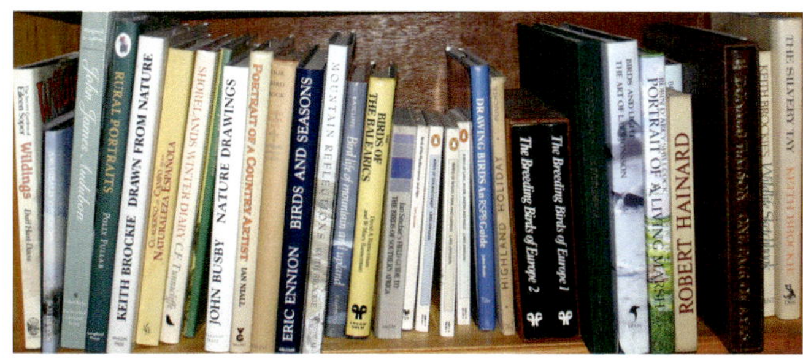

7.1 Bird artists' books in Donald's study

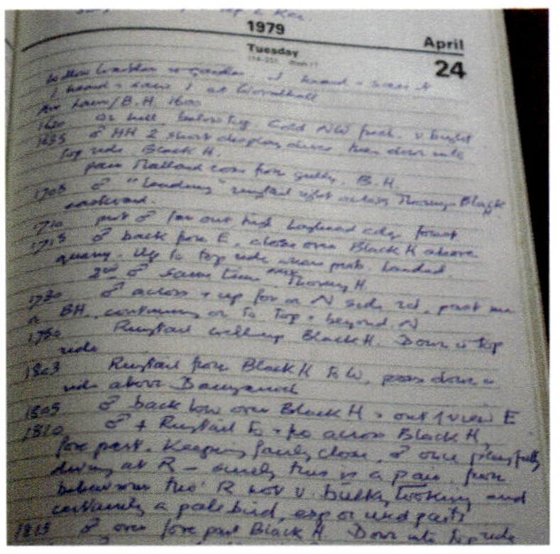

7.2 Donald's meticulous handwriting

where he wished to add or delete words and phrases and where he wanted to express a point in a different way, the result very readable. The manuscript went back to Joan to do the corrections before submission to publishers.

Donald's early mentor was George Waterston of the Edinburgh publishing family. He introduced Donald to Douglas Grant of the Scottish Academic Press, who published his first book, *Birds of Moor and Mountain*. He built a strong relationship with the redoubtable Trevor and Anna Poyser, as a writer of *The Hen Harrier* and illustrator of several books in their series of monographs. His more personal memoirs, *A Bird Artist in Scotland* and *One Pair of Eyes* were taken on by specialist publishers. He built a good relationship with them, for example Nigel Ede at Arlequin Press, the publisher of *One Pair of Eyes*. His last book was published by Ian Langford, who he had met when the latter was working in nature conservation in Galloway, running a natural history bookshop in Wigtown and setting up his publishing business.

Reviews at the time of publication

Published reviews of Donald Watson's books are reproduced here to give a flavour of how his paintings and writing were viewed at the time of publication. These complement the essays in other chapters of this book. Also added is a review of the 2017 reprint of *The Hen Harrier*.

The Oxford Book of Birds

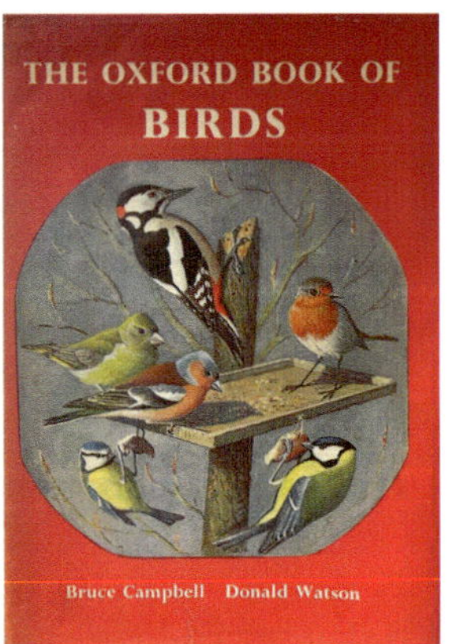

7.3 Donald Watson painting: cover of *The Oxford Book of Birds*

> This new book is of special interest to Scottish ornithologists. The text is by Bruce Campbell and illustrations by Donald Watson, and those of us who have been eagerly waiting the result of this most interesting partnership will not be disappointed … To illustrate an entire series of British birds is a tremendous undertaking, and in this book our own Scottish artist, Donald Watson, joins the very few who have achieved it. Each species is painted with characteristic skill against its natural background, and Scottish readers will soon spot the well-known shape of the Isle of May far out on the horizon on one of the plates. It is almost inevitable in painting such a lengthy series that there should be a certain unevenness of execution. My own preference is for his water birds, in which I think he is unsurpassed, though I am less happy about some of the smaller birds. There is no doubt that in this book the marriage of text and illustrations is a particularly happy one … Certainly a must for all who are interested in birds in all their many aspects.

Olive T. Thompson[1]

> The main part of this book consists of 96 coloured plates each illustrating three or four species of British birds in their natural settings and showing flight patterns and sex, age and seasonal differences where appropriate ... Additional black and white plates show eight American passerines that have been recorded in Britain and Ireland, and the flight patterns of ducks and some waders. Donald Watson's pictures are delightful and have the great merit of so obviously being painted by an artist who knows his birds in the field – and who knows and can paint that field also. The colour reproduction is excellent ... Everyone will have his own favourites, but for myself I would choose the Little Owl where the artist has exactly caught this bird's frown of suspicious disapproval ... At the price I do not know of another work that gives such an authoritative, full and all round account of the lives of so many birds.
>
> R.K. Cornwallis[2]

Cornwallis was a farmer in Lincolnshire who played an active role in the local nature conservation management, writing a number of books on the birds of the area and playing a key role in the governance of many bodies including the BTO. He is described in his obituary as 'outstanding both as an amateur ornithologist and practical conservationist'. I have not been able to discover who Olive T. Thompson was.

Looking back on these reviews and handling my copies of the main book and the pocketbook, I think their assessments are fair and accurate. If I can show a bias as neither an artist nor an ornithologist, I feel that this is Donald's most remarkable work. I have the good fortune to own a selection of his paintings, together with all of his books and many of those he illustrated; the one I treasure most is a plate from *The Oxford Book of Birds*. Paintings of birds of similar species in their habitat setting was a master stroke. It was not new, but Donald took it to a new height with both birds and their surrounding habitats and scenery. Bird books seem not to stand the test of time, as there are advances in publishing technology and there is strong competition from newer bird observation books on the market. It is also clear from correspondence between Donald and Oxford University Press that when they decided to put this book and others on wildlife in a new series, they were not making any commitments for reprinting once the current stock was gone. This book is readily available on the web and has become more of a collector's item than one to use as a modern-day bird guide. That is purely because of the number of guidebooks on British birds, not a comment on the quality of Donald's illustrations.

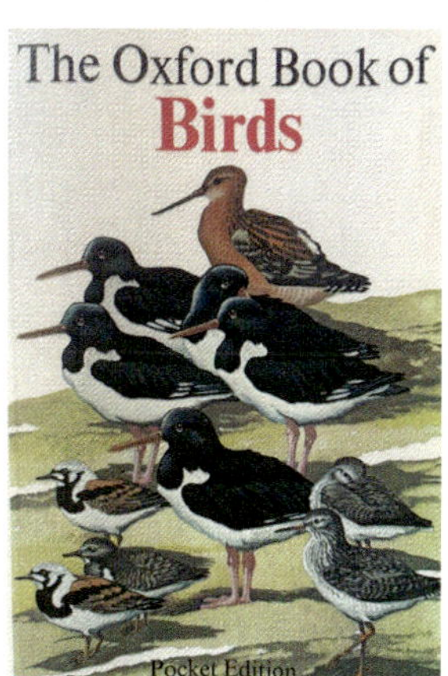

7.4 Donald Watson painting: cover of pocket edition of *The Oxford Book of Birds*

The Oxford Book of Birds Pocket Edition

> This is a miniature replica of the well-known *Oxford Book of Birds* ... Donald Watson's beautiful, coloured illustrations have reproduced extremely well in the smaller format, and for these alone this useful reference book should be well worth its modest price.
>
> Olive T. Thompson[3] (Note the price was £1.35).

Birds of Moor and Mountain

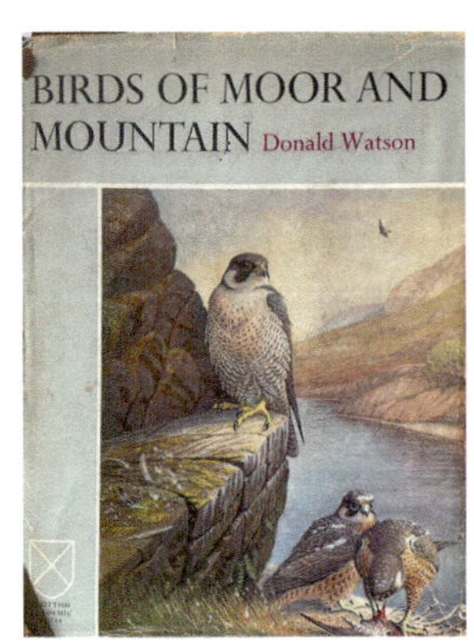

7.5 Donald Watson painting: cover of *Birds of Moor and Mountain*

It is now almost ten years since Donald Watson's first major literary venture, when he provided the illustrations for *The Oxford Book of Birds*. This attracted a lot of favourable comment at the time, but although one admired the artist's ingenuity in packing a number of species onto the one page against a habitat background which maintained a high level of plausibility, one felt that his instincts were for a broader canvas. In this new book he is given space to do himself justice. Twenty five of his paintings are reproduced in colour (the quality of the reproductions is excellent) and a further 15 in black and white. There are also a number of attractive line drawings to adorn the text.

Donald Watson's paintings are well enough known to readers of this journal, and his admirers will not be disappointed by this latest selection. His interest clearly lies as much in the bird's environment as in the bird itself, and the atmosphere of the Galloway moors comes over very convincingly in many of these paintings. They make one very ready to support the author in regretting the steady encroachment of forestry plantations over the hill ground, and one echoes the hope that some balance can be preserved between forestry and moorland so that a very distinctive type of scenery is not lost completely.

The paintings are outstandingly successful in capturing the character of the bird, and they carry the immediate conviction (as for instance in the painting of the teal) that this is an actual event which has been faithfully remembered and recorded. Inevitably one thinks of Donald Watson primarily as an artist, but the text of this book is every bit as distinguished as its illustrations. About 50 species are dealt with at length, and each of these is given two or three pages of comment, including quite detailed plumage description ... Those who have been privileged to go goose hunting with Donald Watson will be particularly pleased to find that there are full accounts of the three local species (Greylag, Whitefront and Bean). He has been living in Galloway for over 20 years, and this book is a remarkable tribute to his activity during this period. Of particular interest is his study of the communal roosting of Hen Harriers, and this is well described along with an excellent account of the breeding behaviours of this splendid bird.

Reading these accounts, one is repeatedly impressed by the breadth and depth of the author's knowledge of his subject, intrigued by the fresh ideas and suggestions he throws out, and by the variety of his personal observations and the sensitive way in which these are expressed. The artist in Donald Watson is just as evident in his writings as it is in his paintings. Altogether, then, this is a most distinguished edition to the literature, and it is a matter of particular satisfaction to us that it should have been made during the author's reign as President of the Scottish Ornithologists' Club.

Dougal G. Andrew[4]

Dougal Andrew was a lawyer in Edinburgh, but his passion was birdwatching. He had a deep interest in and knowledge of birds and their behaviours. He was involved in the operation of the Scottish Ornithologists' Club for many decades.

It is pleasantly appropriate that the appearance of Donald Watson's book should coincide with his final year as President of the Scottish Ornithologists' Club, as this is an outstanding publication of high quality written and illustrated by a man who is both a very talented artist and a competent field ornithologist. Although Donald Watson is probably better known in the former capacity, the text of this book (dealing with 49 species in detail) combines personal observation and record with a readable account of current scientific work and is not simply an album of coloured plates. Indeed, in the text alone this is a most useful compendium of information on mountain and moorland birds.

The majority of people buying this book will do so for its artistic content. As an artist, the publishers say that he has been most influenced by the work of Bruno Liljefors with its insistence on the faithful portrayal of birds and mammals in their correct environment. If any other comparison or attempt to trace the influence of other artists is necessary, it could be said that in some of the paintings, for example the Merlin and Peregrine, his style resembles that of D. M. Reid-Henry, with the meticulously drawn feather-by-feather accuracy of the birds set against a sharply defined rocky background. These opinions, however, are by no means expressions of disparagement of Watson's work and it is much truer to say that, as has obviously been his goal, he has now successfully developed a characteristic style of his own, one eminently suited to the area in which he works and to the subjects of his book – that is to say, a detailed study of his bird on a broad canvas, with a true accurate and recognisable habitat background. As Watson paints his birds exactly as he has seen them in the field, the results are sometimes rather startling until one remembers that all observations are not made at high noon on a fine day.

Many of us already familiar with Donald Watson's paintings and have followed the development of his style, but there is another and hitherto unnoticed facet of his art, the delightful black and white endpieces scattered throughout this book. These deserve special mention, for they are exquisitely done in a lively manner and would on their own establish an artist's reputation.

Everyone with an interest in bird art *should* have a copy of this book, but for those who do not buy it for the sake of the plates will find it well worth having for the summaries

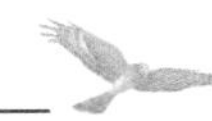

of contemporary studies and personal observation unrecorded elsewhere. There is also a good bibliography which is a useful reference to work on Scottish birds.

Ian D. Pennie[5]

Ian Pennie was a GP based for most of his career in Sutherland. He wrote extensively on birds published in Scottish bird magazines. Ironically, his obituary was written by the other reviewer of this book, Dougal Andrew. Like Donald Watson, he was a president and later an honorary member of the Scottish Ornithologists' Club.

'In some ways', declares Donald Watson in the introduction to his *Birds of Moor and Mountain*, 'this is a very personal book.' This individuality is indeed what gives it its special appeal. It is apparent not only in the illustrations but in the text. As a painter of birds in their haunts Mr Watson owes much to the great Swedish mammal and bird painter Bruno Liljefors, but his style is markedly his own. Similarly, though he has drawn extensively on the recent specialist literature, in particular for the essays that preface the notes on appearance, haunts and distribution, migration, calls, food and mating habits of the 60 species he deals with, they are full of his own personal observations and impressions. Mr Watson is to be congratulated on putting together one of the most attractive, informative and readable books that have been published in recent years.

J.K. Adams[6]

Adams was a reviewer of books for *Country Life*.

This book is first of all a picture book and a delightful one. The plates give the opportunity to share the artist's vision of some of the birds of the wilder places of Britain. My vote would go for the Slavonian grebe, and I like to think I know the loch where they were painted, and the black-necked grebe as the winner among tail pieces. Mr Watson's vision is sometimes unusual and always interesting. I was at first puzzled by the background of the painting of the 'pass' of hen harriers until I realised that just so would a young plantation of deep plough look from the air. The landscape backgrounds to some of the birds come out well from the Chinese test that one would be able to go for a walk in any landscape, and one could walk for miles from the knoll where his red grouse are feeding. This is not only a picture book. The text which accompanies each plate is quite brief, but always to the point, always based on personal knowledge and often stimulating to further observation. Mr Watson is not skilled only with the brush and pencil; he has a pleasant turn of phrase.

Peter Hartley[7]

Peter Hartley is a retired paintings restorer and latterly a poet of birds.

The appearance of this long awaited book will give pleasure to many north of the Border where Donald Watson has long established his reputation as a leading bird artist. His book is like a breadth from the old days when ornithologists concentrated on the living birds, their lives and their habits, and it shows Mr Watson in new light as a good writer too. The author's claim that this is very personal book is not a disadvantage but part of the book's charm for Mr Watson is able to capture the romance of the birds' world and to describe the environment in which his subjects live as only an observer with a strongly developed artistic sense and love of nature could do.

The personal anecdotes are never dull reading and the part of the essays devoted to descriptive matter err on the side of brevity when compared with the thirty-odd lines describing appearance, haunts, distribution, migration, voice, food and nesting, the result of long hours spent near his Galloway home or in the islands of the Hebrides, painting and studying his subjects.

Mr Watson pays a well-deserved tribute to the outstanding Scottish naturalists from whose writing he has himself gained so much: Seton Gordon the doyen of Scottish ornithologists, Desmond Nethersole-Thompson and Adam Watson.

Expectant readers will not be disappointed with the twenty four full colour plates and fourteen monochromes which have been well produced by Hislop and Day of Edinburgh with their usual care. If in one or two backgrounds the water is of an almost unbelievable vivid hue, we may allow an artist's licence to make a telling picture. One or two of the plates have a sombre effect in contrast to the clear definition of the others, but all of the backgrounds are bound to evoke happy memories for those who know what Scottish scenery can offer.

David Bannerman[8]

From the records available, this is the most widely reviewed of Donald Watson's books, both in the bird literature in Scotland and Britain, and in the wider review literature such as *The Times Literary Supplement*, *The Field* and *The Guardian*. The reviews demonstrate the wide and high regard in which he was held as a bird artist and writer. Given these comprehensive reviews there is little more to add, although they were written half a century ago. There is likely to be more detailed ornithological knowledge of the some of the 61 species described and inevitably the distribution will have changed as a result of many factors, perhaps most of all land use, a point made poignantly about afforestation by Hartley. Nevertheless, as with other of Donald's books illustrated with his paintings, the combination is a unique blend of comprehensive, accessible and informative text and superb black-and-white and colour reproductions.

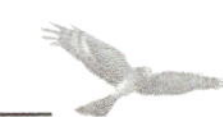

The Hen Harrier

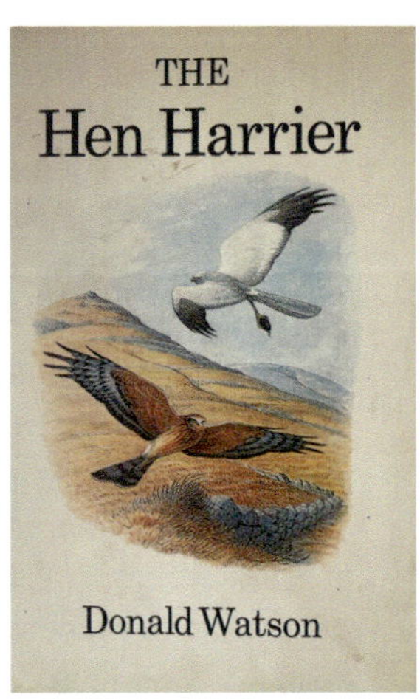

7.6 Donald Watson painting: cover of *The Hen Harrier*

> *The Hen Harrier* by Donald Watson enhances the reputation of the publishers still further, and it must have been a great delight to them to have a good author who is also a good artist. This book is beautifully illustrated throughout, with many black and white pictures and sketches and four coloured plates. Living as I do in Orkney, it is easy to become obsessed with this magnificent bird of prey and Donald Watson's book is the result of such an obsession. The author's love affair with harriers started in France in 1937, continued in several parts of the world and culminated in a study of Hen Harriers nesting in his home country of southwest Scotland. He has obviously read everything he can lay his hands on – the bibliography contains over 280 references – and corresponded with everyone with an interest in these birds … . In the concluding chapter, Donald Watson thoughtfully and reasonably, discusses the opposing views concerning protection or shooting of what he describes as 'this controversial bird'. I hope that those who hate harriers – as well as those who love them – will read this book. The increasing demand for improved agricultural land and the increasing value of that land may pose big problems for moorland nesting birds in the future and these demands will be difficult to resist. That some birds also have to face the guns, traps and poisons of people who feel (probably mistakenly) that they pose a threat to their ability to kill large numbers of grouse seems quite unacceptable in these prosperous times. The author says that his case for the defence of the Hen Harrier rests on how well he has told the story of its life. I conclude that he is a first-rate advocate.
>
> David Lea[9]

David Lea was the RSPB officer for the Orkney Isles and was resident there for many years. With its well-known areas of moorlands with apparently successfully breeding hen harriers, he was well versed in their ornithology but also in the management of the birds and their habitat where grouse shooting was a rare occurrence.

> The Hen Harrier, your latest book, which I have just finished reading, is the most important complete work of a single species in the past few years. The delightful drawings and the text full of accurate information which reveal an uncommon gift of observation in the author and ornithologist.
>
> Alfredo Noval[10]

Review of reprint, 2017

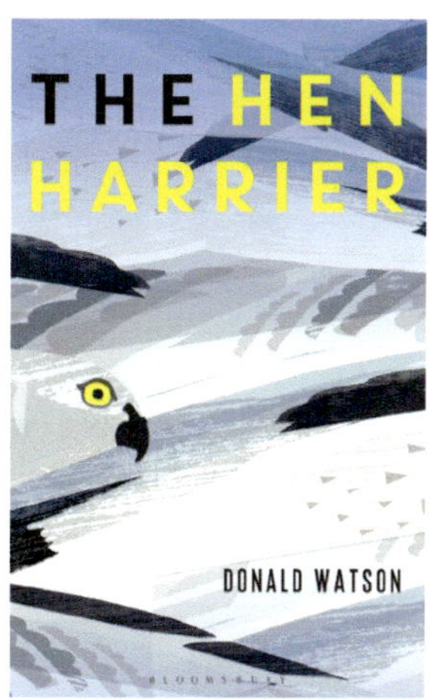

7.7 Cover of reprint of *The Hen Harrier* by unknown artist (Bloomsbury)

> This is a classic book. Donald Watson was a fine artist, and this book contains most of the original edition's drawings and the colour plates. They show Watson's skill at depicting birds in their landscapes and as portraits. Why re-issue a book from the 1970s now? Well, first of all the interest in Hen Harriers is higher than ever before and second hand copies of this Poyser volume are both rare (probably because, like me, owners wouldn't want to part with them) and expensive. But the book also deserves a wider audience now. I've re-read the whole volume and there are very few places where the book feels dated. The information is still a useful source, the anecdotes are still interesting, and the artist's insights are fascinating. This is also partly an account of a field study, and it gives a good flavour of how it feels to be studying a birds of which the author was clearly very fond.
>
> Watson's study of forest-nesting Hen Harriers was breaking new ground at the time, and it remains a fine record of this aspect of their ecology.
>
> Even then, the Hen Harrier was a controversial bird and Watson sets out a lot of arguments and issues that still occupy us four decades later.
>
> Mark Avery[11]

Mark Avery is a former RSPB conservation director and now an active commentator on ornithological issues in part on illegal activities, as well as very active blogger and writer on environmental issues.

He summarises well why Donald Watson's hen harrier book is still relevant. The study was so comprehensive, and in some respects ground-breaking – particularly his analysis of breeding and communal roosting and his detailed study of the species in south-west Scotland – that new research has neither overtaken Donald's analysis nor challenged his findings. Given that the hen harrier was his special bird for painting, for study and for campaigning, no one who has succeeded him to date has the range of attributes which are so admirably covered and displayed in his book. This is clearly a masterpiece, and even if another scientist were to produce a new version, it would be hard to surpass the quality and range of scraperboard sketches and drawings and the colour plates, including the brilliant depiction of the food pass on the jacket of the book. More specifically, there remains a significant issue of raptor persecution, particularly in areas where there are grouse moors in northern England and in many parts of Scotland. The figures for persecution remain high; the population is being artificially suppressed to well below half what it might be without illegal activity (see Chapter for full treatment).

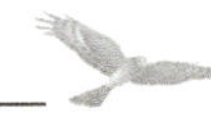

A Bird Artist in Scotland

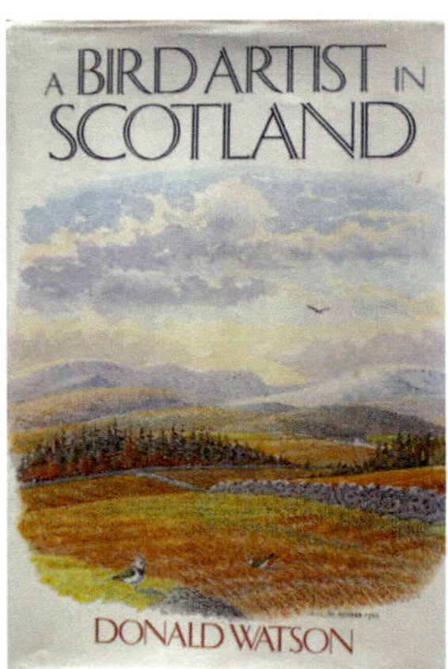

7.8 Donald Watson painting: cover of *A Bird Artist in Scotland*

My earliest recollection of the work of Donald Watson is of poring over his plates in *The Oxford Book of Birds*. It was the only book in our school library illustrating more than just adult plumages. My next encounter came in Poyser's *Birdwatchers' Year*, in which Donald Watson's year was my favourite: a compelling account of a year in south west Scotland, masterfully illustrated with some fine scraper boards.

A Bird Artist in Scotland is a book in two parts. The first section comprises five chapters in which Donald Watson relates his progress from early bird drawing to the present day – with lively accounts of Scottish artists' scene (including tea with Thorburn!) and his wartime experiences – and gives an insight into his working methods.

The second section, covering perhaps two thirds of the book, is an account of a year of Donald Watson's observations and thoughts in Galloway, presented as select entries from a diary. In that respect, it is very like the earlier work in *Birdwatchers' Year*, but with the years covered being some 18–20 years apart, the content is somewhat different: the first written when afforestation was in its infancy, the second when the hills are being invaded wholesale. It is written, as before, with acute observation, and a deep understanding of the habitat and its present problems. It is far from a gloomy account, for Donald Watson still gains much pleasure here both as an artist and as a naturalist, and this he passes on to his reader.

As one would hope, barely a page seems to pass without a 'moment-capturing' half-tone, scraper board or colour plate to delight the reader. They are full of atmosphere, with bold but skilful treatment of colour and light, giving great depth and form. The paintings represent work from throughout the artist's life, and many appear 'tighter' in style than those that I have seen at recent Society of Wildlife Artists' exhibitions.

The inclusion of a list of birds of Galloway may seem a little odd, but once you have read the book (and I hope you do) you will find it is every bit as much about Galloway as it is about the artist.

All in all, a splendid book, well produced, and a must for all interested in bird art and Scotland.

Alan Harris[12]

Alan Harris is well known illustrator of over 80 books and magazines, with his special attribute of meticulously accurate illustrations for field guides. His style is quite similar to Donald's, depicting birds in their habitat setting with great accuracy.

Finally, Derek Ratcliffe, a close friend of Donald, was an eminent nature scientist who spent many days in the field with him. In Derek's autobiography, *In Search of Nature*, he wrote of *A Bird Artist in Scotland*:

> To anyone who knows Galloway, it is a most evocative appealing account which will stir good memories and excite a desire to return. To those who do not, it will awaken their interest and illuminate their future acquaintance.[13]

This is a book of more historical importance, focusing in part on Donald's career as an artist and in part on the birds of Galloway from his diary. It gives an insight into his work as an artist and the influences he came under. It demonstrates his acute observational skills as a bird observer, and his meticulous documentation of what he saw in diaries, notebooks and sketchbooks. It is obvious from his many comments that he was deeply concerned about the management of the land and the effect of land use changes on the landscape and on the birds.

One Pair of Eyes

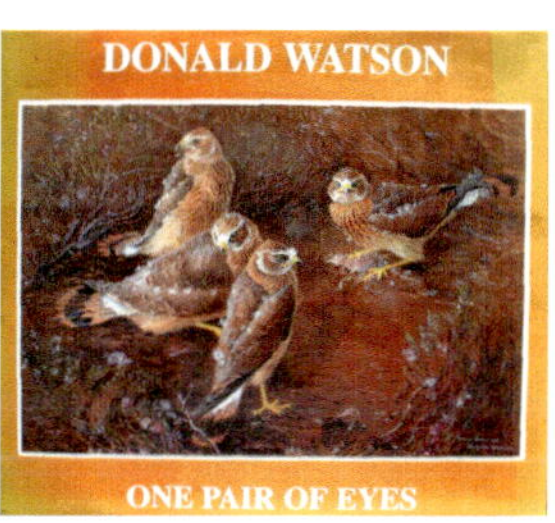

7.9 Donald Watson painting: cover of *One Pair of Eyes*

> This book is another quality limited edition from Arlequin Press, this time featuring the paintings and drawings of Donald Watson. The 80 or so paintings span his career, and most are previously unpublished. The text is also by Donald Watson and is mainly about birds and his Galloway surroundings; the anecdotes, often prompted by the paintings, make a good read. Always a strong advocate of working directly from life, his loose 'on-site' landscapes reveal a delightful spontaneity and freshness, with a vibrant use of colour. Happily, these qualities translate to the tighter studio works. In most, his birds are skilfully 'incidental' focal points. Being a limited edition, this book is expensive. Nevertheless, it is warmly recommended.
>
> Alan Harris[14]

If you are at all interested in Donald Watson's writing and his artistry this is the book you must have. Although it was an edition limited to 1,000 copies, it is still readily available for purchase on the web at a price that is reasonably affordable to the keen collector of bird books. From the dust cover, showing a brood of hen harriers almost fledged, to the frontispiece and endpiece of his sketches of kestrels, you will not be disappointed by the amount and the quality of the illustrations. The reproductions are first class. Far from restricting his paintings in the field and in the studio to Galloway, this book demonstrates his wide travelling around Scotland and further afield to Andalucia, Mallorca, France and, of course, the Seychelles, where Jeff was undertaking his PhD fieldwork on the indigenous kestrel. The landscape format, at 30cm × 26cm, allows large reproductions of previously unpublished paintings, adding further to the attraction of the book. Given his previous books, the diversity of species depicted should be of no surprise.

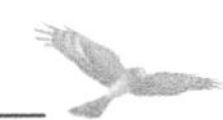

In Search of Harriers

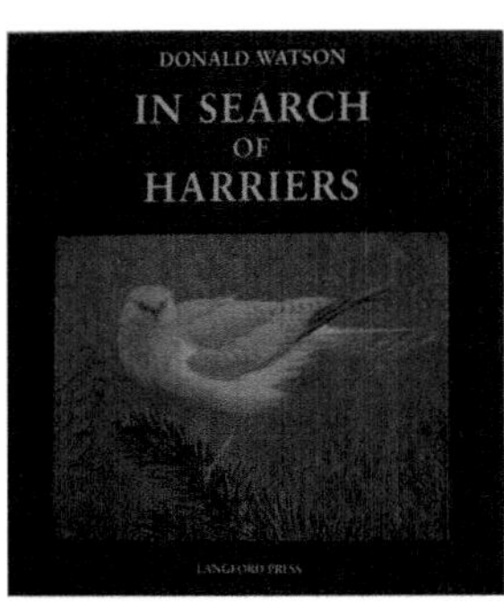

7.10 Donald Watson painting: cover of *In Search of Harriers*

If I had to pick my five favourite bird artists, Donald Watson would definitely make the final cut – following Archibald Thorburn, whose work influenced Watson in his early days as an art student. Both of these men loved raptors, and Watson's particular fascination with harriers has resulted in this splendid book. Watson had in fact completed writing the text before his death in 2005 and his friend and publisher, Ian Langford, has now ensured that the book has made it into print.

Watson illustrated over 30 books, and his characteristic scraperboard images of birds are really memorable. The drawing technique requires the artist to use sharp knives and tools to etch the image into a thin layer of white China clay that is coated with black ink, and for me Watson used this technique to great effect. A few examples are in this book, which mainly features his watercolours that again are so distinctive. While his individual bird paintings can be very pleasing, personally I prefer his landscapes in which the birds are not the main feature. They are really evocative, and for me nobody's art can better the way he conveys the dull light of a cold Scottish moorland where you can spend hours seeing nothing, and then suddenly a Hen Harrier or Merlin appears before you, and the long wait is worth this reward. If that's the kind of birding you enjoy, then you'll like this book.

Watson's interest in harriers goes back to the mid-1940s when in India he was lucky to watch Pied and Pallid Harriers at close quarters. Back in Scotland he then began studying harriers in detail right up till his death. This book takes some excellent examples of his work, and paintings appear on almost every page. Hen, Montagu's and Pied Harriers share the space with others including Short-eared Owl, Merlin, Peregrine, Kestrel, Golden Eagle and Whooper Swan, with a few smaller sketches of passerines thrown in.

Of course, each painting has a story behind it and often we are told this together with other information based on the author's extensive knowledge based on fifty years of study. Watson's fascination for the Hen Harrier led to his monograph of the species published in 1977 by Poyser. This would make a great present for a raptor enthusiast, while those who love wildlife art will enjoy the images, most of which have not been published before.

Keith Betton[15]

Keith Betton is professional birder and PR consultant. He has travelled extensively to see birds around the globe. He has a long engagement on the boards of bird charities in the UK.

'Why paint harriers?' Donald Watson asks in the introduction to this book, and responds: '[B]riefly the answer must be that all harriers are beautiful, wonderfully graceful and a joy to watch in flight[16] ... a cock harrier of either species (Hen or Montagu's) can certainly bring an arresting focal point of life to a spacious landscape and sky'.[17]

Writing of the hen harrier skydiving, he says 'on a fine sunny day the brilliantly white upper parts, jet-black wing ends compel the eye to follow every twist in its tortuous flight'.[18]

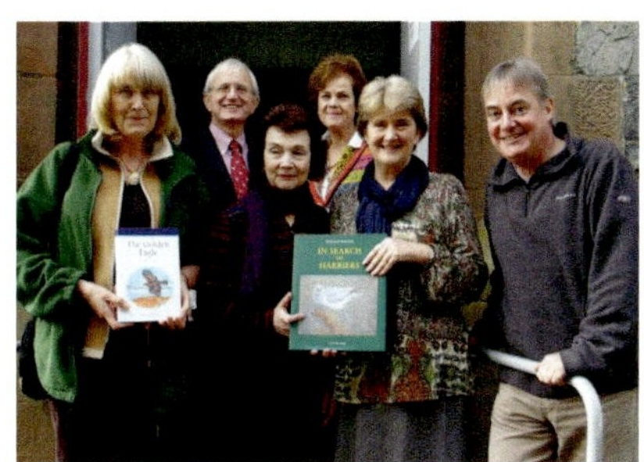

7.11 The launch of *In Search of Harriers*, l to r: Vanessa Watson, Roger Crofts, Pam Richardson, Cathy Agnew, Louise Watson and Des Thompson.

This posthumously published book gives insights into Donald Watson's passion for harriers, their study and protection. The focus is on hen harriers, but also discusses other harriers. The format, 30cm × 24cm, allows space for the reproduction of colour images, a *forte* of Donald's books and of Ian Langford's inspiring approach to publishing. Whether the would-be purchaser is a bird expert or a lover of bird art or a liker of coffee-table books with a message, this is a book that would satisfy a wide range of interests. Given the continuing interest in and concern about the persecution of the hen harrier, this book should have a wider appeal today. It is readily available for purchase from the web.

Overview

Donald Watson's writing style is unique. He manages to marry many aspects in his books. He is faithful to the work of his predecessors, having read widely and corresponded with those of his generation. He has been out in the field, in many places accompanied by many birders, as befits an observer and recorder of birds and their behaviour and a painter *en plein air*. He is therefore able to give the reader a real flavour of being out in the wilder areas of Britain with him. His observations and his reminiscences of these occasions give his writing a very distinctive and insightful flavour.

Words about his writing style come to mind such as: open and accessible; perceptive and illuminating; lyrical and entrancing; revealing and challenging. Displaying his scholarship and his acute knowledge of birds and their habitat settings and the wider landscapes, he is able to lead the reader into thinking more deeply and widely about birds and their habitat. At the same time, he is able to drive home his messages about the beauty of birds in the wild and the challenges that human attitudes and behaviour cause to threaten their survival in the wild and fundamentally change their habitat and the wider landscape.

Re-reading all of Donald's books in preparing this chapter, I am yet again struck by his easy style. It is informative of his field observations. It is engaging to the extent of the reader feeling part of the scene he is describing. It also gives an insight into his personality – infinite patience in wanting to observe the habits of his favourite birds, the hen harriers, when other people would have long given up in disconsolation. This style is not one of the diarist, but one of the acute observer, telling his story, putting over information and thereby engaging and absorbing his reader.

His style is also one of the artists able to describe the colours in the scene. For example,

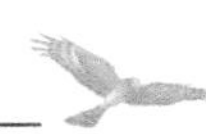

> where the blue cloud shadows were flying loosely across the madder brown slopes of the big hill beyond the burn, but the brown cock harrier was a poor substitute for the silver grey bird at the other site.[19]

This finely demonstrates his unique combination of artist and bird observer – his hallmark being placing birds in their landscape setting.

I will end this chapter with two quotes from Donald's writing, demonstrating his acute observation of the hen harrier in its landscape setting.

> The Hen Harrier is, to my mind, the most elegant and fascinating of our birds, but compared with eagle, peregrine, or osprey it arouses little public acclaim and is actively disliked on grouse moors. I have followed the fortunes of a few pairs in the quiet uplands of Galloway for 20 seasons and have also enjoyed the slow pageant of their winter roost gatherings. In early spring the arrow-head silhouettes of a pair in lazy flight above dark forest or moor never fail to set a tingling in anticipation of visual delights ahead, like the first frenzied sky dance of a displaying male and the neat aerial food pass between the pair. In bright light an adult male could be momentarily mistaken for a gull, from his silvery blue-grey plumage relieved by black wingtips, while the bulkier female is as brown as a buzzard apart from her brilliant white tail-base. The sudden appearance of a harrier in low questing flight brings a compelling focus of life to a wild and spacious landscape. Owl-like it hunts by hearing as well as sight, capturing its prey by surprise.[20]

And finally:

> Her deep-set dark amber eyes were offset by rippling white eyebrows and cheeks, the latter contrasting sharply with her russet brown ear coverts, bordered by the wavy fretted pattern of the neck ruff.[21]

What marvellous writing! It needs no further commentary.

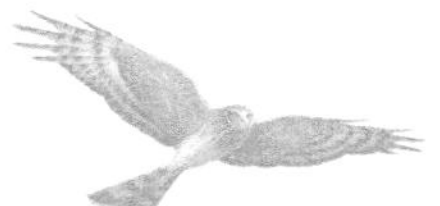

Eight
A conservation campaigner

ROGER CROFTS

> The future of the Galloway countryside and its wildlife does not carry much weight with politicians and bureaucrats. Some of us, and not only those who live here, think it is very precious.[1]

Describing Donald Watson as a conservation campaigner may seem out of character with a mild-mannered and thoughtful person. However, the following quotes from his book *A Bird Artist in Scotland* paint a different picture of his views at an early age. He stated that T.A. Coward's *Birds of the British Isles and their Eggs* was the treasured guide of his older brother Eric and himself from their early teens: 'His writings taught me the essentials of conservation as it is known today.'[2] He commented on the land around the family house in Surrey, where he lived until aged 12, as being bird-rich commons, but went on to observe how it became unrecognisable as the commons were ploughed up for wartime agriculture. Visiting Arran in 1933, aged 15, he noted that there were no buzzards, as they had been probably shot by gamekeepers, and that 'hen harriers had been persecuted out of existence'. Half a century later, in the later 1980s, his letters to politicians – particularly to Ian Lang, the local MP, about the march of plantation forestry over the Galloway landscape (see below), and to the Inquiry Reporter, W.D. Campbell, about the proposed test drilling for high level radioactive waste burial around Mullwharchar[3] – and his comments about raptor persecution in his books demonstrate that he had clear views. These were derived from what he was observing as detrimental changes to the land and landscape, and habitats and species in Galloway. His views were undoubtedly reinforced by conversations and correspondence with his friend Derek Ratcliffe, the campaigning chief scientist of the Nature Conservancy Council. Ratcliffe has stated that

> Donald Watson was one of the few people to stand up for nature conservation in this part of Scotland, which he did frequently and to good effect, and during his long residence he witnessed, with some misgivings, the transformation of his chosen country by afforestation.[4]

This chapter describes Donald Watson's views, seeks to place them in the context of the time he was writing and seeks to assess whether the situation has changed over the intervening years and how he might have reacted at the present time.

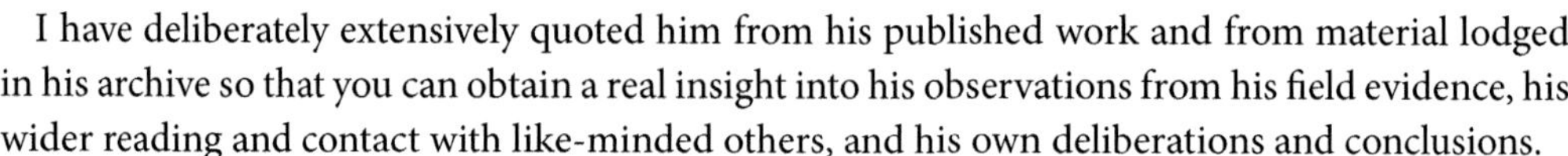

I have deliberately extensively quoted him from his published work and from material lodged in his archive so that you can obtain a real insight into his observations from his field evidence, his wider reading and contact with like-minded others, and his own deliberations and conclusions.

His general observations

He commented on the impact of livestock grazing and specifically trampling by livestock on the nests and eggs of ground-nesting birds, and on the lack of carrion for birds such as ravens. He was also critical of the collecting of eggs, especially those of raptors as prized species for collections and onwards sale. He was more positive about raising the level of Loch Ken as part of the hydro scheme, as it provided more attractive habitat for wildfowl.[5]

> The loss of the corn stacks, then so common, must have dealt a severe blow to many birds in winter.[6]

> Looking at many fields near my home, which were good for lapwing nests only 10–15 years ago, it is all too obvious how they have changed adversely for them. Now in May they look like lush green lawns, heavily fertilised and without field flowers, well on their way toward the first early cut of silage. Research has shown that silage grass has grown too tall for lapwing chicks to feed in successfully by the usual time of hatching. Compared with the old flowery hay meadows, monoculture fields of rye grass are likely to be impoverished of the insect life which is an important part of lapwing food.[7]

> The decline of the Black Cock in Galloway is most likely due to trampling and grazing by deer and sheep thereby reducing their food supply.[8]

He was very conscious of the bad habits of gamekeepers, saying that 'old habits die hard in some places', and noting that the death of red kites from poisoned baits were still occurring despite the fact that these birds are carrion feeders.[9]

In *Birdwatchers' Year* he stated that at the end of July

> I went to a distant grouse moor with two ladies to see a startling discovery they had made. It was a Crow Trap of the usual type, but they had heard from a forestry worker that it was apparently being misused ... I went with them and examined the trap thoroughly. I counted nearly forty dead birds, mostly fairly fresh, few long dead. There were at least twenty-five Mistle Thrushes and four Ring Ousels, all juveniles, two Cuckoos, a Blackbird and some remains of Red Grouse and Greyhen ... I contacted the RSPB immediately and the police have been informed. Now today, after the RSPB and the police visiting and photographing the trap, seeing the keeper's employer, a Duke, I am told that there is no case for prosecution. Apparently, the trap is standard 1½" mesh and there are nine others like it on the estate.[10]

Not all was negative. Donald Watson was called in as a hen harrier expert to guide the relocation of a hen harrier nest with female on eggs to make way for construction at the Clyde submarine base at Coulport on Loch Long, as reported in *The Times*.[11]

Donald Watson reserved his main critique for afforestation and for raptor persecution. The remainder of this chapter will therefore focus on these two issues. For each one, I quote and paraphrase what Donald said and did, place it in the context of the time, and assess whether the situation has changed.

Afforestation and its effects: Donald Watson's views

Derek Ratcliffe commented that in Donald's book, *One Pair of Eyes*,

> the thoughtful essays include a very fair account of forestry and its effects, a subject which must touch the thoughts of any naturalist in the region.[12]

Donald became aware in the early 1950s of the effects of conifer planting on birds, their habitats and the landscape. He wrote a paper for the Scottish Wildlife Trust, pleading for 'the retention of enclaves of open ground to be left in forests'. He notes that 'it cut no ice with the foresters at the time, ostensibly for economic reasons'. Continuing, he writes in the early 21st century that 'at last this is happening, as forests are being restructured and large areas clear felled'.[13] Whether this is continuing at the present time is highly debatable, as large swathes of ground are often replanted with the same species, with no gaps left and hard plantation edges.

In December 1987 Donald Watson wrote the following letter to his local MP, Ian Lang:[14]

> May I urge you when you are in Galloway to take a look at the land on the north side of the A702 road between Corriedoo and Holmhead, also the road around by Lochinvar Loch, Glenshimmeroch and near Butterhole Bridge? I am very concerned about the increase of conifer afforestation in this area. Most of it is private sector forestry. I have spoken to many local people and visitors who are horrified at what has been happening. I have been resident in Dalry for over 36 years as an artist and naturalist. The A702 road has always been my favourite approach to Galloway with incomparable views of the Rhinns of Kells and Cairnsmore of Carsphairn as you near Dalry. It must be the route whereby visitors have their first impressions of Galloway. The minor road to Lochinvar is also very popular, both with hill walkers and those who travel by car.
>
> Over the years I have lived here with the inexorable advance of the conifer afforestation and noted the mainly adverse changes in landscape quality and wildlife it has brought. I put it to you, as my M. P., that there is now a desperate need to take steps to make it less attractive to hill farmers to sell land for planting and for wealthy absentees, massively helped by tax advantages and subsidies, to acquire land for plantations. The Forestry Commission went a long way towards changing the character of the Galloway landscape irrevocably long ago, but in the 1950s, they could argue that they provided a lot of rural employment (much less now). While they often planted quite ruthlessly (especially in the early years) they acquired a protective attitude to wildlife where it did not conflict with their commercial aims, and I have generally found the Commission helpful regarding access to the forests for legitimate interests or study. I have read recent publications questioning the economics and other aspects of forestry, but I was interested to learn that

the one clearly profitable area of the Forestry Commission's activity is in the providing of tourist/amenity facilities. Apparently, financial cutback has prevented these being developed as they might be.

I have no doubt that the private forestry companies give most cause for concern today. Everyone knows the problems of the Flow Country in Caithness and Sutherland. Many of the same arguments against large scale upland planting apply in Galloway. What worries me most of all is that we are now at the stage where there will soon be very little open moor left below 100 feet. It is true that many tourists from urban areas are happy with the facilities that the Commission offer, but an increasing number are complaining about the monotony of conifer plantations. How boring it is to walk along forest roads through tunnels of maturing Sitka and difficulties of the access to the higher hills.

Generally speaking, private forestry does nothing to attract the public and there is usually no one on hand locally who can easily be asked about access etc. Younger people than I will see the A702 turned into a Sitka tunnel. I remember it when I could walk for miles on both sides of the road over sheep country with Curlews and Golden Plover [...] hardly ever out of earshot in spring and early summer.

In the past I have played a small part in the establishment of some areas particularly rich in upland vegetation or wildlife as SSSIs or in one case a National Nature Reserve. These cannot go far enough for obvious reasons. I am not a hill farmer but if last month's Galloway cattle sales are anything to go by, there are good prospects for hill cattle, and I know sheep farms which seem prosperous. Admittedly, I am a bit of a specialist on ornithology and could give you a comprehensive list of uplands birds lost when the plantations arrive. It does, of course, include the Red Grouse and research in Argyll must indicate that our very few Golden Eagles are in danger. Foresters quote research suggesting there is a larger biomass of birdlife in the forests than on the open moor, but this is invalidated because most of the birds in plantations (like Chaffinches, Willow Warblers, Thrushes etc) are widespread and abundant elsewhere.

I have taken the A702 as a prime and local example of what I am concerned about. A senior employee of Economic Forestry has complained to me that their particular afforestation scheme is 'cowboy' work with ploughing taken much too close to water courses. You will be well aware of the widespread concern about increased acidity, and loss of fish stocks in granitic areas. In last week's *Galloway News* alarm was expressed about the high level of aluminium in local water. It seems to be agreed that the spread of conifer plantations is contributory in these matters. Galloway would of course be enriched in many ways if more hardwoods were planted, and I know that efforts are being made but in the upland forests they are never likely to be more than peripheral.

The large number of people who have protested against the proposed forestry schemes on Criffel are an indicator of what many more feel, but are too inarticulate to voice. Up

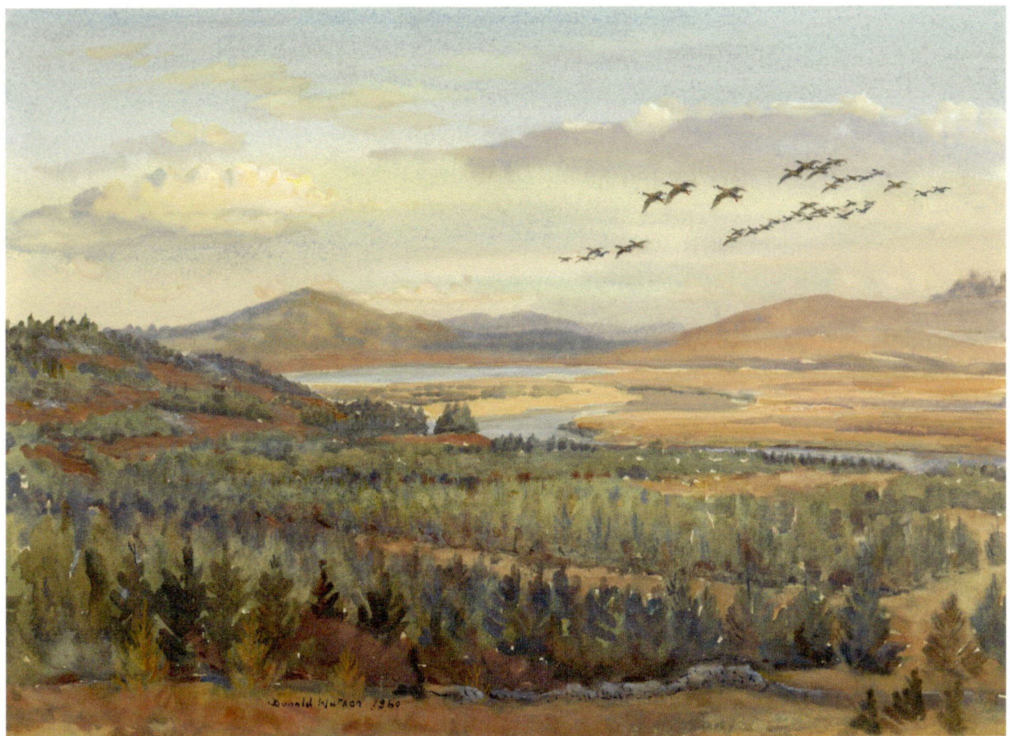

8.1 Donald Watson painting of forestry encroachment in north Galloway, 1960

> here in The Glenkens, I think there is an even greater need to challenge the advance of the forests. There may soon be little left to defend.

I have deliberately quoted Donald's letter in full because it gives an insight into the issues as he perceived them, both personally and from discussions within the community. I have no evidence of Ian Lang's response other than a polite reply! However, on the political front matters were being reconsidered, as I know personally from my postings in the Scottish Office during this period (see below). Derek Ratcliffe helped to persuade Donald to make his views known to politicians and he maybe advised Donald on the drafting, but that is immaterial. The letter clearly expresses Donald's views. Suffice to say, his observations, as an acute observer of the effects of afforestation on birds and on the wider landscape of Galloway countryside, are telling.

This letter reflects a cumulation of his growing concerns about afforestation and its effects. This is evident from the correspondence between Donald Watson and Derek Ratcliffe over a 30-year period from the early 1970s.[15] Specifically, they expressed early concerns about the encroachment of forestry plantings on the western slopes of the Rhinns of Kells onto the watercourses feeding the Silver Flowe, the patterned blanket bog protected as a National Nature Reserve. Similar concerns were expressed about afforestation around Airie Flowe near Mossdale, an important roosting area for hen harriers in winter. In the 1980s they noted the decline of ravens because of afforestation (bearing in mind that Ratcliffe authored the classic monograph on that bird in the Poyser series[16]). Donald's views became more evident in the 1980s as a result of all the disputes between afforestation and nature conservation, as part of a broader dispute between economic development and environmental protection which I discuss in the next section. Ratcliffe, wearing his Nature Conservancy Council hat, openly challenged the Forestry Commission and in 1985 apparently wrote a paragraph-by-paragraph rebuttable of the Commission's paper. Donald was well aware of these arguments and, encouraged by Ratcliffe, wrote the letter quoted above to the local MP. He also made clear his views in his many references to the detrimental effects of afforestation on birds and landscape in *A Bird Artist in Scotland*. Significantly, this book was published in 1988 at the height of the afforestation versus nature conservation arguments. The salient statements from that book are as follows:

> Alas, more and more of these favourite moorland birds (wheatear) will find their upland nesting grounds destroyed forever by the forestry plough.[17]

> On the south side of the road here (New Galloway to Clatteringshaws) well-grown conifer plantations – Sitka spruce with patches of larch – clothe the hill down to the Knocknairling Burn. A few years ago, when the trees were small and had not extinguished a rich growth of heather and bog myrtle, stonechats benefitted from them.[18]

> Perish the thought that when the wheatears do arrive on these hills (Galloway) they will find many of their best territories furrowed by the forestry plough. They are one of the first birds banished by afforestation.[19]

> Now it is afforestation and improved sheep husbandry with little carrion available that seems to explain the absence of pairs (of ravens) from so many traditional sites.[20]

> Crows and foxes which predate on eggs have increased in numbers with the plantations, so birds do not nest near the plantation edge.[21]

> The disappearance of the dunlin nest near Loch Skerrow is probably due to afforestation.[22]

> These clear-felled areas do have the merit of opening up the countryside for a few years, but (during the early years) they resemble nothing so much as a First World War battlefield, chaotically littered with brash and tree roots which foresters presumably hope will depress the growth of natural vegetation liable to compete with second generation tree planting.[23]

> Now I regret my complaints that foresters do nothing to make clear felled ground 'visibly acceptable'. Hideous though it is, I would much rather they left it as it is to provide good nest sites for owls – and possibly harriers too.[24]

> Oak and birch woodlands in Glen Trool are good for small insectivorous birds such as Pied Flycatcher, Redstart and Wood Warbler. I was sorry to see that part of the wood had been underplanted with Sitka spruce.[25]

Talking of the High Bridge of Ken area, he says

> The present mixture of afforestation and sheep walk in this glen suits both these big predators (Buzzard and Hen Harrier) and they should be safe enough from persecution here. It would be a great loss to the landscape if the open slopes of Dodd Hill disappeared under conifers.[26]

In Galloway in the 1960s hen harriers were nesting in the lush growth beneath the trees in conifer plantations, and Donald Watson painted the scene. This accords with his observations of the cycle of change noted below:

> Looking back at the dates of nests within the forest blocks it is clear that these are generally only suitable for Hen Harrier nesting for the first period of not more than about 15 years.[27]

Derek Ratcliffe substantiated this point, stating:

> Donald had made a special study of the Hen Harrier, which recolonised Galloway from the late 1950s, and I admire his skill in findings its nests … He followed a favourite pair

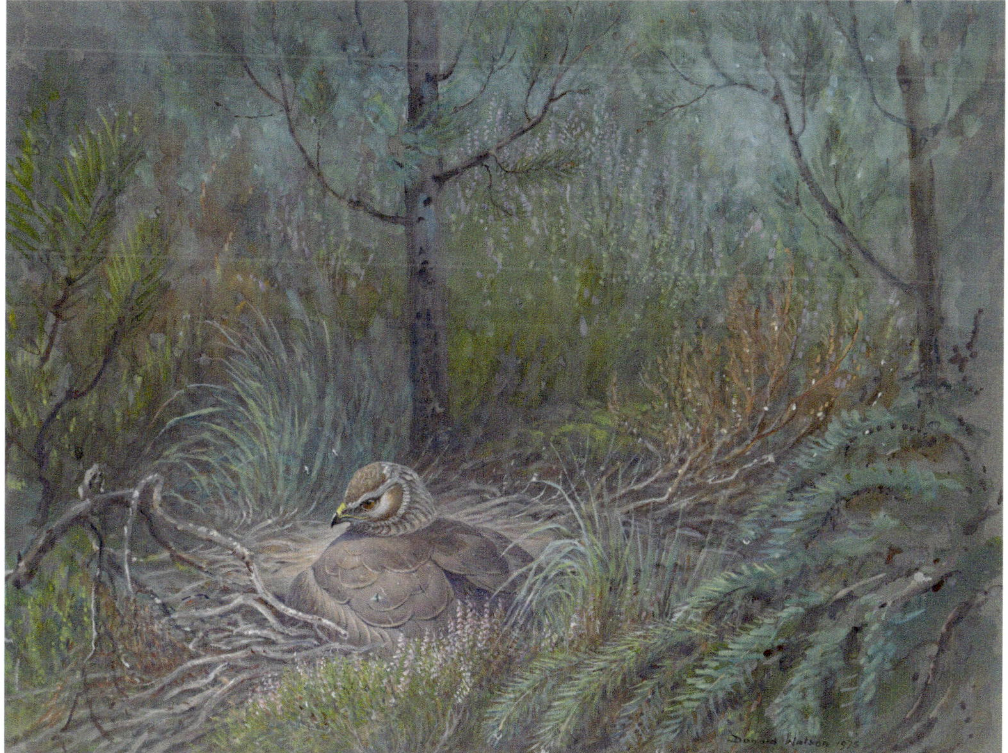

8.2 Donald Watson painting: Hen Harrier in forestry plantation ride, 1975

> for years, but was disappointed when the Stewartry harriers dropped out one by one, when their forest nesting habitat became too tall.[28]

Earlier in the decade Donald Watson and Derek Ratcliffe saw the encroachment of afforestation in Galloway and observed the effects over time on bird habitats, nesting areas and supply of food. Ratcliffe quotes his observation in *In Search of Nature* as follows

> Upland Galloway has been transformed from the almost treeless state of my youth … I have already noted the adverse effects on the numbers and breeding success of Golden Eagles and Ravens. Other birds have been more affected. Golden Plover have declined to very low numbers and most remaining pairs are high above the forest limits.[29]

He notes that a balance between losses and gains depends on the stage in the cycle from sheep walk to closed-canopy plantation forestry. He defines the cycle of the relationship between forestry plantation growth and the effects on habitat and bird, which both he and Donald had observed. Firstly, sheep are cleared off the ground, which results in the loss of carrion for birds such as ravens and golden eagles. With the preparation of the ground for planting and for the first 10–15 years after planting, small birds increase. Once the canopy closes, bird numbers decline, partly because nesting sites are no longer available and partly because there are fewer small mammals available as food. This led Sir Arthur Duncan to conclude that 'what the Forestry Commission has done to Galloway is absolutely criminal'.

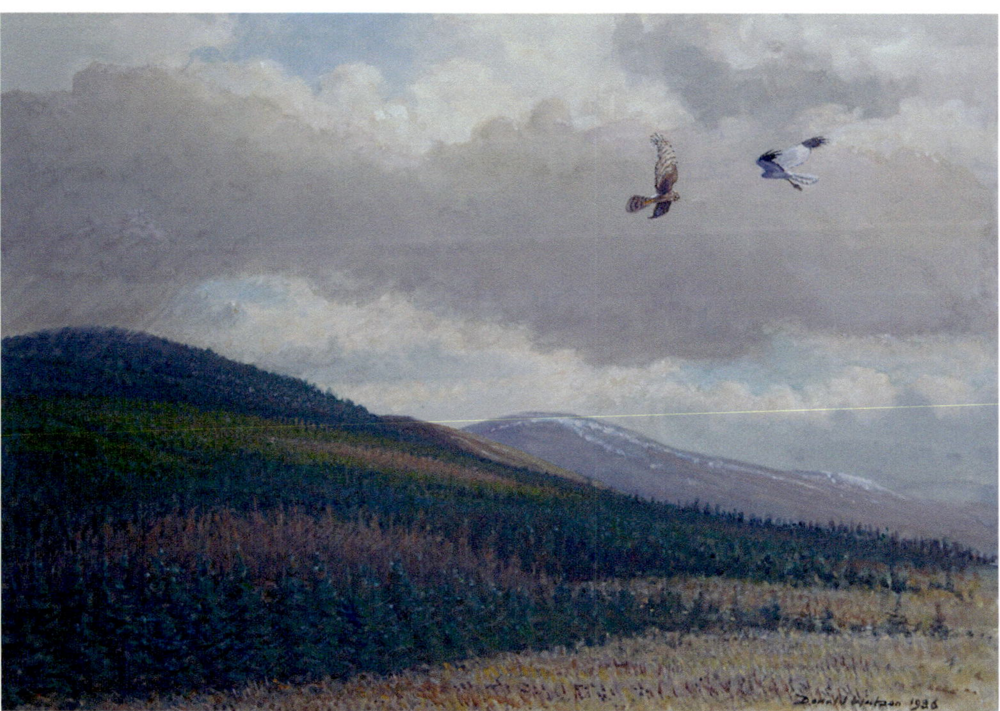

8.3 Donald Watson painting: Hen Harrier pair flying over forestry plantation, 1986

One case was causing Watson and Ratcliffe great concern: the Grade 1 nature site of Merrick-Kells (the grading used in the Nature Conservancy Council's Nature Conservation Review, 1977). Both men decided to lobby; Donald wrote to John Davies of the Forestry Commission, the conservator for South Scotland, and Derek Ratcliffe wrote to his Nature Conservancy Council colleague, Sandy Kerr, the regional director for West Scotland. Donald wrote in sadness rather than anger

> It was the first time I had seen the high level planting at close quarters. I decided that I really must write to you to say how much this saddened me and to ask what is the reason for taking the forest so high … There is also some loss of habitat for the small high level population of breeding Golden Plover – a bird which has already lost a vast amount of lower nesting ground to afforestation. My own experience suggests that the present top limit of planting even encroaches on the breeding habitat of the very rare dotterel.[30]

Ratcliffe argued on the point of principle of 'the extension of the plantations within the boundary of the Grade 1 site'. The reply from John Davies to Donald stated the Forestry Commission's position: they were doing an experiment the results of which would be invaluable not only in Galloway but in other parts of Scotland. This response gave limited assurance, and the following statement could only have been read with incredulity by Ratcliffe: 'we just do not know where tree growth will stop but believe it will be well below the 2300 feet plantation we have made. The Good Lord will etch in this for us'.[31] Oh dear! The planting was not removed, and the upper limit of afforestation was never modified as a result of Donald's and Derek's representations. As on many occasions, the fear that the Nature Conservancy Council was no match for the Forestry Commission seemed to be substantiated.

The context at the time

It is fair to say that in the 1980s forces were aligned in a battle of nature versus forestry. Although this had been brewing for some time, it was brought to a head by a number of factors. First and best known to all, as mentioned by Donald Watson – no doubt also briefed by his son Jeff, who was working in the chief scientist's team at the Nature Conservancy Council – were the tax breaks available to those who invested in forestry. The situation on incentives was made worse by the existence of a wheeze consisting of 'compensation for profit forgone'. This meant that those stating that they wished to plant trees where the Nature Conservancy Council objected to them were entitled to compensation even though the proposers had never actually intended to plant trees. The UK Government, through the lead Environment Ministry, was clearly uncomfortable – but nothing like as uncomfortable as the lead Forestry Minister, the Secretary of State for Scotland and his junior ministers and officials in the Scottish Office. The government took action: – the 'income forgone' ability closed, the tax breaks halted, the senior figures in the Forestry Commission retired off, new management brought in from overseas, and nature conservation reorganised from a Great Britain body to country agencies, including the establishment of Scottish Natural Heritage. By the time these steps had been taken much government money had been wasted and much environmental damage done.

The worst exemplification of the tax breaks was in the Flow Country of Caithness and Sutherland. Here, following experiments by the various arms of the Forestry Commission, plans

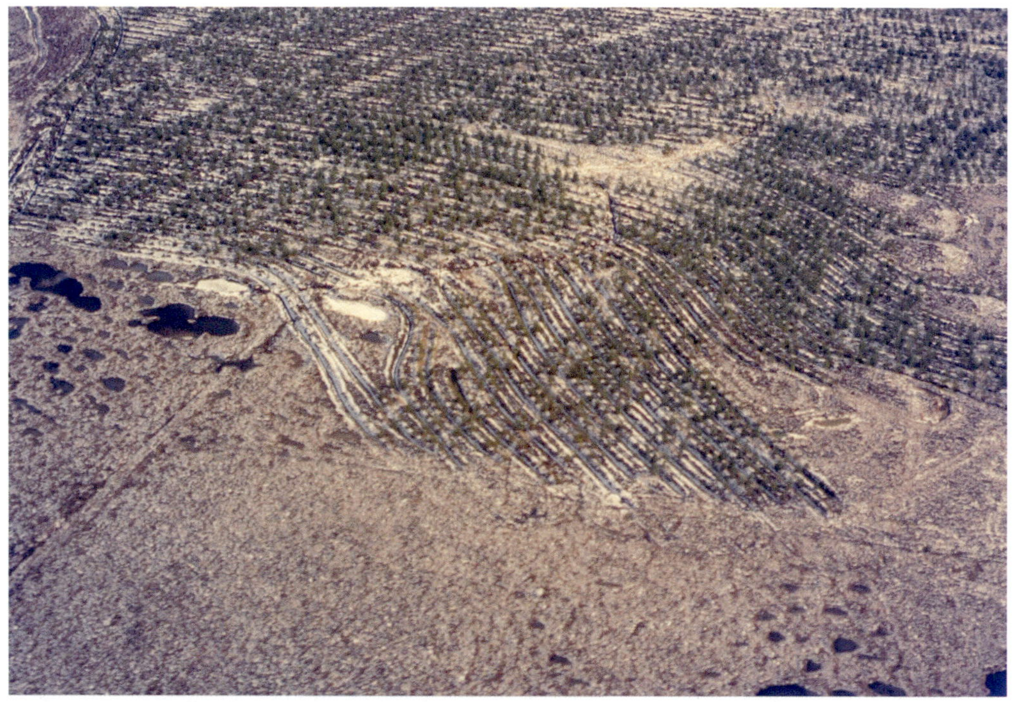

8.4 Flow Country: aerial photo of forestry ploughing and planting into wetlands

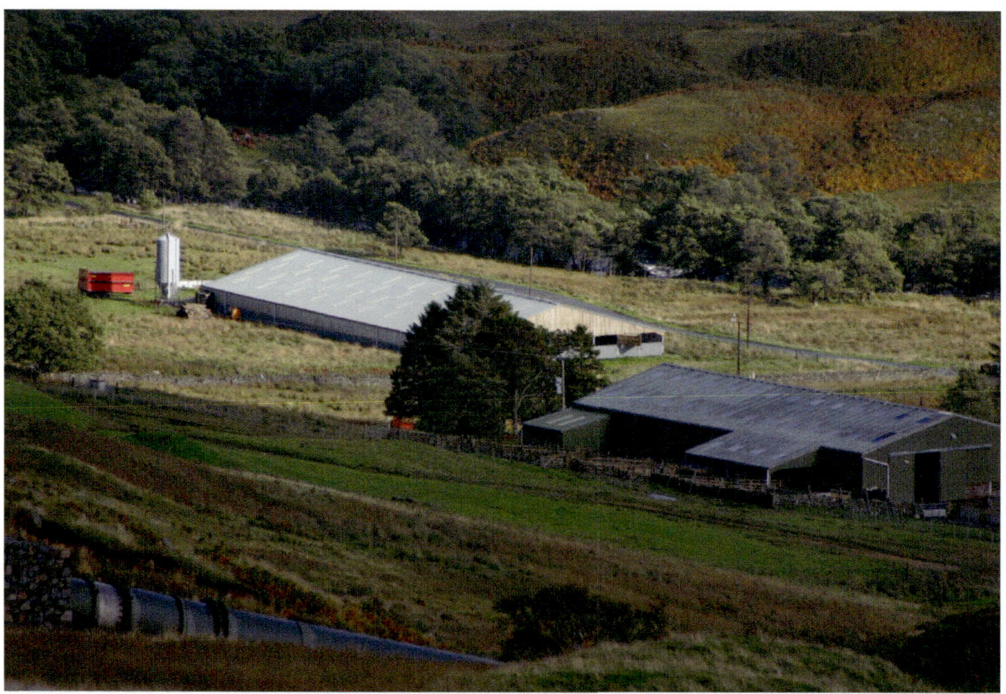

8.5 Glen Lochy sheep shed built with compensation from NCC

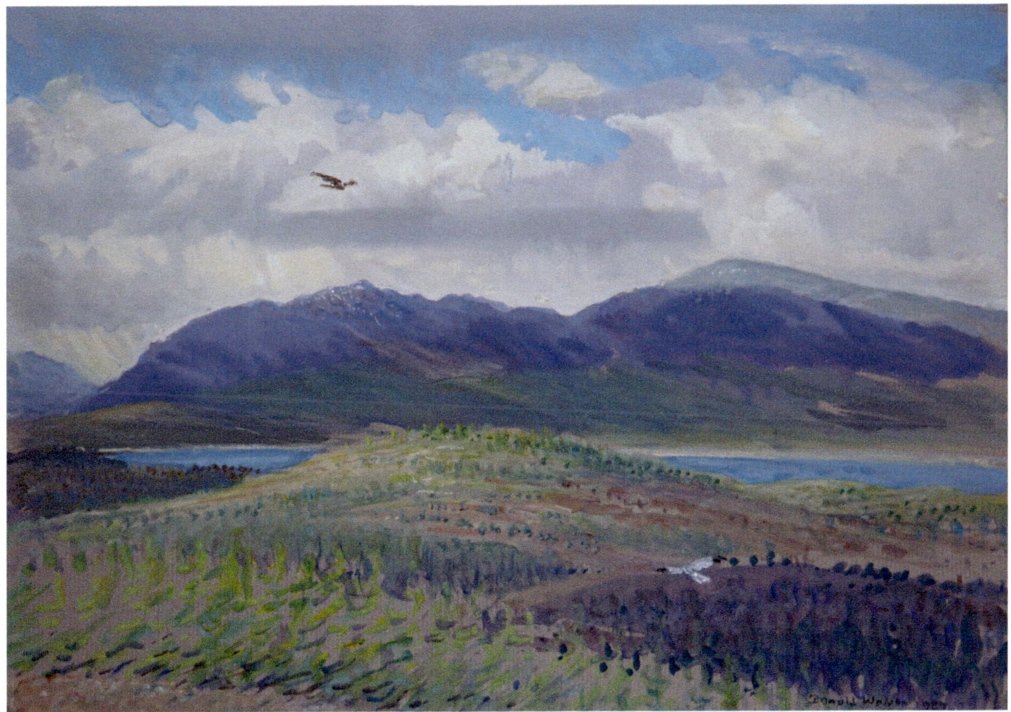

8.6 Donald Watson painting: The march of the conifers, 1987

for planting conifers on the peatland were well advanced. Sitka spruce was the predominant species, with lodgepole pine as the nurse crop. This approach was strongly supported by economic interests, particularly the Highlands and Islands Development Board and the Highland Regional Council. It made sense to them, as it would create jobs, the latest silver bullet in the regeneration of the Highlands. It would help to meet the government's newly established tree-planting targets of 10,000 hectares a year.

Commercial forestry companies, led by Fountain Forestry, began the planting. Rich celebrities made even more money. The Nature Conservancy Council was caught out, as it had not properly appraised the value of the whole of the Flows by the time the Nature Conservation Review, led by Derek Ratcliffe, was completed in the late 1970s. This was a classic example of the old paradigm of the focus on nature protection sites, rather than the protection of whole ecosystems.

The worst exemplification of the 'profit forgone' was in Glen Lochy, one of the largest sheep farms in Europe, owned by a leading Fife-based farmer, John Cameron. He wanted to plant windbreaks to give his various sheep hefts shelter from the weather. The Nature Conservancy Council staff in Scotland failed to see the possibilities of habitat gain, resulting in a £1.2 million claim, a large part of which had resulted from the delays by the NCC staff in Scotland in dealing with the case.

The Nature Conservancy Council was preparing its approach to forestry.[32] In Scotland, a movement was getting under way to use the statutory planning system to provide guidance and encouragement to the local authorities who were producing *Indicative Forestry Strategies*; I signed a circular issued by the Scottish Environment Ministry.[33] At the same time, a book assessing the

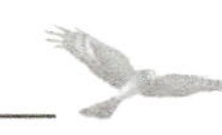

interactions between afforestation and birds was published by leading scientists, one in the RSPB and one in the Forestry Commission;[34] they showed conclusively that afforestation in Galloway had resulted in the reduction of feeding and breeding territories for raptor species.

The complacent attitude in the Forestry Commission is exemplified by an article written in the 1980s by John Davies, the forestry conservator for the South Scotland region of the Forestry Commission:

> As a result of the great post war planting programmes, most of our forests are very uniform. Within 10 years their structure will change remarkably due to felling and the large holes that are bound to be torn in them by the wind.

Donald had a copy of this manuscript,[35] and no doubt considered that the writer's aspirations were nowhere to be seen on the ground in south-west Scotland. Sadly, that continues to be the case today.

Has the situation changed?

The cumulative effects which Donald was concerned about have occurred most especially in The Glenkens area of Galloway and in eastern Dumfriesshire. The recent reintroduction of the old planting targets and the biased application of the Forestry Grant Scheme towards commercial afforestation have made matters worse.[36] Donald Watson would have been horrified at the landscape changes and at the reduction in the open moorland habitat that is so important for the range of raptor and upland species he was used to seeing. One has to conclude that since his time there has been little progress, despite his and Derek Ratcliffe's efforts and the lobbying by many following in his footsteps. There are maybe positive omens in the emerging Scottish Government policy of an integrated approach to land use change with recognition of the need for more multiple objectives, recognising the twin crises of climate change and biodiversity loss. In reality, however,

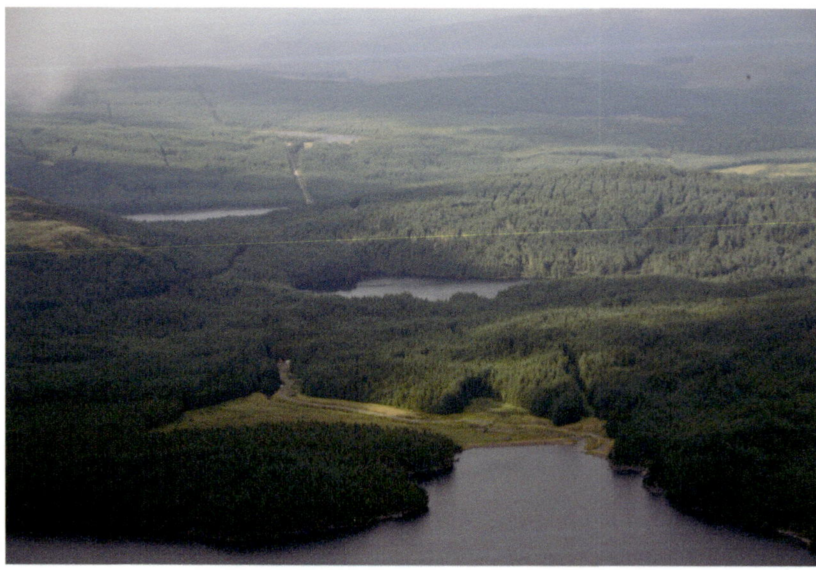

8.7 Extensive commercial forestry in The Glenkens this century

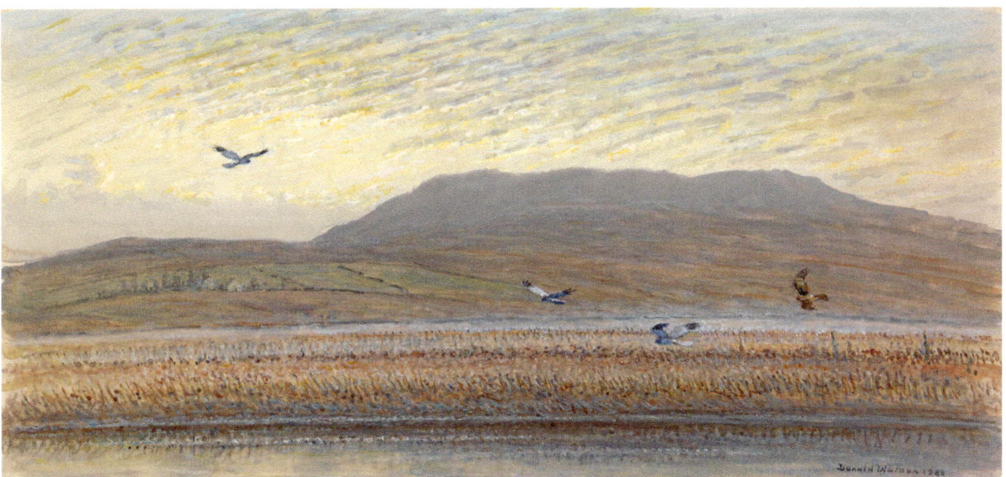

8.8 Donald Watson painting: Airie Flow Hen Harrier roost

there is no obvious change, so we shall have to wait and see whether the policy rhetoric is translated into meaningful action on the ground, which Donald so clearly argued for 35 years ago.

Sporting land management and raptor persecution: Donald Watson's views

Donald had strong views on the persecution of raptors, particularly hen harriers. This should be of no surprise given his field observations and his reading of the scientific and conservation literature. This was backed up by the many conversations with shepherds with whom he had built up excellent relationships, and by his suspicions of the activities and attitudes of gamekeepers, as his books make clear. For example, he states 'more than once the shepherds told me keepers would have shot the harriers if they had not known that the nest was being watched'.[37] This led him to press the Nature Conservancy Council to be more robust in its response to forestry planting grant applications, in order to protect hunting and foraging areas and roosts, and to extend the boundaries of SSSIs to include such areas.[38]

He did not take the accounts of others about raptor persecution as a given; rather, he used his detailed knowledge of the life cycle and feeding habits of hen harriers. This is well set out in the early chapters of *The Hen Harrier*. This knowledge gave him an unrivalled ability to decipher the accounts of others, which he found were often based on anecdote exaggerated to suit their opinions. He was therefore able to evaluate critically the factors that earlier writers had attributed to the regional increases and decreases of the hen harrier throughout the British Isles. He noted that it was regarded as 'vermin' by owners and gamekeepers and was already ripe for removal, despite the fact that he considered that there was probably statutory protection of the bird from the 16th century. He also considered that changes in land use, with clearance and improvement for agriculture from the 17th century, meant that birds of prey were pushed onto the higher ground of uncultivated moorland, marshland, peatland and bog. He observed from his reading of the documentary evidence from the 19th century that hen harriers survived in areas where grouse moors were non-existent and where there was a plentiful supply of voles, such as the southern areas of the Western Isles, and in Orkney and on Arran. He noted that where there was no persecution and no muirburn there was more food available for all levels in the food

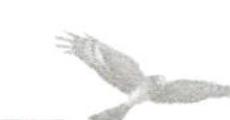

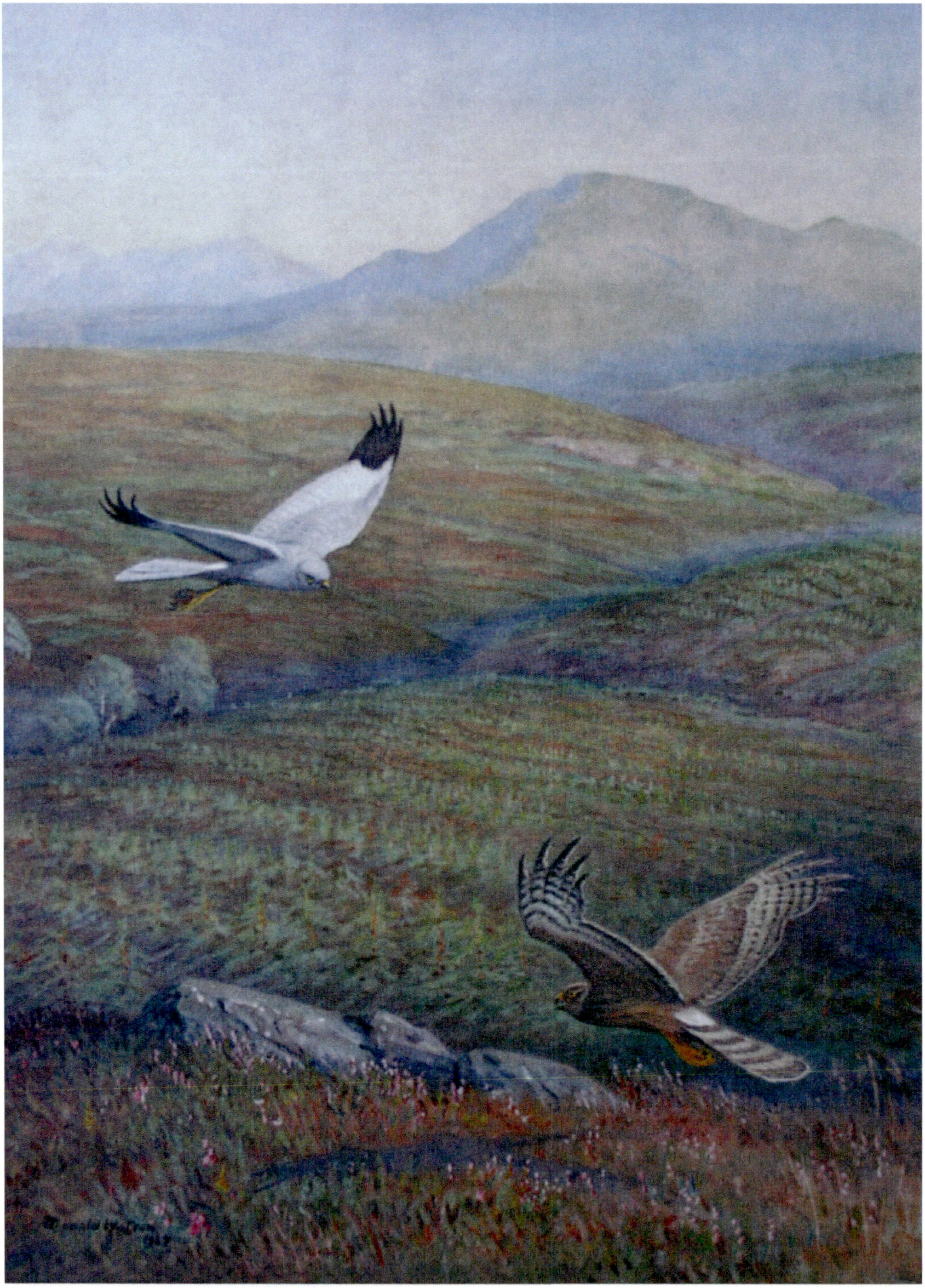

8.9 Donald Watson painting: Hen Harriers over moorland

web and hence a stable, if not rising, population of prey animals, such as voles the item of diet of hen harriers. He also speculated that in areas where there was a rising population near to grouse moors whether this meant that owners and keepers had become less tolerant. His notes that his real interest in this negative interaction occurred in his early years in The Glenkens:

> Strangely it was the attempted breeding of a pair of even rarer Montagu's Harriers in a young conifer plantation at Corriedoo, near Dalry, in 1953 (sadly the female was caught in a gin trap placed at the nest) that first alerted me to keep a special look out for nesting harriers.[39]

> As game keepering intensified through the nineteenth century both eagles became rare, and the last White-tailed Eagles in Galloway bred at Cairnsmore of Fleet about 1866. Golden Eagles apparently ceased to breed there regularly well before then, but a pair nested unsuccessfully in 1905. Several times egg collecting prevented them rearing any chicks.[40]

> A few days ago I saw a male (HH) hunting over prime grouse moor in Dumfriesshire where he would have little chance of long term survival, a pair with a nest even less.[41]

> Hen Harriers were showing signs of increase by 1962, but keepers were becoming aware of this. Louis Urquhart and I decided to call on Mrs Murray-Usher, the formidable landowner of Castramont. She listened to us patiently and later gave her keepers orders not to kill harriers.[42]

Commenting on the Muirkirk uplands in eastern Ayrshire, he observed an increase in the hen harrier population from the 1960s, but noted 'sadly, as the harriers increased, subsequent keepers began killing them, as their employers wanted'. However, he notes that a new regime, agreed between Scottish Natural Heritage and RSPB and the landowners and keepers, had been established as part of the EU protection mechanism of Special Protection Areas under the EU Birds Directive.[43]

Back in 1965 the head keeper of the Stair Estate in Wigtownshire said that he regarded hen harriers as 'his worst vermin', despite them being legally protected. Donald reported finding a pole trap illegally set in hen harrier territory and reported it to the police, who in turn forced all of the traps to be removed.[44]

There is a certain paradox when Donald says

> I often used to ponder the irony that, but for grouse shooting, most of what I liked best in this landscape would disappear and be replaced by conifer forest, or something worse.[45]

He did, however, take a balanced view of the causes of hen harrier declines, citing the action of gamekeepers alongside cold weather in the breeding season, muirburn reducing the availability of nesting sites, tree planting reducing nesting, roosting and feeding areas, disturbance from walkers, and lastly threat from nearby golden eagles.[46] He frequently cited poor heather management and muirburn at the wrong season. His observations were based on patient looking from a distance and a preference for catching and ringing birds, rather than shooting them, for study. Indeed, few of his paintings are of dead birds and those that are were mainly the result of road kill or natural mortality.

His and colleagues' observations from the specially built hide are reported, and indicate that hen harriers' main food were small passerines rather than grouse chicks; the numbers of the latter are often exaggerated by sporting interests to suit their case.[47]

It is important to record what Donald Watson wrote in the last chapter of *The Hen Harrier*, subtitled 'a controversial bird'. He stated:

> whether or not Hen Harriers continue to inhabit this world is a matter of indifference to the great majority of mankind'.[48] … [I]n countries such as Britain, where a small but influential section of the population is intensely keen on game shooting, birds of prey are often still treated as vermin and the Hen Harrier is apt to be placed in the forefront of this category[49] … [W]hat happens to the Hen Harrier on a grouse moor is undoubtedly more likely to be decided by personal opinion of the damage and disturbance it might cause to game, than by consideration of its status under the law.[50]

He continues by quoting an article in the *Shooting Times* and, having analysed the implications that allow gamekeepers to make their own decision irrespective of the legality of the matter, observes that a growing chorus from this small, privileged community was demanding change in the law to allow hen harriers to be killed where they are proven to be preying on grouse. He refutes this argument from his field evidence of hen harrier prey, and suggests that it is most likely that only weakling grouse are preyed upon. He blames the economic value of grouse shoots as determined by the cost per grouse shot, and argues his case for the continuing protection based on his and his colleagues' careful observation. Although at the time he was writing hen harrier numbers were increasing, habitat loss, agricultural pesticides, disturbance and other causes of decline meant that protection was still needed. He concludes his seminal work by saying

> it cannot be denied that direct human destruction has been, and regrettably still is, a major hazard as far as harriers are concerned.

Donald Watson and Roger Clarke, his co-worker and observer from the specially built hide, were certainly concerned about the continuing persecution of hen harriers in the mid-1990s. They wrote

> the need for action to find a solution to the confrontation between grouse interests and harrier conservation is clearly becoming much more urgent, not the least because of the inclusion of the Hen Harrier on the Red List of as a species of the highest conservation concern in the UK. It is clear that special measures are required now to fulfil the UK's responsibility for conservation of its resident Hen Harrier.[51]

The context at the time

There was a debate through the 1970s, 1980s and 1990s about the status of the hen harrier alongside the claimed economic importance of grouse shooting. It is fair to say that despite working parties and dialogue no significant changes were made. This was largely a result of the lack of political will within the UK Parliament to legislate, given the strong opposing forces, especially the landowning fraternity in the House of Lords. Even the advent of the Scottish Parliament with its devolved responsibilities for nature conservation did not fundamentally change the situation over this period.

In government, if there seems to be no meeting of minds between the factions and there is a lack of political will to move matters forward, it is a tradition to establish a working party. That is what happened next: the Secretary of State for the Environment for the UK, supported by the Secretary of State for Scotland, established the Moorland Working Group. Through this means the opposing sides were in at least some sort of dialogue.

Earlier, the plight of raptors had led to the establishment of volunteer-led raptor study groups around Scotland joining together as a lobby force. One route taken was to try to establish through scientific research what was actually happening on grouse moors. The original Langholm Report[52] did not really settle the matter despite the efforts of the researchers and the high-level steering group. One finding did emerge, however: that hen harrier takes of red grouse when the latter's numbers were low did reduce sporting bags. But it raised the question of whether the low numbers of red grouse were really due to predation by hen

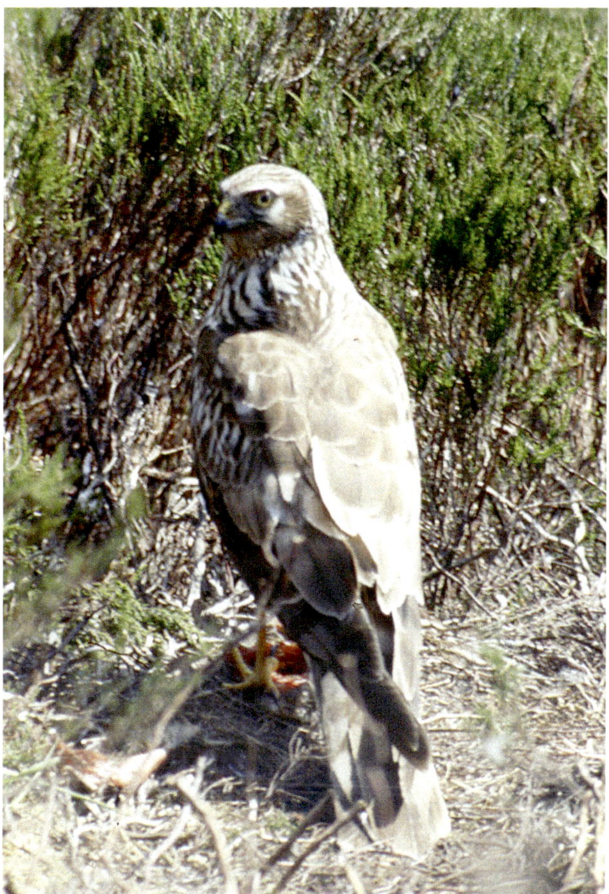

8.10 Hen Harrier with grouse chick on nest, Langholm Moor

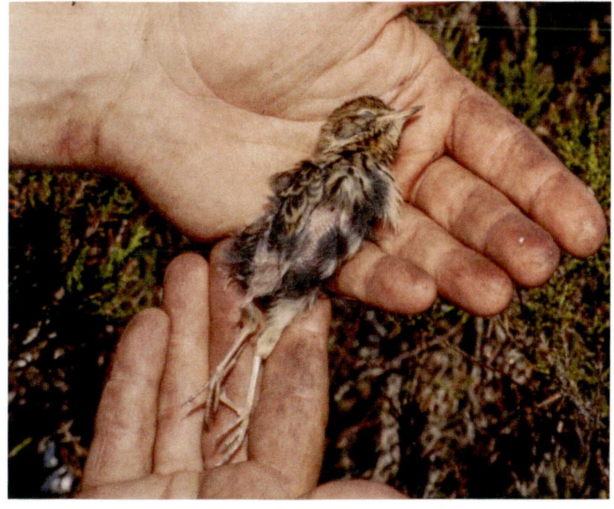

8.11 Meadow pipit, the usual Hen Harrier food

harriers or to other factors such as poor moorland management – including overgrazing and poor muirburn practice from which heather did not recover – as well as the effects of disease and weather on mortality. In addition, the known fact that the main feed sources of hen harriers were meadow pipits and voles, as Donald's earlier work had demonstrated, needed to be considered. Perhaps, as Donald Watson himself had wondered, there was dubiety in the allegiance of some of the scientists. Donald was clearly concerned about the direction of some of the scientific work undertaken by those with close links to the Game Conservancy. This concern is obvious from a reply by Steve Redpath in 1987 seeking to reassure Donald that his research was both objective and independently funded.[53]

It remains debatable whether the Langholm Moor was the most appropriate site. Grouse bags had declined continuously from the 1920s, as shown on a graph in the Buccleuch Estate office in Langholm. This was made obvious to me on a visit to the moor in the company of Ian Newton, the world's leading raptor scientist, who showed me the remnants of heather moorland where grouse butts strode across a now grassy landscape.

Undeterred, Scottish Nature Heritage and the Joint Nature Conservation Committee, supported by Buccleuch Estates, determined to experiment with what they called diversionary feeding. This entailed feeding hen harrier chicks with white mice bred in research laboratories, in the hope that this would deter the male from taking red grouse chicks to feed his young. The experiment worked to the extent that predation of grouse chicks declined. But questions remained about both the efficacy and the practicality of carrying out the practice in the proximity of all grouse moors where hen harriers were successfully breeding.

Another approach was to take a more species-protection route. Since 1954, with the passing of the Protection of Birds Act,[54] killing specified wild birds such as hen harriers has been illegal. This

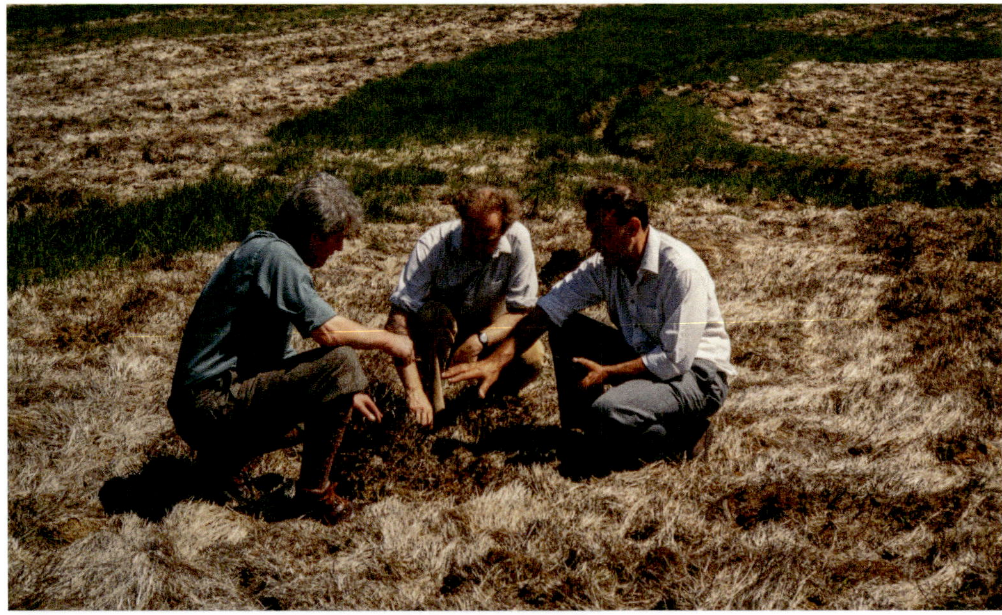

8.12 Landowners and scientists debating grouse moor management

includes those raptor species likely to prey on birds such as grouse – that is, all species of eagle and of harriers, goshawk, hobby and merlin. The EU Directive on Wild Birds of 1979 placed a much more stringent protection on those birds listed in its annexes, including the hen harrier. However, the persecution continued, and the Directive proved to be a paper tiger, as the law enforcement authorities did not have the manpower to implement it. More significantly, it was extremely difficult to provide evidence of the persecution culprits' identity that would stand up in court.

Suffice to conclude that despite all of these efforts and legal requirements the problem was not resolved.

Has the situation changed?

Not really, as recent reports attest.[55] Hen harriers are ten times more likely to die or disappear in areas dominated by grouse moors than elsewhere. From the population increases since the 1940s through to the 1970s, the bird has seen a steady decline to the extent that in the 1990s it was placed on the UK Red List for endangered species. In the last decade the situation has worsened, with UK trends showing a decline.[56] Records indicate 23 suspicious disappearances of hen harriers in Scotland that were satellite-tagged between 2004 and 2021.[57]

Writing in 2010 a group of experts on the raptor protection concluded that

> progress requires continued dialogue between the main stakeholders and a risk analysis based on improved understanding of the costs, acceptability, legality, feasibility and the environmental, economic and social consequences of following alternative approaches.[58]

The authors explain that there are two distinct types of approaches – enforcement and consensus. Expert though these authors were, I cannot help thinking – and I am sure that Donald Watson would agree – that this statement, while reflecting the consensus at the time, made the solution much more complex and more difficult to arrive at. It seems to me to have copped out on coming up with a solution. But in reality it reflected the lack of political will at the time to take decisive action. That was to come later.

It is often difficult to disentangle the reasons for changes in policy and proposals for new regulation. Do they result from objective observation and analysis by dispassionate scientists? Or do they result from a long-standing perception of one side against the values and practices of the other? In the case of raptor persecution, I judge it is a combination. One side demands total protection and a strong enforcement regime, including legal action. The other side demands the ability, if not the right, to control birds regarded as vermin – birds that reduce the production of red grouse chicks on grouse moors. Derek Ratcliffe, writing in a draft letter dated 1995, stated accurately that 'the issue is most fundamentally not about facts and science, but about value judgements and political influence'.[59] Ultimately, the scientific evidence is that raptor numbers are suppressed in those areas in and around grouse moors, as the material quoted below attests.

To move matters forward, the Scottish Government commissioned an independent Review of Grouse Moor Management,[60] chaired by the eminent geographical scientist, Emeritus Professor Alan Werritty. Its task was to examine the environmental impact of grouse moor management practices such as muirburn, the use of medicated grit, and mountain hare culls, and advise on the option of licensing grouse-shooting businesses. The key conclusion was that if there was no

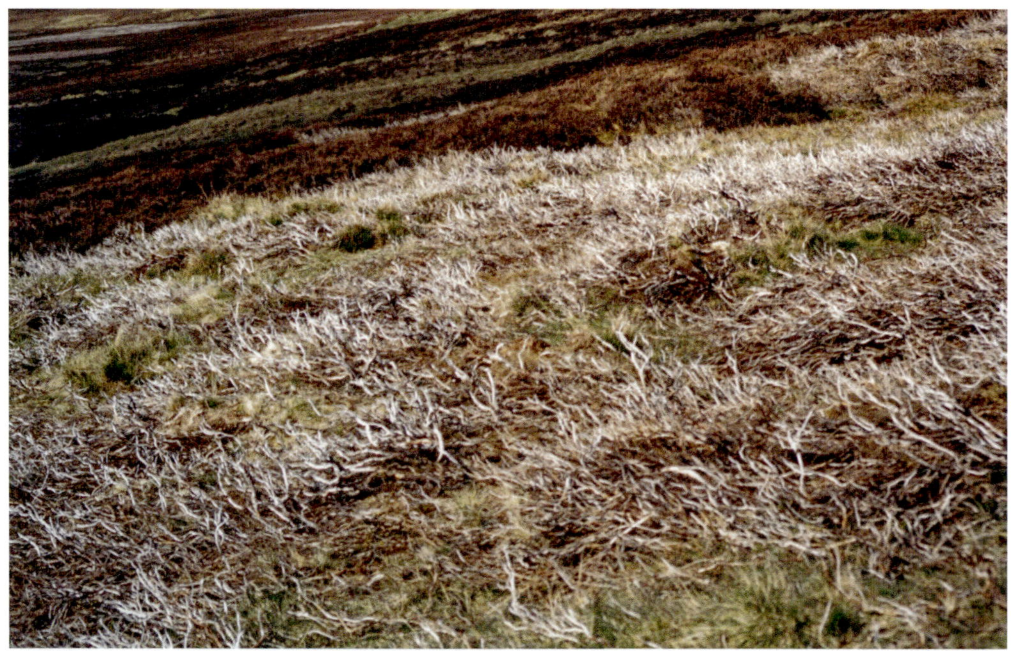

8.13 No heather regeneration following overhot muirburn

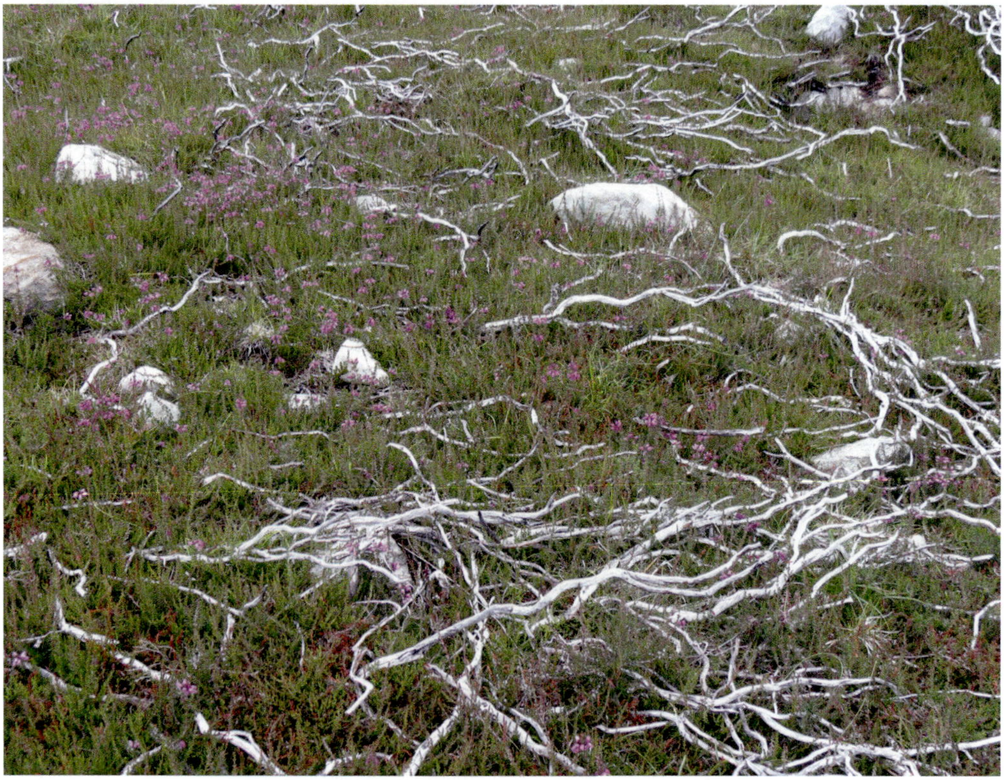

8.14 Heather regeneration following effective muirburn

marked improvement in the ecological sustainability of grouse moor management a licensing scheme should be introduced for the shooting of grouse. The chairman considered that this action should be implemented as soon as possible, whereas the majority of the committee felt that a five-year trial period of the *threat* of licensing was preferable. From those recommendations, and particularly the clear advice of its chairman, the Scottish Government consulted formally in late 2022 on its policy intention to introduce a statutory licensing system for grouse moors.

The sides remained ranged against each other. The situation is not dissimilar to that when Donald Watson was lobbying. It is obvious that vested interests in the grouse-shooting fraternity both deny that they are creating a problem and will lobby hard to stop any licensing system. Countering their viewpoint is the view which Donald Watson would have registered with. It comes from scientific experts who are Fellows of the Royal Society of Edinburgh writing in its response to the Scottish Government consultation on grouse moor management. The statement, which I quote in full below, was drawn up by the world's leading raptor scientist, Professor Ian Newton FRS, in consultation with other raptor scientists, including Professor Jeremy Wilson, the head of research at the RSPB, and Alan Werritty.

> This Bill came about largely because of the continued killing of legally-protected raptors, which are much valued by the public at large. Over the past century, all these species (and others) have increased from the low levels they reached through persecution in the late 19th and early 20th centuries. However, the increase has occurred mainly on land not managed for Red Grouse. Recent research has shown that continuing persecution on managed grouse moors is still limiting the numbers and distributions of several species in Scotland (and other parts of Britain), notably Golden Eagle, Hen Harrier, and Peregrine Falcon, and, more locally Goshawk and Red Kite. In the case of all of the aforementioned species, illegal killing has been sufficient to affect numbers over wider areas.
>
> The evidence of this decline is unequivocal and comprises the following:
> - greater disappearance of nesting pairs, lower breeding densities or reduced occupancy of apparently suitable traditional territories on grouse moors compared with other areas;
> - reduced nest success compared with other areas;
> - reduced adult survival compared with other areas;
> - reduced age of first breeding, reflecting the removal of adults from nesting territories and their replacement by birds in immature plumage;
> - greater levels of disappearance of satellite-tracked birds on grouse moors than elsewhere; and
> - the finding of poisoned baits and traps, and shot or poisoned carcasses of raptors.
>
> Since the publication of the Werritty review, the persecution of birds of prey has continued in Scotland, at least to judge from the numbers of carcasses found and reported to the RSPB during 2020–21 (the Covid years), with 26 confirmed bird of prey persecution incidents in Scotland in 2020 (part of the worst year for such incidents ever recorded by RSPB, UK-wide) and 17 in 2021.

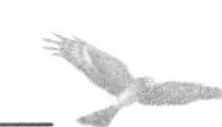

> On the basis of past research, we accept that some level of predator control is a legitimate part of management for shooting of grouse, and there is evidence that other ground-nesting birds, including wader species of conservation concern, are currently maintaining their numbers in Britain chiefly in areas where predators are controlled. In other words, there are wider benefits of some predator control. However, the key predators involved are foxes, crows, and mustelids, all of which can be legally controlled. For this reason, we would not recommend the complete banning of all predator control, as some have suggested, but rather are in favour of greater enforcement of the protective legislation that exists for birds of prey. The licensing of grouse moors is likely to provide a breakthrough in achieving this outcome.[61]

The Scottish Government has decided to move matters forward as the cabinet secretary, Mairi Gougeon, announced to the Scottish Parliament in November 2020, stating:

> After taking into account all of this evidence I have reached the conclusion that there is a need for greater oversight of the practices associated with grouse moor management, including muirburn and the culling of mountain hares. The key recommendation put forward in the Werritty report – is that a 'licensing scheme be introduced for the shooting of grouse'. This is a recommendation that I accept.
>
> ....
>
> Despite our many attempts to address this issue, every year birds of prey continue to be killed or disappear in suspicious circumstances on or around grouse moors. Since 2007, the Scottish Government has undertaken a range of measures to tackle wildlife crime, including: the introduction of vicarious liability; a poisons disposal scheme and restrictions on licences for those operating on land where it is suspected that wildlife crime has taken place.
>
> The fact that raptor persecution continues in spite of all these measures suggests that, while regulation from within the grouse shooting industry can be an important factor in driving behavioural change, self-regulation alone will not be enough to end the illegal killing of raptors, and further intervention is now required.[62]

I have no doubt that Donald Watson would have supported these statements from his own detailed and objective observations and reading of the scientific literature. The Scottish Government accepted the need for legal change and put forward legislative proposals in 2023. These were approved by the Scottish Parliament as the Wildlife Management and Muirburn (Scotland) Act 2024 which, *inter alia*, established a licensing system for killing and taking wild birds[63]. If properly enforced the Act should reduce the persecution of raptors, including the hen harrier, in and around grouse moors. As a result, hen harriers should achieve the biologically determined populations, rather than those illegally set by humans.

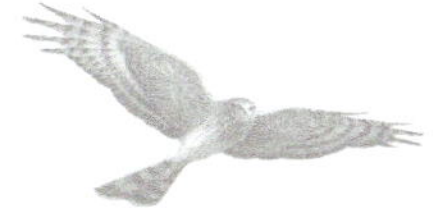

Nine

Watson Birds – a legacy project

ROGER CROFTS

> Your Watson Birds vision, ingenuity and determination makes these things happen. It is amazing. It is inspiring that, once again, something in Dumfries and Galloway is happening which might not have seemed probable.
>
> The Duke of Buccleuch,
> Watson Birds Patron

Watson Birds is a celebration of Donald Watson's outstanding contributions across so many fields of endeavour related to birds. The intention is that his legacy should act as a stimulus to younger generations. The project specifically aims to encourage activity linking birds, nature and the arts across all abilities and all generations. This chapter defines the project, describes the various elements and identifies the challenges for the future.

In summary, Watson Birds holds periodic festivals in Galloway, organises scientific talks and artistic concerts, and works with poetry and birdsong projects. Internationally outstanding research on raptors is recognised through the Watson Raptor Science Prize. Walking and riding trails linking birds and the changing landscape based in Galloway seek to stimulate participants' reaction in music and song, in poetry and prose, in painting and drawing, and in photography and filming, so that these perceptions can be shared and stimulate others. Our website, www.watsonbirds.org, provides more details of our activities. Watson Birds is a component of The Glenkens Community & Arts Trust.[1]

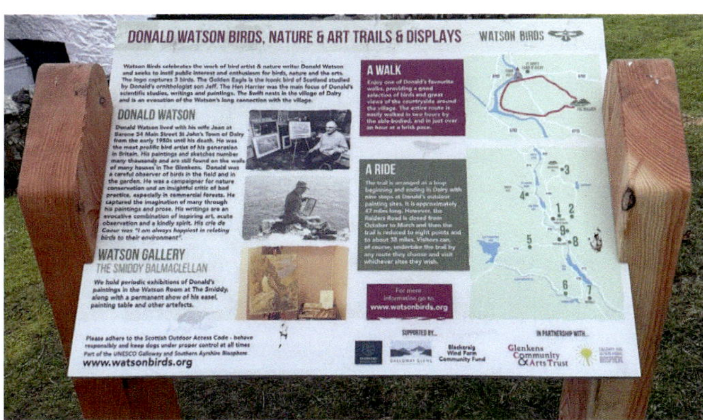

9.1 Interpretation board in the grounds of the Town Hall, Dalry

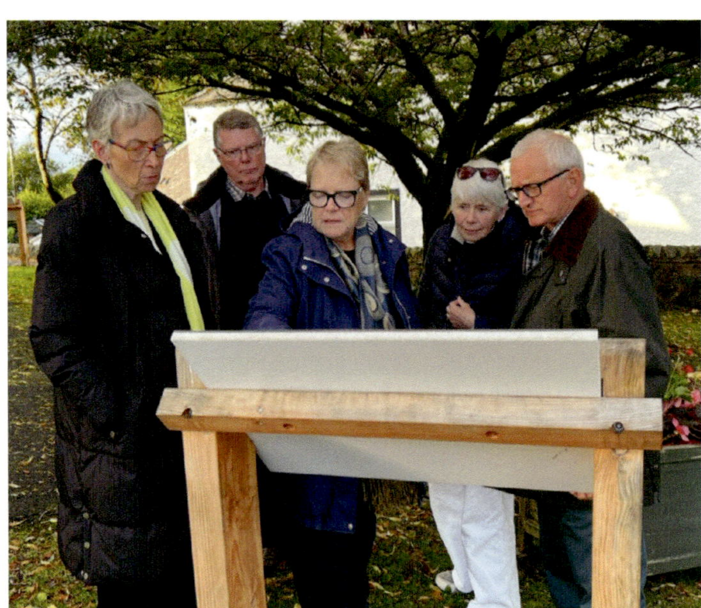

9.2 Visitors planning their Watson Bird activities

Why Watson Birds?

As the originator of Watson Birds and its current director I should explain at the outset why this project was established.

I met Donald and his wife Joan only once. It was at the launch of their son Jeff's outstanding monograph *The Golden Eagle* at the Battleby Conference Centre of Scottish Natural Heritage near Perth. Donald had provided some of his Highland landscape paintings, complete with a golden eagle, in the first edition. That day was a fitting climax of the professional relationship between father and son, each inspiring the other and each being proud of the other, as Vanessa Watson has described in Chapter 4.

In 2007, my late wife Lindsay and I bought a house in St John's Town of Dalry, just down Main Street from the Watson family home. It was just before Jeff died, all too young, and after Donald and Joan had died. I was fortunate to have worked for a decade with Jeff at Scottish Natural Heritage, where he was a thoughtful, creative and forward-looking director with a high reputation as an ornithological scientist alongside these attributes. I treasure a handwritten card from him of his father's painting of Tynron village welcoming us to the village. Sadly, Jeff died before we were able to venture into the countryside of The Glenkens together, although we did spend precious time together on the Black Isle and in Easter Ross. Arriving in the village, we began to understand the continuing status and standing of his parents there, and the reach that his father still had in the wider bird and wildlife art community. It seemed fitting, therefore, that Donald's life and legacy should be celebrated. Hence, with the support of Donald's daughters and Chris Rollie, a neighbour who knew Donald and the family well (see Chapter 5), my wife and I established Watson Birds as a component project within The Glenkens Community & Arts Trust (GCAT), with the strong help and support of Cathy Agnew (the enterprising founder Chair of GCAT) and Gill Khosla (the astute businessperson and trustee overseeing GCAT finances).

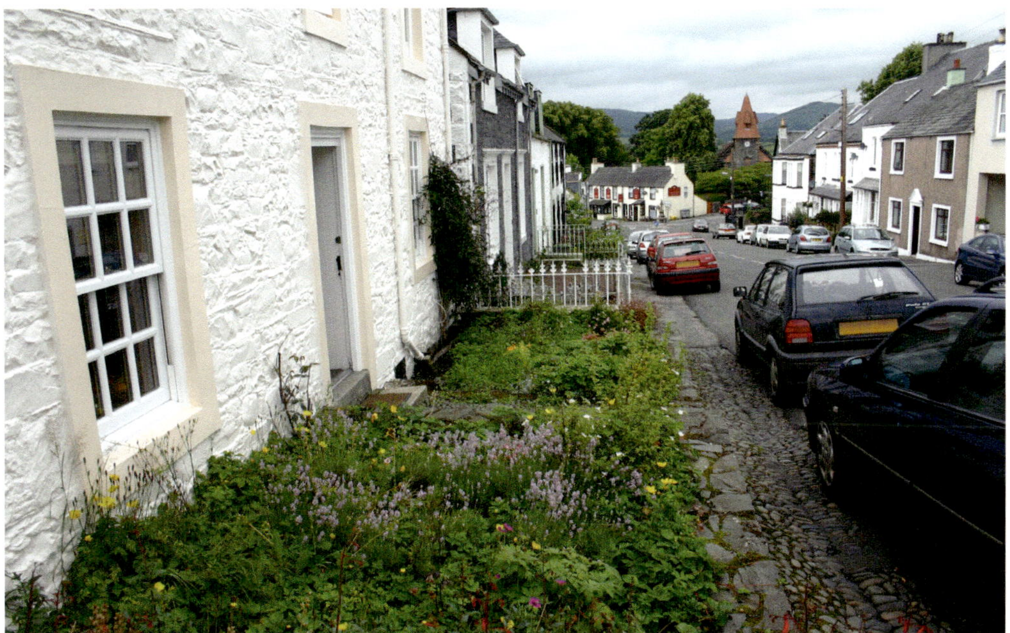

9.3 Looking down Main Street, Dalry

I am a strong believer that celebrating people's lives and their contribution is not a passive and backward approach, but rather one that can inspire and stimulate younger generations. When I talked to third- and fourth-year students at Dalry School, asking them what their ambitions were, and whether they thought they could emulate Donald and Jeff, I certainly found that to be the case. Their responses were very positive.

In the village at the time, however, the atmosphere was not all that positive – as, sadly, in so many rural communities. The local pub/hotel in the heart of the village was closed. There were concerns about Dumfries and Galloway Council's commitment to retaining the four-year secondary school. Would one or both of the shops, together with the post office and the garage, all survive? Inevitably, the ageing community members, comprising many who had lived there all of their lives, were worried for their and their families' futures.

Since then, matters have turned round. There is now a vibrant and younger community and younger retirees alongside older residents who are still active. More jobs have been created through renewable energy. There are new owners of the shop. The garage has been converted into shop and vehicle refuelling point for the passing trade along the main road. The pub/hotel has progressive new owners gaining awards for their cuisine and ales. A charity shop serves the village, and its takings are fed into community projects including this book. The purchase of the Watsons' home by an active family provides an opportunity to make a link to Donald.

External factors have certainly helped. The building of new houses in the village for rental and purchase has resulted in a positive shift in the demographic profile and new youngsters for the nursery and the primary school. The acquisition and refurbishment of existing houses by the Pamela Young Trust (established, before Pamela died, by a close friend of Donald and Joan), a locally run social housing scheme, has provided much-needed accommodation. The establishment of The Glenkens Community & Arts Trust as a facility throughout the area has allowed new projects, like Watson Birds, to find a home, along with intellectual and administrative support. The establishment of the Galloway and Southern Ayrshire UNESCO Biosphere has put the area on the international map. The five-year programme of the Heritage Lottery Fund – the Galloway Glens Landscape Partnership – has brought money to the area and stimulated projects in it. And community benefit funds have been made available from wind turbine owners with decisions delegated locally to The Glenkens & District Trust, which has also facilitated the implementation of a local strategy and action programme.

What has this got to do with Donald Watson and Watson Birds? I tell this story because those who run a project in a village must not only understand and work with the people and the place, but also proffer them some benefits through activities and engagement, and through funds and volunteering.

There is another personal perspective which I should mention. I have the good fortune to own a selection of Donald's paintings bought from the family, and a copy of all of his books and many of those he illustrated. Of all of these items, the one I treasure most is a plate from *The Oxford Book of Birds*.

What is Watson Birds?

Our aim throughout has been to celebrate Donald Watson's achievements and to inspire people in the study of birds and their habitat, and in linking birds, nature and the arts in any way they feel appropriate.

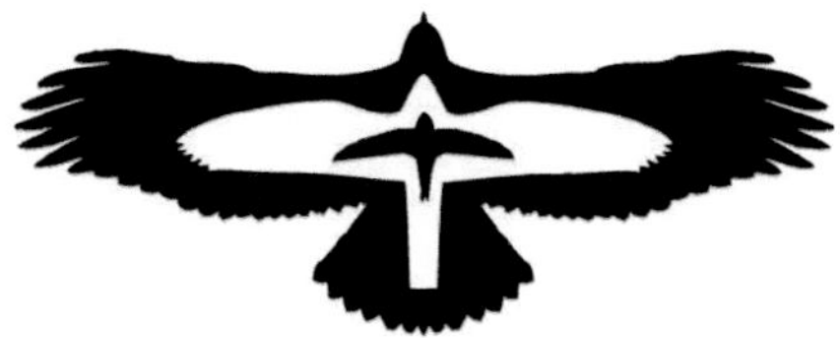

9.4 Watson Birds logo

At the outset the project had two components, one a capital project and one a series of activities and events. The Watson Bird Centre was to be based in the Watsons' family home. Watson Birds Celebrations would comprise a range of events and activities for a variety of interests and reflecting Donald's own diverse interests.

Our logo comprises three birds imposed on each other. The golden eagle is the iconic bird of Scotland, studied by Donald's ornithologist son Jeff, who published the classic monograph on the subject. The hen harrier was the focus of Donald's scientific studies and paintings, and is depicted in his last book, *In Search of Harriers*, and his monograph, *The Hen Harrier*. The swift builds its nests in the tower of Dalry Town Hall and is an evocation of the Watson family's long connection with the village.

Nesting boxes have been installed in that tower to accommodate the swifts, and nesting boxes for other birds have been installed around Dalry as part of our ambition to make Dalry The Bird Town.

Recognising scientific excellence

Scientific excellence was a hallmark of Donald's work, as reflected in his work on the hen harrier, and also by Jeff's work on the Seychelles kestrel and the golden eagle. The Watson Raptor Science Prize was therefore initiated. Its aim was to recognise outstanding raptor science published in peer-reviewed, internationally reputable journals. A panel to select the winners and runners-up was established, led by Des Thompson, the eminent upland scientist (and incidentally a son of

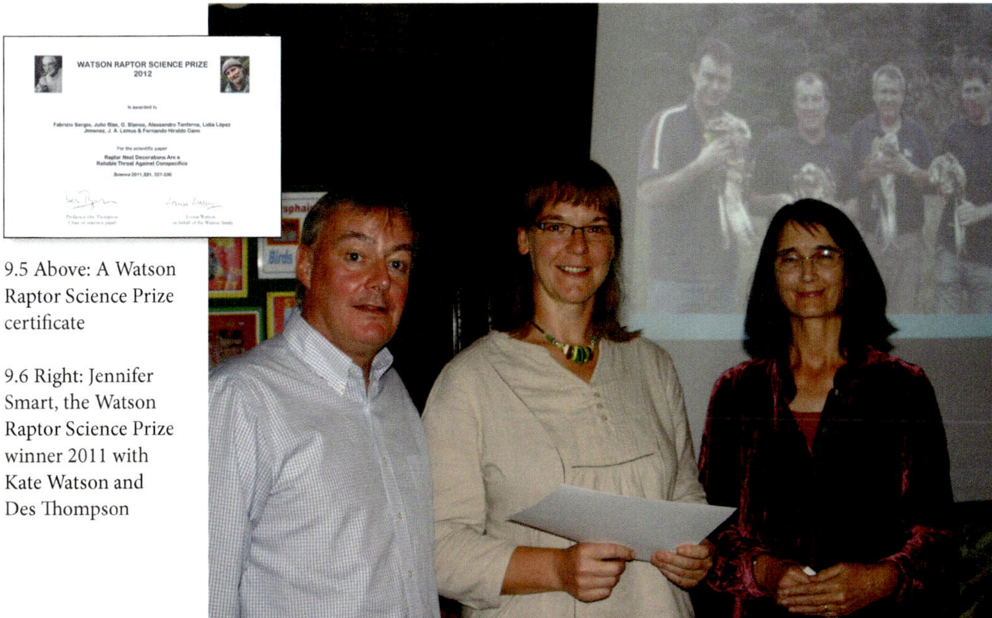

WATSON RAPTOR SCIENCE PRIZE
2012

is awarded to

Fabrizio Sergio, Julio Blas, G. Blanco, Alessandro Tanferna, Lidia López Jimenez, J. A. Lemus & Fernando Hiraldo Cano

For the scientific paper

Raptor Nest Decorations Are a Reliable Threat Against Conspecifics

Science 2011,331, 327-330

9.5 Above: A Watson Raptor Science Prize certificate

9.6 Right: Jennifer Smart, the Watson Raptor Science Prize winner 2011 with Kate Watson and Des Thompson

the Nethersole-Thompsons whose books Donald illustrated); Ian Newton, the most distinguished raptor scientist of his generation; and Steve Redpath, a raptor scientist at Aberdeen University. The prize was given annually for seven years from 2011 to 2017, after which it was decided that the amount of work annually was too onerous for any panel. It will be resurrected at a future date when new panel members volunteer and a less onerous formulation is put in place.

The winner and runners-up were asked to give a public talk about their research at an event, either at the Watson Bird Festivals based in St John's Town of Dalry or at another suitable scientific event.

The winners and runners-up were as follows:

- The 2011 prize was awarded to Jennifer Smart and colleagues at RSPB for their paper on illegal killing of the recently reintroduced red kites in Scotland.[2] Although the reintroduction of red kites to the UK has been a phenomenal success story, not all populations have increased at the same rate; due to illegal killing the north Scotland population reached only 35 pairs.
- The 2012 prize was awarded to Fabrizio Sergio and colleagues for their paper demonstrating that protection of black kite nests and chicks can be achieved by the use of foreign objects to decorate the nests.[3] The runner-up in 2012 was for a paper led by Arjun Anwar, demonstrating that higher sheep numbers create greater pressure through foraging on grassland, which is the hunting habitat of hen harriers, and that the reverse is also true; sheep reductions benefit the raptor population.[4]
- The 2013 prize was awarded to Miguel Ferrer and colleagues for their paper assessing the relationship between birds and wind farms, concluding that through careful observation the placing of individual turbines can reduce bird mortality.[5] The 2013 runner-up was Richard J. Evans' and colleagues' review of placenames and other documentary evidence

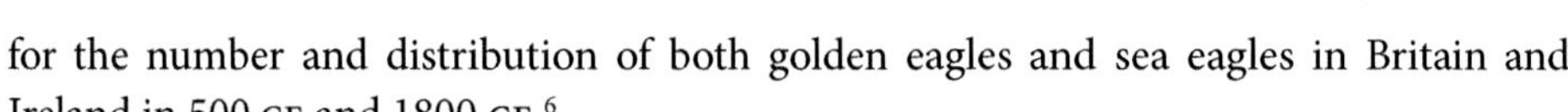

for the number and distribution of both golden eagles and sea eagles in Britain and Ireland in 500 CE and 1800 CE.[6]

- The 2014 prize was awarded to Raymond Klaassen and colleagues for their paper on tracking raptors on their migration routes, demonstrating that mortality was higher during migration than during stationary periods. They concluded that higher mortality occurred in Africa in spring and in Europe in the autumn, and that it has a marked effect on raptor population dynamics.[7] The runner-up for 2014 was Christiane Trierweiler et al, who had investigated the reasons why raptors overwintering in the Sahel moved between different home ranges, and demonstrated that the availability of their key food, grasshoppers, was the main determinant.[8]
- The 2015 prize was awarded to a team led by a previous winner, Fabrizio Sergio, for their paper showing that migration skills develop gradually over time and that greater age determines the most successful migration tactics.[9] The runner-up was a paper again led by a previous winner, Miguel Ferrer,[10] concluding that translocation programmes with supplementary feeding for wild birds were much cheaper and more publicly acceptable than captive breeding programmes for the same species.
- The winning paper for the 2016 prize went to Sarah Hoy and colleagues,[11] who showed that predation of other predators is age- and sex-selective, and is likely to target those of lower reproductive value. The runner-up was Julian Terraubea and colleagues,[12] who concluded that the best hunters had the most specialised diet. They noted the importance of habitat composition being a major determinant of prey abundance.
- The winner in the final year, 2017, was Anna-Katharina Mueller and colleagues,[13] analysing the interactions between eagle owls, northern goshawks and common buzzards in three regions in Westphalia, Germany. The runner-up was Roberto Muriel and colleagues,[14] examining the implications of the observed dispersal behaviour in eagles for major conservation translocation trials.

In addition to the papers read by winners and runners-up at the Watson Bird Festivals held each year from 2011 to 2014, Watson Birds has held a number of seminars and workshops reporting on raptor science and the bird interest in The Glenkens. These include 'Bird Science Supports Conservation', held in Edinburgh and Dalry, involving leading raptor scientists led by Ian Newton. Earlier a conference on the hen harrier was held in Dalry to celebrate 35 years since the publication of Donald Watson's hen harrier monograph.[15]

Exhibiting the best of local bird and nature art

Donald's painting style evolved over time, as John Threlfall records in Chapter 2, and stimulated him into a bird art career. Inviting professional artists to display their work at festivals was therefore a natural development of Watson Birds. There has been a long-standing community of wildlife artists in the area, including John Threlfall, Lisa Hooper, Frances Godfrey and Paul Collin. In addition, we thought it important to invite other wildlife artists from further afield. Darren Woodhead, who displayed his skills as a speaker while producing a painting, was one of many. Also, we wished to stimulate the younger generation through school projects with the help of their teachers. Susan Bielinski, a peripatetic art teacher and keen conservationist, and Sarah Keast, an Earth scientist turned artist based in Moniaive, led the production of many materials,

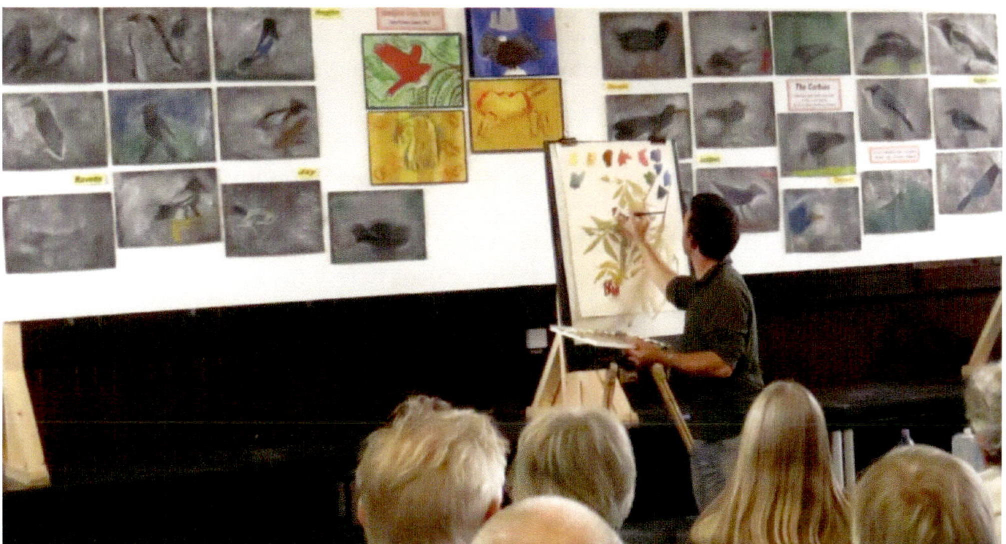

9.7 Watson Bird exhibitions in Dalry Town Hall

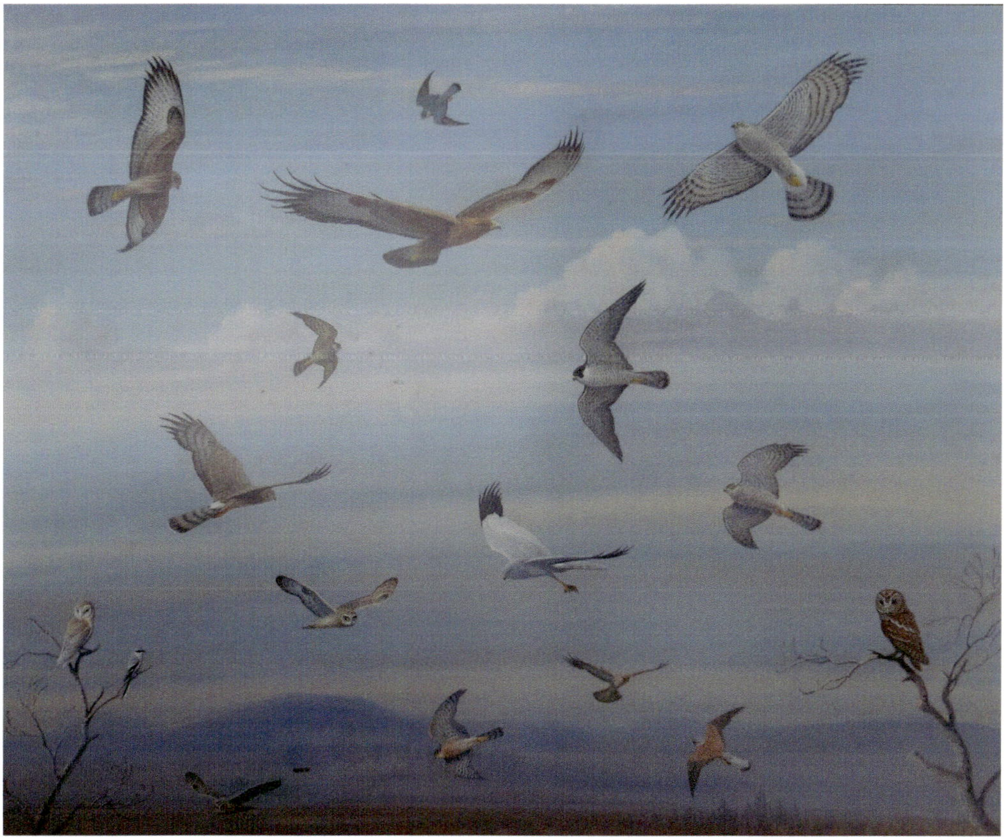

9.8 Donald Watson painting of raptor montage, hanging in Dalry Town Hall

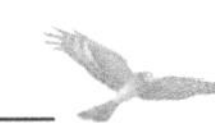

with events held in the town hall of St John's Town of Dalry to display the pupils' efforts to their families, to neighbours and to visitors. Paintings, drawing, sketches, songs and poems were all produced. Some of the results can be found on the website: https://watsonbirds.org/.

We hold periodic exhibitions at CatStrand in New Galloway and in The Smiddy in Balmaclellan. In the last two years we have focused on three themes: Bird Studies, to display Donald Watson's technique and his detailed approach to bird depiction; Watson Trails, displaying reproduction of the main sites illustrated in the brochures mentioned earlier; and Birds and Forestry, displaying Donald Watson's depiction of the march of commercial planting over the Galloway landscape, alongside photographs that I took, showing poor and better woodlands and forestry.

There remains much more we can do to stimulate this activity as well as provide space for local artists to display their work.

One classic canvas of Donald's adorns the walls of Dalry Town Hall. The compilation of raptors in exquisite detail recognises his artistic ability and his long residence in the village.

There follows a story about one of Donald's friends and a collector of his paintings. On his death his daughter, Harriet Denne, donated many items from her father's remaining collection to Watson Birds for our use, following an exhibition at the Wildlife Art Gallery in Lavenham. Her story follows.

> In 1980 my father, Jock Holden, moved to Dalry after my mother died. Although they had previously met, it was then that his friendship with Donald Watson grew as they both shared a love of all things ornithological. And my father's knowledge of birds and their habitats improved enormously under Donald's tutelage.
>
> If Jock was lucky enough, he might be taken by Donald up to the hills to "look for something interesting" ... Black Grouse, Peregrine, Hen Harriers or even an elusive Golden Eagle. Jock admired Donald's work greatly, and I know he was fascinated by the skill and patience he took in making all of his paintings. And he never ceased to be thrilled by the three-dimensional end result, particularly if it depicted the Galloway Hills. He felt that Donald always managed to set his subjects very happily in their chosen habitats and, at the same time, captured the essence and wonderful colours of the Scottish landscape.
>
> My father started building his collection of Donald's works, eventually accumulating around sixty paintings. All of these were hung in Jock's cottage, known locally as 'Donald's gallery', as every possible bit of wall space featured a painting! I remember well my father cheerily reporting 'I've managed to buy a great little sketch by Donald which was half hidden under a pile of scrap paper on the studio floor!'

Encouraging outdoor experiences

Two trails have been established. The Donald Watson Art Trail around The Glenkens is a nine-stop one (eight in the winter) by vehicle, which starts and ends in the centre of St John's

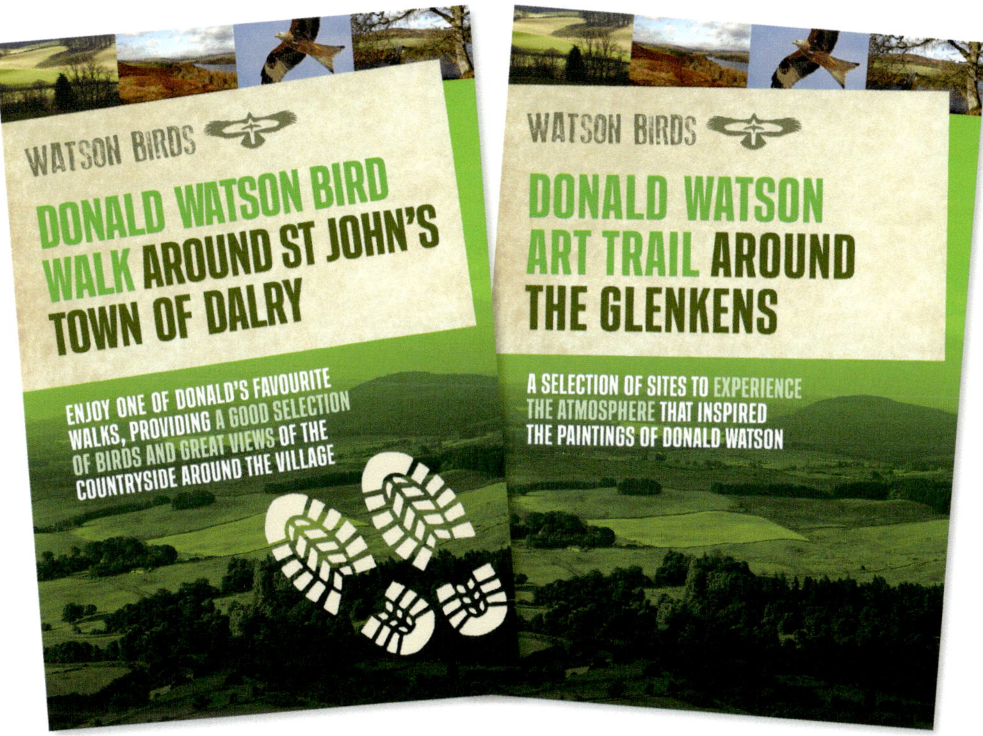

9.9 and 9.10 Trail brochures

Town of Dalry. Users can determine whether they do the whole route in sequence or at their own volition.[16]

The walking trail around Dalry also starts and ends in the centre of the village, at the town hall.[17]

Brochures are readily available for both of the trails from local outlets and from the website. A commentary on the two trails is available for download via a QR code; it is given by Chris Rollie, the very knowledgeable locally based ornithologist, interviewed by Roger Crofts.

The idea of the two trails is to persuade people to go out of doors to observe birds over the seasons and at different times of the day. We hope this will stimulate their reactions to how the use of the land has changed and what effect this has on the landscape.

We are hoping, too, that users of the trails will react to the prompts in the brochures and on the interpretation boards at each of the nine sites on the Donald Watson Art Trail around The Glenkens, to give us their reactions in whatever form suits them: photographs, paintings, sketches, poetry, prose, music etc.

The trails have been well received as one of our patrons, Dame Barbara Kelly, attests:

> Congratulations on this next step in the initiative to celebrate Donald Watson and his love of The Glenkens countryside. The brochures are beautifully assembled and full of fascinating information. There can be no doubt that they and the signing and interpretation of the two trails will encourage local people to appreciate even more

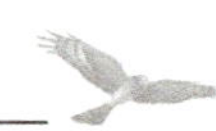

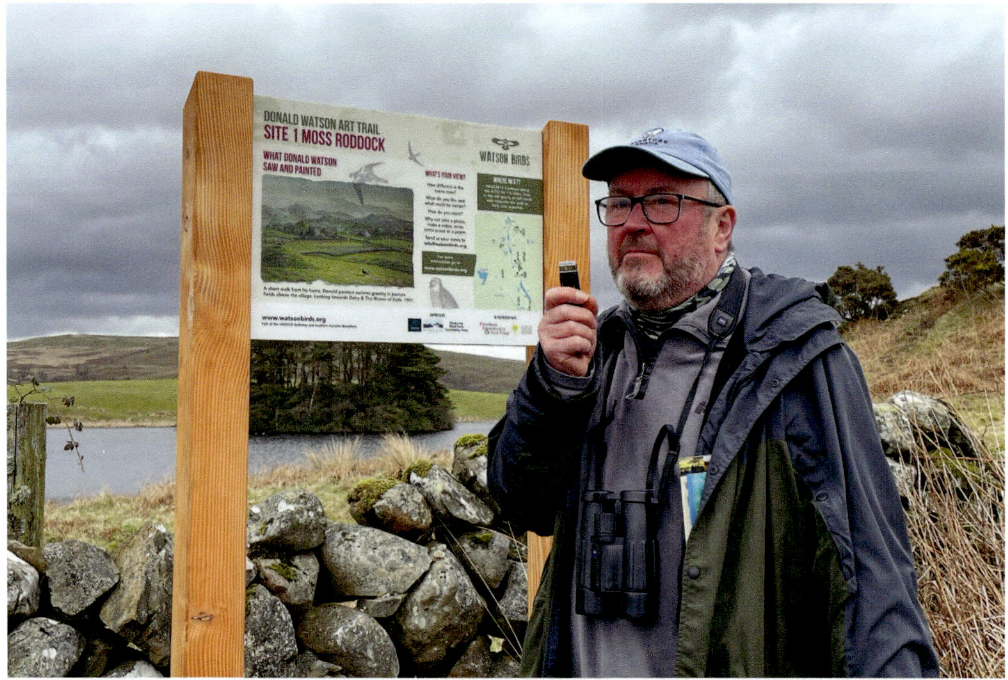

9.11 Chris Rollie recording commentary for the app

their surroundings and take pride in telling visitors about where to go and what to do. The timing of this project could not be better in the midst of the COVID pandemic where it is now widely recognised that there are huge benefits in health and wellbeing for everyone enjoying the outdoor space, contacting nature and the landscape. I look forward to seeing the interpretation boards in place and the signposts around the trails and to hearing Chris on his App. Well done on the development of an initiative bringing significant community benefits.

Using other arts to stimulate interest in nature

Watson Birds has collaborated with poetry and birdsong projects to stimulate interest in the link between nature and the arts.

Peter Cowdrey (co-founder of Planet Birdsong),[18] a worldwide initiative to enhance understanding and appreciation of birdsong, writes:

> After Donald Watson's death in 2005, I was lucky enough to visit his home in St John's Town of Dalry before it was cleared. In his studio there were thousands of pictures of birds, on the walls, in diaries, on easels, on large sheets of tracing paper, and in sketch pads covering his creative life from his early teens to his last few years. The impression was of a whole lifetime observing and sketching birds, wherever Watson was, whatever else he was doing. Not all met with his subsequent approval; some were crossed out and some labelled with the single word 'no'. However, even his most hasty and rudimentary work had an astonishing knack of catching the essential characteristics of a bird's

movement; a cursory glance almost always revealed the bird's identity. This was fortunate since many sketches were unidentified and often the only attempts at classification were tiny loose scraps of old newspaper with semi-legible abbreviations scrawled in pencil.

It struck me that sketches made in the moment, without artifice or intent are in some ways the purest expression of Watson's art. What wasn't apparent was how they could be shared more widely. An opportunity presented itself during lockdown when I was confined to the grounds of Fingask Castle in Perthshire. Life slowed down and my hosts the Murray Threipland's [*sic*] and I decided to produce a short book celebrating how, like many people during lockdown, we were able to dig deeper into the experience and history of landscape through its birds and birdsong. I thought reproductions of some of Watson's sketches would make ideal illustrations. Roger Crofts kindly gave me permission to trawl through cardboard boxes in a warehouse outside Dumfries, eventually whittling thousands of sketches down to a short list of a hundred or so, matching the species mentioned in the book. Photographing them for publication was a challenge, but my hope is that the rough and ready reproductions catch some of the spontaneous spirit of the originals.[19]

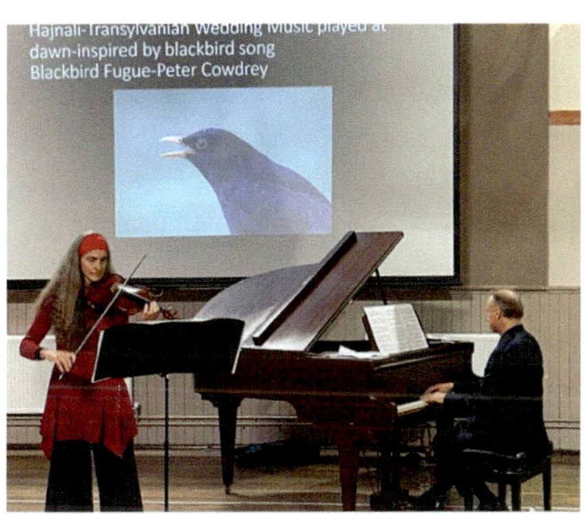

9.12 Conference of Birds Concert

Planet Birdsong's links to Watson Birds date back to September 2011, when our performing group *The Conference of Birds* played at the first Watson Birds Celebration in Dalry Town Hall, exploring bird sound through music surrounded by an exhibition of work by local artists. Sound recordist Geoff Sample was also involved. In September 2021 we performed at Dalry again, after leading a walk along the route of one of the new Watson Trails. On the same day, we ran Planet Birdsong's Birdsong Studio, in which people of all ages were filmed reproducing slowed-down sounds of local songbirds. These were sped up to the original speed, so that participants sounded remarkably like the original birds. I like to think Donald Watson would have approved.

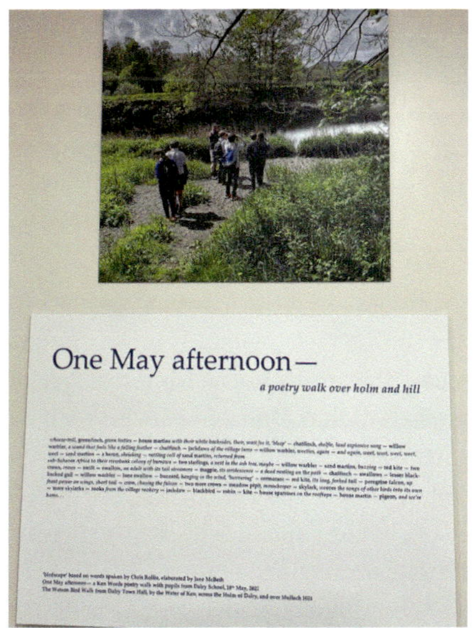

9.13 Ken Words Poetry Workshop output

Jane McBeth, the originator of the Ken Words Writing Project, says that 'Ken Words has at its heart imaginative engagement with sense of place, particularly within the landscape of the Galloway Glens'.[20] It seeks to encourage anyone interested in writing to develop their enjoyment, confidence and

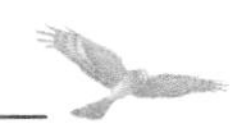

ability through friendly, supportive writing activities and events. Specific events linking birds and poetry have been a series of seasonal walks led by Jane and Chris Rollie. Alongside those who regularly write poems, the project has attracted others who have never written a stanza in their life.

A winter walk around the Watson Trail at Dalry led by Jane and Chris stimulated me to write the following:

Did I see nature today as I was trampling head down along the artificial levee?
Did I see nature today as the highly controlled river rushed by?
Did I see nature today as I saw the intensely grazed fields?
Did I see nature today as I looked at the Sitka spruce monocultures striding over the hills?
Did I see nature as I saw the wind turbines on the hill tops and heard them whirring?
Yes, I experienced nature today!
Yes, I saw it as birds flashed to and fro, perched in tree tops and soared high in the sky.
Yes, I heard it through their mews and chitterings.
Yes, I heard it through the local names of birds and their calls.
Yes, I sensed it in the hues and chromas of browned juncus stalks, purple birch, moss clad oaks and rotting leaves.
Yes, I felt it under my feet as I stood on the upturned ocean bed rocks.
And yes, I envisioned it as I recalled the advancing ice fashioning the drumlins into 'baskets of eggs'.
So yes, I saw and experienced nature today in so many ways.

Stimulating debate on conservation issues

It will be apparent from Chapter 8, on Donald Watson's views on conservation, that the stimulation of debate on issues relating to the land and landscape, and the plants and animals which depend on it, is an intrinsic element of Watson Birds. In addition to the scientific events detailed earlier, Watson Birds collaborated with local interests to hold a one-day workshop 'Imagining our future forests'. As readers will have discovered from Chapter 8, Donald was a passionate opponent of commercial monoculture forestry. The outcome of the workshop is available online.[21]

The Bird Centre proposition

Colleagues working with me in the early days of Watson Birds placed the Watson Bird Centre as their highest priority over the activities programme. Local interests managed to raise funds from private sources, and a local charity sufficient to purchase the family house from the Watson family. Architects provided their ideas for free. The plan was to retain Donald Watson's original studio, to have a library, archive and study area, to have a retail area and shop, and to open up the garden for educational activities and public use.

The Bird Centre ambition was, however, never realised. I should explain why. It is expensive to convert a house into a visitor and study centre, and a stream of finance is needed to meet its running costs. Despite many permutations, the help of consultants funded by EU cash and knowledgeable input from business colleagues, it was not possible to get the sums to work for the

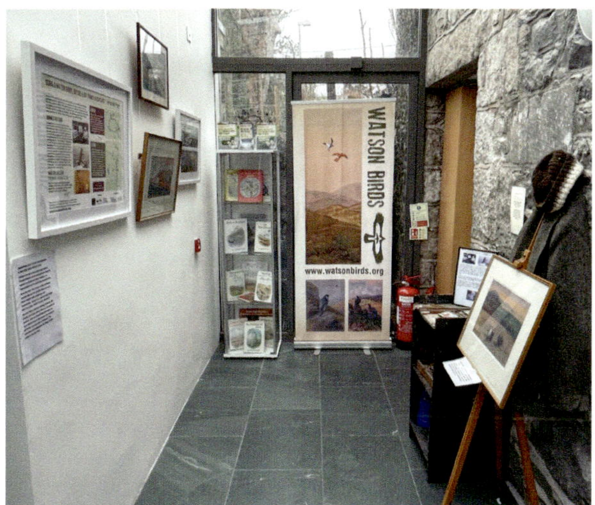

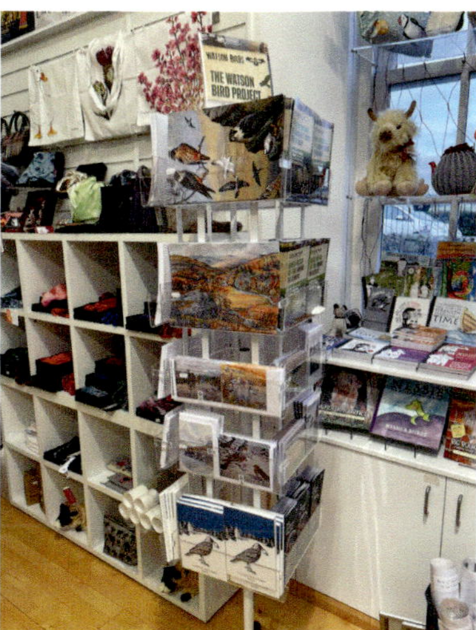

9.14 Left: Watson Birds CatStrand display. 9.15 Right: Watson Birds items for sale in CatStrand shop

conversion and even less for the operation of the proposed centre. It was therefore with reluctance that the house was sold. The new owners have ambitions to open a café and to make part of the garden into a public space. But a range of factors, not least the 2020–21 pandemic, has meant that at the time of writing these ambitions have not yet been realised.

A temporary facility was provided in the nearby village of Balmaclellan through the conversion of the old smithy into meeting rooms, one of which has until recently been designated as the Watson Room to reflect one of the funding sources for the conversion of the building. It will continue to act as a secure store for some of the Watson collection used locally. As the building is not generally open to the public, the permanent exhibition for Donald's work and Watson Bird activities is now housed at the CatStrand, the headquarters of The Glenkens Community & Arts Trust in another nearby village of New Galloway. Here are displayed a selection of the books authored by Donald and those he illustrated, his painting table and easel, and his Harris tweed jacket and his 'toorie' (woollen hat) for those cold days painting in the open air. There is also a revolving exhibition of his paintings covering different themes such as wildlife sketches, birds in the landscape, the phases of his art and the trails around the area. In the shop at the CatStrand are prints of Donald's paintings for sale, A3 and A4 size posters, A5 letter cards which reflect the range of his art, and a series of postcards of birds he created in his mid-teens.

The Donald Watson archive

Donald left a great deal of material. This has now been reviewed and the most important elements retained for use now and in the future.

The main archive is stored in the library at the Scottish Ornithologists' Club headquarters at Aberlady in East Lothian. This archive comprises notebooks and sketch books, diaries, notes for the preparation of his books, correspondence about the exhibitions of his paintings, his published papers, together with around ten of his paintings. Arrangements for *bone fide* researchers to review this material should be made with the librarian at the SOC.[22]

A collection of all of the books authored by Donald, and many of the books he illustrated, has

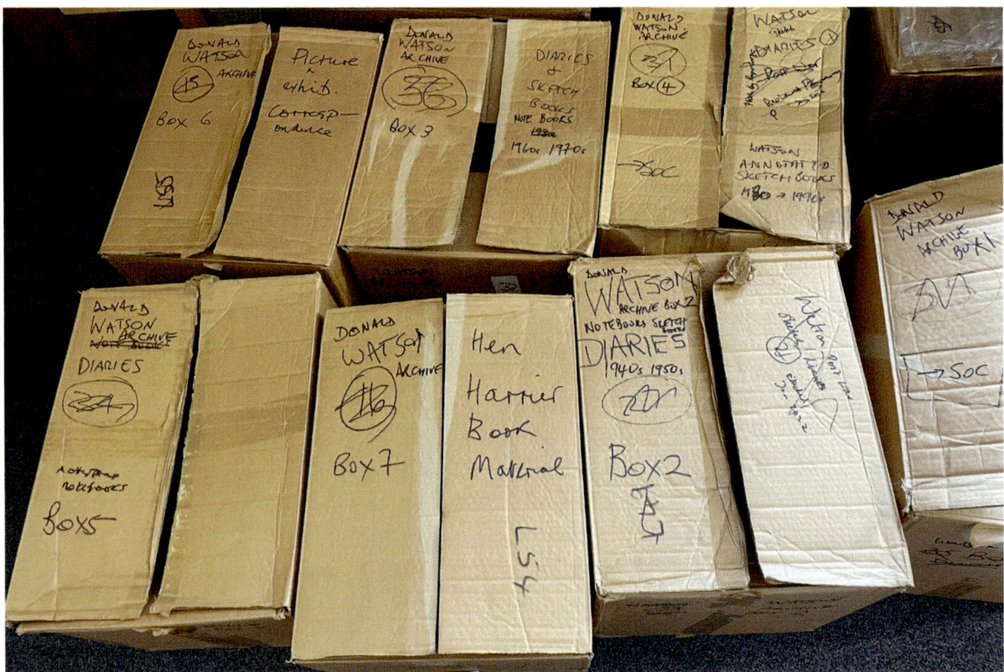

9.16 Watson Archive at SOC HQ

been retained and is on display at the CatStrand. In addition, the project has an extensive picture collection which is catalogued and stored securely for use in exhibitions.

Many hundreds of high-resolution images of Donald Watson's paintings are held by the project for use in publications, exhibitions and other ways.

A large collection of books which Donald had in his studio is available for sale to support the project. These are usually on display at events in The Glenkens.

The future

Watson Birds has aspirations for the future and hopes that there will be sufficient public interest and plenty of volunteers, as well as finances from donors and grants, to make these a reality.

- We hope to gather the reactions from the 2022 trails, then exhibit them at the CatStrand and in Dalry Town Hall to stimulate discussion.
- We plan to organise periodic talks on progress in raptor science with eminent researchers.
- We plan to mount exhibitions each year at the CatStrand and other appropriate venues, using originals or reproductions of Donald's work.
- If there is sufficient interest we shall arrange guided tours around the two trails with expert guides.
- We plan to make available the outcome of the collaborative project with Ken Words on poetry stimulated by Donald's paintings and observations.
- Finally, we hope to obtain approval from Dumfries and Galloway Council for Dalry to be named The Bird Town.

Annex 1: Donald Watson's books, authored and illustrated, plus articles and other published materials

This is a comprehensive list of the books authored and illustrated by Donald Watson. Also listed are his other contributions as a compiler, provider of scraperboard sketches, and author of articles published.

Authored books

Birds of Moor and Mountain. 1972. Scottish Academic Press, Edinburgh.

The Hen Harrier. 1977. T. & A.D. Poyser, Berkhamsted. Second edition 2017. Bloomsbury, London.

A Bird Artist in Scotland. 1988. H.F. and G. Witherby Ltd, London.

One Pair of Eyes. 1994. Arlequin Press, Chelmsford.

In Search of Harriers. 2010. Langford Press, Peterborough.

These are available to purchase online through the normal channels, such as Amazon Books and Abe Books, https://www.abebooks.co.uk

Illustrations in books by others

Donald Watson had illustrations in all of these books. In some he was the only illustrator, in others he was the major illustrator, and in others there were only one or a small number of his illustrations.

Isle of May. 1960. J. Eggling, Oliver & Boyd, Edinburgh.

A Popular Handbook of British Birds. 3rd edition 1962, 4th edition 1968. P.H.D. Hollom. Wetherby, London.

But Hibou Was Special. 1964. Andrew McNeillie. Country Life Limited, 1964.

The Oxford Book of Birds. 1964 and 1972. Oxford University Press, London.

Illustrated British Birds. 1964. Publisher not known.

The Shell Bird Book. 1966. J. Fisher. Ebury Press and Michael Joseph. London.

Ospreys in Speyside. 1969. G. Waterston. RSPB.

Handbook of the Birds of India and Pakistan. 1969–74. S. Ali and S.D. Ripley. Oxford University Press. Oxford.

Birdwatchers' Year. 1973. L. Batten et al. T. & A.D. Poyser. Staffordshire.

A Dictionary of British Bird Painters. 1974. F. Lewis (compiler). J. Lewis Publishers, Leigh-on-Sea.

The Roadside Wildlife Book. 1974. Richard Mabey. David & Charles, Devon.

The Unofficial Countryside. 1974. Richard Mabey. David & Charles, Devon.

Pine Crossbills. 1975. D. Nethersole-Thompson. T. & A.D. Poyser. Staffordshire.

Ladder Book of Birds. 1976. Oxford University Press. Oxford.

The Atlas of Breeding Birds in Britain and Ireland. 1976. J.T.R. Sharrock (ed). Poyser/British Trust for Ornithology.

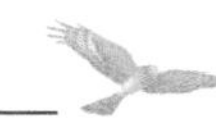

Birds of the Malta Archipelago. 1976. D.A. Bannerman and J.A. Vella-Gaffiero. Valletta Museums Department, Malta.

Birdwatcher at Large. 1979. Bruce Campbell. Dent. London.

The Country Life Book of Birds of Prey. 1979. Gareth Parry and Rory Putman. Littlehampton Book Services.

Greenshanks. 1979. D. and M. Nethersole-Thompson. T. & A.D. Poyser. Staffordshire.

The Peregrine Falcon. 1980. D.A. Radcliffe. T. & A.D. Poyser. Staffordshire.

The Common Ground: A place for nature in Britain's future? 1980. Richard Mabey. Arrow Books with the Nature Conservancy Council.

Bird Habitats in Britain. 1982. R.J. Fuller. T. & A.D. Poyser. Staffordshire.

Birds of the Balearics. 1983. D. and M. Bannerman. Croom Helm. Beckenham, Kent.

Enjoying Ornithology. 1983. Ronald Hickling (ed). T. & A.D. Poyser. Staffordshire.

Country Matters. 1984. I. Niall. Gollancz. London.

A Dictionary of Birds. 1985. Bruce Campbell and Elizabeth Lack (eds). T. & A.D. Poyser. Staffordshire.

Waders. 1986. D. and M. Nethersole-Thompson. T. & A.D. Poyser. Staffordshire.

Twentieth Century Wildlife Artists. 1986. N. Hammond. Croom Helm. Beckenham, Kent.

Drawing Birds. John Busby. 1986. RSPB. Sandy, Bedfordshire.

Birds in Scotland. 1986. Valerie M. Thom. T. & A.D. Poyser. Staffordshire.

The Atlas of Wintering Birds of Britain and Ireland. 1986. P. Lack (ed). Poyser/British Trust for Ornithology.

Farming and Birds. 1986. R.J. O'Connor and M. Shrubb. Cambridge University Press.

The Hawkwatcher. 1989. D. Orton. Unwin Hyman. London.

Bird Walks in Dumfries and Galloway. 1989. D. Watson and R. Hawley. RSPB.

Birds of Galloway. 1989. Scottish Ornithologists' Club.

Tomorrow Is Too Late. 1990. D. Attenborough. MacMillan/Allen Publishing.

Forest Merlins in Scotland: their requirements and management. 1992. J. Orchel. The Hawk and Owl Trust. Wheathampstead.

New Atlas of Breeding Birds of Britain and Ireland. 1994. Gibbons, Reid and Chapman. T. & D.A. Poyser. Staffordshire.

The Golden Eagle. Jeff Watson. 1997. A. Black, London.

Jackdaws and Other Friends. 2022. A.M. Threipland. Fingask Castle, Perth, UK.

In addition, there are many line drawings in *British Birds*, *Scottish Birds* and *The Countryman*. Digital images of these have been made.

See also https://www.the-soc-org.uk/about-us/art-gallery/art-of-donald-watson

Illustrations for the Nature Conservancy nature reserves brochures for Shetland. 1969.

Cover designs for Orkney Bird Report 1984–95; hen harrier pair, British Birds, SOC Scottish Bird Report.

The Countryman: many scraperboard sketches.

British Birds and *Scottish Birds*: many scraperboard sketches to illustrate articles written by others. This includes the cover for *British Birds* 70 (7) July 1977 Barn Owl.

Calendars with his paintings

Curwen Press calendars each year 1976–1981.

Society of Wildlife Artists (Lloyds Bank) 1992.

Other outlets

Chocolate box top for C.J. Cousland & Son, Edinburgh 1953.

Medici Society card. 1955.

Christmas cards George Waterston & Sons, Edinburgh. 1954.

Scottish Society for the Prevention of Vivisection: envelope illustration. 1972.

Compiler

SOC Dumfries and Galloway Region Bird Report, 1988, 1989, 1990

SOC Dumfries and Galloway Stewartry and Wigtown Districts Bird Report, 1985, 1986

Articles published

Watson, D. 1955. Lesser white-fronted geese in Kirkcudbright. *British Birds*, 48, 323–325.

Watson, D. 1956. Lesser white-fronted geese in Kirkcudbrightshire. *British Birds*, 49, 227.

Watson, D. Date unknown. Mostly about goosanders. *Ornithology*, pp.13–15.

Watson, A.D. and Dickson, R.C. 1972. Communal roosting of hen harriers in southwest Scotland. *Scottish Birds*, 7, 24–49.

Watson, D. 1980. David Armitage Bannerman – obituary. *British Birds*, 73, 26–29.

Watson, A.D. 1981. Bird watching in Galloway. *Scottish Birds*, 11, 188–193, 257–262.

Watson, D. 1986. Bean geese in south-west Scotland. *Scottish Birds*, 14, 17–24.

Watson, D. 1997. Memories of a Galloway Moor: the invited essay. *Birds*.

Boyd, H., Bell, M.V. and Watson, A.D. 2000. Spring weather and the migration of geese from Scotland to Iceland. *Ringing and Migration*, 20, 153–165.

Clarke, R. and Watson, D. 1996/97. The Hen Harrier Winter Roost Survey. *The Raptor*, 41–45.

Isle of May. *Country Life*. 16 June 1950.

Ospreys cover. *Country Life*. 25 August 1960.

Rearing an Injured Siskin. *Country Life*. 31 December 1964.

Birds of the Scottish Moors. *Country Life*. 21 April 1966.

Hen Harriers. *Country Life*. 15 February 1969.

Hen Harriers. *Country Life*. 1979.

Short-eared Owls. *Birds*. Autumn 1982.

Annex 2: Exhibitions and paintings in collections

A list of all of the exhibitions where there is evidence in the archive that Donald Watson exhibited his paintings.
* indicates a one man show

Arundel, Sussex

The Arun Art Centre 1968

Bermuda

1968

Billingshurst, Sussex

RSPB/Sotheby's 1990

Bristol

Frost & Reid Bristol 1952 and 1954 (selling to the USA)

Castle Douglas

McGill Duncan Gallery 2019

Dublin

Irish Society for Protection of Birds/RSPB 1969

Dumfries

Blacklock & Farries 1959*
Dumfries 1951
Farries 1988*
Gracefield Art Gallery 1993*
Dumfries and Galloway Fine Arts Society 1956
Royal Infirmary 1997*

Edinburgh

Doig, Wilson & Wheatley 1949*
New Gallery (for Scottish Ornithologists' Club) 1947
Gallery Paton 1976*
Royal Society of Arts, date unknown

England touring exhibitions

Contemporary Bird Painters 1960

Folkestone

Kent & Folkestone Arts Centre, date unknown

Glasgow

Ian McNicol Galleries 1950, 1958*

Glenkens, Galloway

Glenkens Summer Art Exhibition 1999

Haddington

Peter Potter Gallery 1980

Henley-on-Thames

Berkshire, Buckinghamshire and Oxford Naturalists Trust, Century Galleries 1970

Kirkcudbright

Harbour Cottage Gallery 1969
Tolbooth Art Centre 1997, 1999*

Lavenham Suffolk

Wildlife Art Gallery 1993*, 1995, 1996*, 1999*, 2010*, 2013*

Lloyds Bank 1991

London

Abbot & Holder 1994
Moorland Gallery Bond Street London
Rowland Ward Piccadilly 1949*
Tryon Gallery Dover Street London late 1960s
Walkers Gallery 1957
Unknown gallery 1955

Ludlow

William Marler Fine Art 1975

Luxembourg

Musée d'Histoire Naturelle 1988

Newcastle

Northumberland Gallery 1952*

Oxford

Ashmolean Museum 1966
Oxford Gallery 1970

Stroud, Gloucestershire

Stroud Festival 1976

Threave, Castle Douglas

National Trust for Scotland 1986

Toronto, Canada

Royal Ontario Museum 1976

Winchester

Skipwith Gallery 1978

Various locations

BTO Conferences

Various locations around England 1954, 1962, 1963 (Chester), 1965 (Swanwick), 1966 (Swanwick), 1967 (Swanwick), 1981, 1982

Scottish Ornithologists' Club

Various Scottish locations for Annual Conferences – Perth: 1958; North Berwick: 1966, 1978, 1979 , 1980, 1981, 1982, 1983; Dunblane: year not known.

Society of Wildlife Artists

usually on tour around England 1960 (12 locations), 1966 (8 locations), 1967 (8 locations), 1968, 1970 (9 locations), 1971 (7 locations), 1972, 1979 (Sheffield), 1980, 1983, 1990 (Slimbridge),

Wildfowl and Wetlands Trust

Martin Mere, Lancashire, 1985, 1995

Paintings in collections

Clydesdale Bank, Glasgow
Dumfries & Galloway Council Gracefield Arts Centre and elsewhere
Edward Grey Institute of Field Ornithology, Oxford
National Trust for Scotland, Threave Castle, Galloway

Select bibliography

Avery, M. and Leslie, R. 1990. *Birds and Forestry,* T. & A.D. Poyser, Staffordshire.

Bannerman, D. 1983. *The Birds of the Balearics.* Croom Helm. Beckenham, Kent.

Baxter, E.V. and Rintoul, L.J. 1953. *The Birds of Scotland.* Oliver and Boyd, Edinburgh. 2 vols.

Baxter, J.M. and Galbraith, C. (eds). *Species Management: Challenges and Solutions for the 21st Century.* Scottish Natural Heritage and The Stationery Office, Edinburgh.

Campbell, B. and Watson, D. 1964. *The Oxford Book of Birds.* Oxford University Press, Oxford.

Clare, J. 1827. *The Shepherd's Calendar.*

Clare, J. 1830s. *The Midsummer Cushion.*

Delamain, J. 1928. *Why Birds Sing.* Gollancz, London.

Gordon, J.G. (Mearns, R. and Rollie, C. (eds)). 2016. *Birds of Wigtownshire.* The Bookshop, Wigtown.

Hammond, N. 1986. *Twentieth Century Wildlife Artists.* Croom Helm, London.

Mearns, R. and Rollie, C. 2016. *Jack Gordon's Birds of Wigtownshire 1890–1935.* Picto Publishing.

Nature Conservancy Council. 1987. *Nature Conservation and Afforestation in Britain.* Nature Conservancy Council, Peterborough, England.

Newton. I. 1979. *Population Ecology of Raptors.* T. & A.D. Poyser, Staffordshire.

Nicholson, E.M. 1926. B*irds in England – an account of the state of our birdlife and a criticism of bird protection.* Chapman & Hall. London.

Nicholson. E.M. 1927. *How Birds Live-a brief account of bird life in the light of modern observation.* Williams and Norgate, London.

Redpath, S.M. and Thirgood, S.J. 1997. *Birds of prey and Red Grouse.* The Stationery Office, London.

Rollie, C. and Mearns, R. Arthur Duncan Transactions of the Dumfriesshire and Galloway Natural History and Antiquarian Society (Vol XX1V), which also contain notes from Hough's notebooks (1903–1914) contributed by G.F. Scott-Elliot.

Ratcliffe, D. 1980. *The Peregrine Falcon.* T. & A.D. Poyser. Staffordshire.

Ratcliffe. D. 1997. *The Raven.* T. & A.D. Poyser. Staffordshire.

Ratcliffe, D.A. 2000. *In Search of Nature.* Peregrine Books, Leeds.

Ratcliffe, D. 2007. *Galloway and the Borders.* New Naturalist 101. Harper Collins, London.

Thompson, D., Birks, H. and Birks, J. 2015. *Nature's Conscience – the life and legacy of Derek Ratcliffe.* Langford Press, Peterborough.

Threipland, A.M. 2022. *Jackdaws and other friends.* Fingask Castle, Perth.

Watson, J. 1997 and 2010. *The Golden Eagle.* T. & A.D. Poyser, Black Publishers, London.

Watson, J. Unpublished PhD thesis on Seychelles Kestrel. Aberdeen University.

Acknowledgements

This publication has been produced with the generous support of the Scottish Ornithologists' Club (SOC) through its Birds of Scotland Fund www.the-soc.org.uk. Support from The Glenkens Community Shop Fund is also acknowledged. Grateful thanks to these donors. Donald's daughters, Pam, Louise and Kate, have supported this work, as has Jeff's widow, Vanessa. I am also grateful to my co-authors for their contributions and their insights into Donald and his work and the photographs selected.

Thanks to the Watson family for permission to reproduce Donald's paintings.

Thanks to Keith Whittles and his colleagues at Whittles Publishing for turning the manuscript into such a magnificent publication.

Thanks also to Caroline Petherick for expert copy editing.

I acknowledge the continuing interest and support of The Glenkens Community & Arts Trust's past and present trustees and staff, and many friends and colleagues in The Glenkens. Thanks to Erica Caldwell for continuing support.

My late wife, Lindsay, supported all of my work on Watson Birds over the years, and without that I could never have carried on.

Roger Crofts

St John's Town of Dalry

Louise Watson gives grateful thanks to *The Galloway News* for permission to reproduce the photo on page 33, and also to the family of her late cousin, Roger Watson, for permission to reproduce the photo on page 4. She is also indebted to her sisters, Pam Richardson and Kate Watson Forbes, for commenting on the chapter – and to Kate in particular for her editorial improvement.

Des Thompson specifically wishes to acknowledge the support of The Leverhulme Trust.

Notes to the chapters

Chapter 1

1 Cornwallis, R.K. (1964). Review of *The Oxford Book of Birds* in *British Birds* 57 (11).
2 Undated manuscript lodged in Donald Watson's archive at the Scottish Ornithologists' Club.
3 Annex 2 lists exhibitions of Donald Watson's paintings.
4 Watson, D. (2010). *In Search of Harriers.* p.8.
5 Watson, D. (1964). *One Pair of Eyes.* p.41.
6 Undated manuscript lodged in Donald Watson's archive at the Scottish Ornithologists' Club.
7 All of these materials are lodged in the Donald Watson archive at the Scottish Ornithologists' Club.
8 Undated manuscript lodged in Donald Watson's archive at the Scottish Ornithologists' Club.
9 Donald Watson's library contained books of paintings by many bird artists; Liljefors and Tunnicliffe were prominent in the collection.
10 See Annex 1.
11 See Annex 1.
12 *Birdwatchers' Year.*
13 Ratcliffe, D.A. (2007). *Galloway and the Borders.*
14 Undated manuscript lodged in Donald Watson's archive at the Scottish Ornithologists' Club.
15 Undated manuscript lodged in Donald Watson's archive at the Scottish Ornithologists' Club.
16 Threipland, A.M. (2022). *Jackdaws and other friends.*
17 Hammond, N. (1986). *Twentieth Century Wildlife Artists.*
18 Letters from Stanley Cursiter to Donald Watson lodged in Donald Watson's archive at the Scottish Ornithologists' Club.
19 Undated manuscript lodged in Donald Watson's archive at the Scottish Ornithologists' Club.
20 Peter Holt.(2008). Notes on visits to Donald and Joan Watson at their home in Dalry, near Castle Douglas and at the Wildlife Art Gallery, Lavenham. Lodged at Scottish Ornithologists' Club.
21 Undated manuscript lodged in Donald Watson's archive at the Scottish Ornithologists' Club.
22 *One Pair of Eyes*, p.8.

Chapter 2

1 Quoted in this chapter.
2 All of Donald Watson's publications are listed in Annex 1.
3 *A Bird Artist in Scotland.*
4 *A Bird Artist in Scotland.*
5 *A Bird Artist in Scotland.*
6 Bannerman, D. (1983). *The Birds of the Balearics.*
7 *A Bird Artist in Scotland.*
8 *A Bird Artist in Scotland.*
9 *A Bird Artist in Scotland.*
10 Hammond, N. (1986). *Twentieth Century Wildlife Artists.* Croom Helm, London, UK, p.219.

Chapter 3

1 Stated in this chapter.
2 *A Bird Artist in Scotland*, p.41
3 *A Bird Artist in Scotland*, p.45
4 *A Bird Artist in Scotland*, p.43
5 *A Bird Artist in Scotland*, p.46
6 *A Bird Artist in Scotland*, p.24
7 *A Bird Artist in Scotland*, p.29

Chapter 4

1 Watson, J. (1997). *The Golden Eagle.* p.2.
2 Watson, J. (1997). *The Golden Eagle.* p.2.
3 Watson, J. (1997). *The Golden Eagle.* p.3.
4 *In the Company of Eagles*, Film, ITV Granada, 2004, based on Watson, J. 1981.
5 Watson, J. (1992). Population Ecology: Food and Conservation of the Seychelles Kestrel (Falco Araea) on Mahé, PhD, University of Aberdeen.
6 https://www.nature.scot/doc/naturescot-commissioned-report-193-conservation-framework-golden-eagle-implications-conservation-and
7 Watson, J. and Whitfield, P. (2002). A conservation framework for the golden eagle *Aquila chrysaetos* in Scotland. *Journal of Raptor Research*, 36 (1 Supplement), 41–49.
8 Whitfield, D.P., Fielding, A.H., McLeod, D.R.A., Haworth, P.F. & Watson, J. (2006). A conservation framework for the golden eagle in Scotland: refining condition targets and assessment of constraint influence. *Biological Conservation*, 130, 465–480.

Chapter 5

1 Chris Rollie, this chapter.
2 See Annex 1 for complete list of Donald Watson's publications.
3 *A Bird Artist in Scotland*, p.11.
4 See Chapter 9 for details of the Watson Trails.

5 Baxter, E.V. and Rintoul, L.J. (1953). *The Birds of Scotland.*
6 Nicholson, E.M. (1926). *Birds in England.* (1929). *How Birds Live.*
7 Mearns R. and Rollie, C.J. (2016). *Jack Gordon's Birds of Wigtownshire 1890–1935.*
8 Hough, T.B. 1903–1914. In G.F. Scott-Elliot's Notes Regarding Bird Life in the Stewartry. Transactions of the Dumfriesshire and Galloway Natural History and Antiquarian Society 1918–19, Vol 6 (Series III) pp.48–65.
Duncan, A.B. (1945–46). List of the Birds of the Stewartry of Kirkcudbright Part I. Transactions of the Dumfriesshire and Galloway Natural History and Antiquarian Society 1945–46. 24 (Series III) 129.
Duncan, A.B. (1946–47). List of the Birds of the Stewartry of Kirkcudbright Part II. Transactions of the Dumfriesshire and Galloway Natural History and Antiquarian Society 1946–47. 25 (Series III) 44.
In the Transactions of the Dumfriesshire and Galloway Natural History and Antiquarian Society (Vol XXIV), which also contain notes from Hough's notebooks (1903–1914) contributed by G.F. Scott-Elliot.
9 See Bibliography for details.
10 *A Bird Artist in Scotland*, p.85.
11 Clare, J. (1827). *Shepherd's Calendar.* Op cit.
Clare, J. (1832). *Midsummer Cushion.* Op cit.
12 Delamain, J. (1932) *Why Birds Sing.* Op cit.
13 *One Pair of Eyes*, p.18.
14 *A Bird Artist in Scotland*, p.129.
15 *One Pair of Eyes*, p.15.

Chapter 6

1 *The Hen Harrier.* p.13.
2 *The Hen Harrier.* p.16.
3 *The Hen Harrier*, p.167.
4 *The Hen Harrier.* p.266.
5 *The Hen Harrier.* p.260.
6 *The Hen Harrier.* p.261.
7 Wotton, S.R., Bladwell, S., Mattingley, W., Morris, N.G., Raw, D., Ruddock, M., Stevenson, A.C. and Eaton, M.A. (2018). Status of the Hen Harrier *Circus cyaneus* in the UK and Isle of Man in 2016. *Bird Study*, 65(2), 145–160. https://doi.org/10.1080/00063657.2018.1476462 .
8 *Op cit.* Wotton et al (2018).
9 Haworth P.F. & Fielding, A.H. (2009). An assessment of woodland habitat utilisation by breeding hen harriers. Report to SNH (Project no. 24069). Scottish Natural Heritage, Battleby.
10 Scottish Forestry. (2018). Scotland's Forestry Strategy 2019-2029. https://forestry.gov.scot/publications/373-scotland-s-forestry-strategy-2019-2029
11 Redpath, S.M. and Thirgood, S.J. (1997). *Birds of prey and Red Grouse.* The Stationery Office, London.
12 Redpath, S.M. and Thirgood, S.J. (2009). Hen harriers and red grouse: moving towards consensus?, *J. Appl. Ecol.*, 46, pp. 961-963.
13 Anon (2000). *Report of the UK Raptor Working Group.* JNCC, Peterborough.
14 Etheridge, B., Summers, R.W. and Green, R.E. (1997). The effects of illegal killing and destruction of nests by humans on the population dynamics of the hen harrier *Circus cyaneus* in Scotland. *The Journal of Applied Ecology*, 34:1081–1105.
15 Final report of the Langholm Moor Demonstration Project (2008–2017). Project website provides background materials and links to publications http://www.langholmproject.com/index.html.
16 Redpath, S., Amar, A., Smith, A, Thompson, D.B.A., and Thirgood, S. (2010). People and nature in conflict: can we reconcile hen harrier conservation and game management? In: *Species Management: Challenges and Solutions for the 21st Century* (eds. J.M. Baxter and C.A. Galbraith), pp.335–350. TSO Scotland, Edinburgh.
17 Fielding, A., Haworth, P., Whitfield, P., McLeod, D. and Riley, H. (2011). A conservation framework for hen harriers in the United Kingdom. JNCC Report No. 441, JNCC, Peterborough.
18 http://jncc.defra.gov.uk/pdf/UKSPA3_Hen%20Harrier%20Circus%20cyaneus%20(breeding).pdf
19 http://jncc.defra.gov.uk/pdf/UKSPA3_Hen%20Harrier%20Circus%20cyaneus%20(non-breeding).pdf
20 *Op cit.* Wooton et al. (2018).
21 Project Skydancer website https://www.rspb.org.uk/our-work/conservation/conservation-and-sustainability/safeguarding-species/skydancer/about-the-project/
22 *Op cit.* Wotton. (2018)
23 https://www.gov.scot/publications/grouse-moor-management-group-report-scottish-government/ (The Werrity Report).
24 https://www.parliament.scot/bills-and-laws/bills/wildlife-management-and-muirburn-scotland-bill/overview
25 Ratcliffe, D.A. and Thompson, D.B.A. (1988). The British uplands: their ecological character and international significance. In: M.B. Usher and D.B.A. Thompson (eds). *Ecological Change in The Uplands*, pp. 9-36. Blackwell, Oxford; Ratcliffe, D. (1990). *Bird Life of Mountain and Upland.* CUP, Cambridge; Newton, I. (2020). *Uplands and Birds.* Collins, London.
26 Watson, D. (1977), *The Hen Harrier.* Thom, V. (1986). *The Birds of Scotland.* Poser, Calton.
27 Balfour, E. (1957). Observations on the breeding biology of the hen harrier in Orkney. *Bird.* Notes 27(6-7): 177-183, 216-224.
Later publications from work on Orkney with James Cadbury, and work there continued to 1981 by Nick Picozzi, and later by Arjun Amar and colleagues.
See: Amar, A. & Redpath, S. (2005). Habitat use by hen harriers *Circus cyaneus* on Orkney: implications of land use change on this declining population. *Ibis* 147: 37-47.

Amar, A., Picozzi, N., Meek, E.R., Lambin, X. & Redpath, S.M. (2005). Decline of the Orkney Hen Harrier Circus cyaneus population: do changes to demographic parameters and mating system fit a declining food hypothesis? *Bird Study* 52: 18-24.

28 Sharrock, J.T.R. (1976). *The Atlas of Breeding Birds in Britain and Ireland.* Poyser, Berkhamsted.

29 Watson, D. (1977). *The Hen Harrier.* Poyser, Berkhamsted.

30 Picozzi, N. (1978) Dispersion, breeding and prey of hen harriers (*Circus cyaneus*) in Glen Dye, Kincardineshire. *Ibis*, 120, 498–504.

31 Stroud, D.A. (2003). The status and legislative protection of birds of prey and their habitats in Europe. In: D.B.A. Thompson, S.M. Redpath, A.H. Fielding, M. Marquiss and C.A. Galbraith. *Birds of Prey in a Changing Environment*, pp. 51-84. TSO, Edinburgh. https://www.academia.edu/85426755/The_status_and_legislative_protection_of_birds_of_prey_and_their_habitats_in_Europe?uc-sb-sw=34382241

32 Bibby, C. J. and Etheridge, B. (1993) 'Status of the Hen Harrier *Circus cyaneus* in Scotland in 1988–89', *Bird Study*, 40(1), pp. 1–11. doi: 10.1080/00063659309477123

33 Redpath, S.M. and Thirgood, S.J. (1997). *Birds of prey and Red Grouse.* Stationery Office, London

34 http://jncc.defra.gov.uk/pdf/UKSPA3_Hen%20Harrier%20Circus%20cyaneus%20(breeding).pdf

35 http://jncc.defra.gov.uk/pdf/UKSPA3_Hen%20Harrier%20Circus%20cyaneus%20(non-breeding).pdf

36 Etheridge, B., Summers, R.W. & Green, R.E. 1997. The effects of illegal killing and destruction of nests by humans on the population dynamics of the Hen Harrier *Circus cyaneus* in Scotland. *J. Appl. Ecol.* 34: 1081–1105. doi: 10.2307/2405296

37 Sim, I.M.W., Gibbons, D.W., Bainbridge, I.P. & Mattingley, W.A. 2001. Status of the Hen Harrier *Circus cyaneus* in the UK and the Isle of Man in 1998. *Bird Study* 48: 341–353. doi: 10.1080/00063650109461233

38 Potts, G. (1998). Global dispersion of nesting hen harriers *Circus cyaneus*; implications for grouse moors in the UK. *Ibis*, 140:76–88. 8.

39 Moorland Working Group (1998). *Good Practice for Grouse Moor Management.* Scottish Natural Heritage, Battleby.

40 Anon (2000). *Report of the UK Raptor Working Group.* JNCC, Peterborough

41 Redpath, S.M., Thirgood, S.J. & Leckie, F.M. (2001). Does supplementary feeding reduce predation of red grouse? *J. Appl. Ecol.* 38: 1157–1168. doi: 10.1046/j.0021-8901.2001.00683.x.
Preceded by Moorland Working Group (1999) Substitute feeding of hen harriers on grouse moors. Scottish Natural Heritage, Battleby.
See later publication: Ludwig, S.C., McCluskie, A., Keane, P., Barlow, C., Francksen, R.M., Bubb, D., Roos, S., Aebischer, N.J., & Baines, D. (2018). Diversionary feeding and nestling diet of Hen Harriers *Circus cyaneus. Bird Study*, 65: 431-443.

42 Scottish Raptor Monitoring Scheme website https://raptormonitoring.org/ Key ensuing reference: Hardey, J, Crick, H., Wernham, C., Riley, H., Etheridge, B. and Thompson, D. (2013). *Raptors: A Field Guide to Surveys and Monitoring.* 3rd Edition. The Stationery Office, Edinburgh.

43 Moorland Working Group (2002). *Scotland's Moorland: the nature of change.* Scottish Natural Heritage, Battleby. Scotland's Moorland Forum https://www.moorlandforum.org.uk/

44 Summers, R.W., Green, R.E., Etheridge, B. & Sim, I.M.W. (2003). Changes in Hen Harrier (*Circus cyaneus*) numbers in relation to grouse moor management. In: D.B.A. Thompson, S.M. Redpath, A.H. Fielding, M. Marquiss, and C.A. Galbraith (eds) *Birds of Prey in a Changing Environment,* pp. 487-498. The Stationery Office, Edinburgh.
This followed from Etheridge, B., Summers, R.W. & Green, R.E. (1997). The effects of illegal killing and destruction of nests by humans on the population dynamics of the hen harrier *Circus cyaneus* in Scotland. *J. Appl. Ecol.* 34: 1081–1105. doi: 10.2307/2405296

45 Sim, I.M.W., Dillon, I.A., Eaton, M.A., Etheridge, B., Lindley, P., Riley, H., Saunders, R., Sharpe, C. & Tickner, M. (2007). Status of the Hen Harrier *Circus cyaneus* in the UK and Isle of Man in 2004, and a comparison with the 1988/89 and 1998 surveys. *Bird Study* 54: 256–267. doi: 10.1080/00063650709461482

46 Final report of the Langholm Moor Demonstration Project (2008–2017). Project website provides background materials and links to publications http://www.langholmproject.com/index.html

47 Watson, D. (2010). *In Search of Harriers – Over the Hills and Far Away.* Langford Press, Peterborough

48 Hayhow, D.B., Eaton, M.A., Bladwell, S., Etheridge, B., Ewing, S.R., Ruddock, M., Saunders, R., Sharpe, C., Sim, I.M. & Stevenson, A. (2013). The status of the Hen Harrier, *Circus cyaneus*, in the UK and Isle of Man in 2010. *Bird Study* 60: 446–458. doi: 10.1080/00063657.2013.839621

49 Redpath, S., Amar, A., Smith, A., Thompson, D. B. A. & Thirgood, S. (2010). People and nature in conflict: can we reconcile hen harrier conservation and game management. In: J.M. Baxter and C.A. Galbraith (eds), *Species Management: Challenges and Solutions for the 21st Century*, pp. 335-350. The Stationery Office, Edinburgh.

50 Raptor Persecution UK Blog https://raptorpersecutionuk.org/about/. Mark Avery provides a lively blog covering a wide range of nature conservation interests, and includes a lot of detail on hen harriers https://markavery.info/blog/

51 *Op cit* Fielding, A. et al (2011)

52 Project Skydancer website https://www.rspb.org.uk/our-work/conservation/conservation-and-sustainability/safeguarding-species/skydancer/about-the-project/
53 Hen Harrier Day website https://www.henharrierday.uk/about-hha/history/
54 Hen Harrier Life Project and other conservation projects heavily involving RSPB website https://www.rspb.org.uk/our-work/conservation/conservation-and-sustainability/safeguarding-species/case-studies/hen-harrier/
55 *Op cit* Wotton et al (2018)
56 NatureScot (2016). Wind farm proposals on afforested sites - advice on reducing suitability for hen harrier, merlin and short-eared owl. Scottish Natural Heritage, Battleby. Guidance withdrawn in August 2024, in order that bespoke advice is given on case-by-case basis. https://www.nature.scot/professional-advice/planning-and-development/planning-and-development-advice/renewable-energy/onshore-wind-energy/wind-farm-impacts-birds
57 Watson, D. (2017) *The Hen Harrier* (2nd Edition, with Foreword by Mark Avery). Bloomsbury, London.
58 https://www.gov.scot/publications/werritty/ and Whitfield, D.P. and Fielding, A.H. (2017). Analyses of the fates of satellite tracked golden eagles in Scotland. Scottish Natural Heritage Commissioned Report No. 982.
59 Cobham, David (2017) *Bowland Beth: The Life of an English Hen Harrier*. Collins, London.
60 https://www.gov.scot/publications/grouse-moor-management-group-report-scottish-government/
61 Murgatroyd et al (2019) https://www.nature.com/articles/s41467-019-09044-w
62 Scottish Government (2020) https://www.gov.scot/publications/scottish-government-response-grouse-moor-management-group-recommendations/pages/1/. The group chaired by Professor Alan Werritty was set up in response to the findings of a report which found that around a third of satellite-tagged golden eagles in Scotland disappeared in suspicious circumstances, on or around grouse moors.
63 Etheridge (2020). *Heads up for Harriers – Image analysis 2015–2019*. NatureScot Research Report No. 1209.
64 Carter, I. and Powell, D. (2022). *The Hen Harrier's Year*. Pelagic Publishing, London.
65 Scottish Parliament website https://www.parliament.scot/bills-and-laws/bills/wildlife-management-and-muirburn-scotland-bill/overview
66 Ewing, S. R. Steven R.E., Thomas, C.E., Butcher, N., Denman, B., Douglas, D.J.T., Anderson, D.I.K., Anderson, G.Q.A., Bray, J., Downing, S., Dugan, R., Etheridge, B., Hayward, W., Howie, F., Roos, S., Thomas, M., Weston, J., Smart, J. and Wilson, J.D. (2023). Illegal killing associated with gamebird management accounts for up to three-quarters of annual mortality in hen harriers *Circus cyaneus*, *Biological Conservation*, Volume 283.

Chapter 7

1 Thompson, O.T. (1965). *Scottish Birds*, 3.
2 Cornwallis, R.K. (1964). *British Birds* 57 (11), 474–475.
3 Thompson, O.T. (1972). *Scottish Birds*.
4 Andrew, D.G. (1973). *Scottish Birds*, 7, 317–318.
5 Pennie, I.D. (1972). *British Birds*, 65 (11), 485–486.
6 Adams, J.K. (1972). *Country Life* 10 August.
7 Hartley, P. (1972). *The Field* 13 July.
8 Bannerman, D. (1972). *The Times Literary Supplement*.
9 Lea, D. (1979). *British Birds*, 72 (8), 402
10 Noval, A. (1977). *El Libro de la Fauna Iberica*. Letter to Donald Watson 07/12/77 lodged in Donald Watson's archive at the Scottish Ornithologists' Club.
11 Avery, M. (2017). Online 09/07/17 Search Results for "review of Hen Harrier Donald Watson" – Mark Avery
12 Harris, A. (1990). *British Birds* 83, 31–32.
13 Ratcliffe, D.A. (2000). *In Search of Nature*. Peregrine Books, Leeds, UK p.131.
14 Harris, A. (1995). *British Birds*, 88, 373.
15 Betton, K. online review In Search of Harriers: Over the Hills and Far Away | NHBS Academic & Professional Books
16 *In Search of Harriers* p.10.
17 *In Search of Harriers* p.12.
18 *In Search of Harriers* p.49.
19 *The Hen Harrier* p.187.
20 The Hen Harrier. *Country Life*.
21 *The Hen Harrier* p.207.

Chapter 8

1 *A Bird Artist in Scotland*, p.139.
2 *A Bird Artist in Scotland*, p.10.
3 Letter deposited in the Donald Watson archive at the Scottish Ornithologists' Club.
4 Ratcliffe, D. (2007), in *Galloway and the Borders*. p.37.
5 *A Bird Artist in Scotland*, p.68.
6 *A Bird Artist in Scotland*, p.134.
7 *A Bird Artist in Scotland*, p.78.
8 *In Search of Harriers*, p.19.
9 *In Search of Harriers*, p.39.
10 *Birdwatchers' Year.*
11 Softly, softly move for rare bird. *The Times* 22 August 1986. Also noted on p.75 in *In Search of Harriers*.
12 Ratcliffe, D. *In Search of Nature*, p.131.
13 *In Search of Harriers*, p.63.
14 Letter deposited in the Donald Watson archive at the Scottish Ornithologists' Club.
15 The correspondence is deposited in the Donald Watson archive at the Scottish Ornithologists' Club.
16 Ratcliffe, D. (1997). *The Raven*.
17 *A Bird Artist in Scotland*, p.138.
18 *A Bird Artist in Scotland*, p.52.
19 *A Bird Artist in Scotland*, p.57.
20 *A Bird Artist in Scotland*, p.57.
21 *A Bird Artist in Scotland*, p.74.
22 *A Bird Artist in Scotland*, p.75.

23 *A Bird Artist in Scotland*, p.64.
24 *A Bird Artist in Scotland*, p.77.
25 *A Bird Artist in Scotland*, p.82.
26 *A Bird Artist in Scotland*, p.132.
27 *A Bird Artist in Scotland*, p.83.
28 Ratcliffe, D. *In Search of Nature*, p.130.
29 Ratcliffe, D. *In Search of Nature*, p.131.
30 Letter deposited in the Donald Watson archive at the Scottish Ornithologists' Club.
31 Letter deposited in the Donald Watson archive at the Scottish Ornithologists' Club.
32 *Nature Conservation and Afforestation in Britain* (1987). Nature Conservancy Council.
33 Scottish Office Circular (1989). *Indicative Forestry Strategies*. Edinburgh.
34 Avery, M. and Leslie, R. (1990). *Birds and Forestry*.
35 Typescript of article deposited in the Donald Watson archive at the Scottish Ornithologists' Club.
36 Royal Society of Edinburgh. (2023). Response to Scottish Forestry consultation on Forestry Grant Scheme. Edinburgh.
37 *The Hen Harrier*, p.176.
38 Letters for example to Sandy Kerr, NCC South West Regional Director, and to Vin Fleming, Assistant Regional Officer, deposited in the Donald Watson archive at the Scottish Ornithologists' Club.
39 *The Hen Harrier*, p.170.
40 *A Bird Artist in Scotland*, p.91.
41 *A Bird Artist in Scotland*, p.62.
42 *In Search of Harriers*, p.26.
43 *In Search of Harriers*, p.71.
44 *In Search of Harriers*, p.73.
45 *The Hen Harrier*, p.187.
46 *The Hen Harrier*, p.194.
47 *The Hen Harrier*. Tables 9, 15 and 18.
48 *The Hen Harrier*, p.261.
49 *The Hen Harrier*, p.261.
50 *The Hen Harrier*, pp.261–262.
51 Clarke, R. and Watson, D. (1996/97). The hen harrier winter roost survey. *The Raptor*, 41–45.
52 Redpath, S.M. and Thirgood, S.J. (1997). *Birds of Prey and Red Grouse*.
53 The correspondence is deposited in the Donald Watson archive at the Scottish Ornithologists' Club.
54 Protection of Birds Act 1954, see Section 1 for protection of birds, nests and eggs, and Schedule 1 for list of birds protected at all times. Protection of Birds Act 1954 (legislation.gov.uk).
55 See the recent RSPB wildlife crime report; p.14 deals with hen harriers. bc2021_report.pdf (rspb.org.uk)
56 British Trust for Ornithology, Facts: the Hen Harrier. Hen Harrier | BTO - British Trust for Ornithology
57 See the recent RSPB wildlife crime report; p.14 deals with hen harriers. bc2021_report.pdf (rspb.org.uk)
58 Redpath, S., Amar, A., Smith, A., Thompson, D S.B and Thirgood, S. (2010). People and nature in conflict: can we reconcile hen harrier conservation and game management? In *Species Management: Challenges and Solutions for the 21st Century*. Baxter, J.M. and Galbraith, C. (eds). Scottish Natural Heritage and The Stationery Office, Edinburgh, pp.335–350.
59 Draft letter by Derek Ratcliffe on behalf of Raptor Study Groups dated 18 September 1995. Deposited in the Donald Watson archive at the Scottish Ornithologists' Club.
60 Independent Review of Grouse Moor Management: ministerial statement - gov.scot (www.gov.scot)
61 RSE-AP-Wildlife-management-grouse-bill-2023.pdf
62 Independent Review of Grouse Moor Management: ministerial statement - gov.scot (www.gov.scot)
63 Wildlife Management and Muirburn (Scotland) Act 2024 (legislation.gov.uk)

Chapter 9

1 Homepage – GCAT
2 Smart, J. et al (2010). Illegal killing slows population recovery of a re-introduced raptor of high conservation concern – the red kite *Milvus Milvus*. http://dx.doi.org/10.1016/j.biocon.2010.03.002.
3 Sergio, F. et al (2011). Raptor nest decorations are a reliable threat against conspecifics. *Science* 331, 2011, 327–330.
4 Amar, A. (2011). *Journal of Applied Ecology*, 48, 220–227. Long-term impact of changes in sheep Ovis aries densities on the breeding output of the hen harrier Circus cyaneus - Amar - 2011 - Journal of Applied Ecology - Wiley Online Library
5 Ferrer, M. et al (2012). Weak relationship between risk assessment studies and recorded mortality in wind farms. *Journal of Applied Ecology*, 49, 38–46. Weak relationship between risk assessment studies and recorded mortality in wind farms on JSTOR
6 Evans, R.J., O'Toole, L. and Whitfield, D.P. (2012). The history of eagles in Britain and Ireland: an ecological review of placename and documentary evidence from the last 1500 years. *Bird Study*, 59 (3), 335–349. http://dx.doi.org/10.1080/00063657.2012.68338.
7 Klassen, R.H.G. et al (2014). When and where does mortality occur in migratory birds? Direct evidence from long-term satellite tracking of raptors. *Journal of Animal Ecology*, 83: 176–184. doi: 10.1111/1365–2656.12135.
8 Trierweiler, C. et al (2013). A Palaearctic migratory raptor species tracks shifting prey availability within its wintering range in the Sahel. *Journal of Animal Ecology*, 82: 107–120. doi: 10.1111/j.1365–2656.2012.02036.
9 Sergio, F., Tanferna, A., De Stephanis, R. et al (2014). Individual improvements and selective mortality shape lifelong migratory performance. *Nature* 515, 410–413. https://doi.org/10.1038/nature13696.

10 Ferrer, M., Newton, I., Muriel, R., Báguena, G., Bustamante, J., Martini, M. and Morandini, V. (2014). Using manipulation of density-dependent fecundity to recover an endangered species: the bearded vulture *Gypaetus barbatus* as an example. *e*, 51, 1255–1263. Using manipulation of density-dependent fecundity to recover an endangered species: the bearded vulture Gypaetus barbatus as an example - Ferrer - 2014 - Journal of Applied Ecology - Wiley Online Library

11 Hoy S.R., Petty, S.J., Millon, A., Whitfield, D.P., Marquiss, M., Davison, M. and Lambin, X. (2014) Age and sex-selective predation moderate the overall impact of predators. *Journal of Animal Ecology.* http://onlinelibrary.wiley.com/doi/10.1111/1365-2656.12310/full

12 Terraubea-Monich, J., Guixé, D. and Arroyo. B. (2014). Diet composition and foraging success in generalist predators: Are specialist individuals better foragers? *Basic and Applied Ecology 15.* 616–624. Interactions between individual diet specialization, foraging success and fitness components: are specialists better (core.ac.uk)

13 Mueller, A.-K., Chakarov, N., Heseker, H. and Krüger, O. (2016). Intraguild predation leads to cascading effects on habitat choice, behaviour and reproductive performance. *Journal of Animal Ecology, 85*: 774–784. doi:10.1111/1365-2656.12493 http://onlinelibrary.wiley.com/doi/10.1111/1365-2656.12493/full.

14 Muriel, R., Morandini, V., Ferrer, M., and Balbontín, J. (2016). Juvenile dispersal behaviour and conspecific attraction: An alternative approach with translocated Spanish imperial eagles. *Animal Behaviour*, 116, 17–29. http://www.sciencedirect.com/science/article/pii/S0003347216001068.

15 Watson Raptor Science Prize - www Watson Birds see sections on 2012 and 2017 events.

16 Watson Birds leaflet_Art Trail

17 Watson Birds leaflet_cicular walk

18 www.planetbirdsong.org

19 Threipland, A. (2022). *Jackdaws and other friends.* Privately published. Copies available for purchase at the CatStrand shop in New Galloway.

20 Ken Words – Writing Project - The Galloway Glens Landscape Partnership

21 Crofts, R. (2023). Imagining our future forests.. *The Geographer.* Royal Scottish Geographical Society. Winter 2023 edition, p.24. .

22 Contact is library@the-soc.org.uk